SCREENING METHODS IN PHARMACOLOGY

VOLUME 1 - PRINCIPLES AND APPLICATIONS

RAO MURALIDHAR

Made with ♥ on the Notion Press Platform
www.notionpress.com

Dedication

I dedicate this book "Screening Methods in Pharmacology: Volume 1 - Principles and Applications" to my beloved brother, **Dr. Akkaladevi Sridhar Rao M.B.B.S., M.D (Anesthesia).** His unwavering commitment to his profession, his simplicity, love, and affection have been a source of inspiration and strength to me throughout my life.

As a doctor, he has dedicated himself to providing compassionate care to his patients and has always gone above and beyond to ensure their comfort and well-being. His professionalism and dedication to his work have been a shining example for me to follow.

Thank you, Annaiah, for your support, encouragement, and blessings. I am grateful to have you as my brother and friend. This book is a tribute to you and all the wonderful things you do.

With love and admiration,

Dr.Akkaladevi Muralidhar Rao

M.Pharm.,Ph.D

Hyderabad

28-02-2023

Contents

"SCREENING METHODS IN PHARMACOLOGY: VOLUME 1 - PRINCIPLES AND APPLICATIONS"

Dr.A.Muralidhar Rao

Published by Notion Press
Notion Press, Inc.
800, West EI Camino Real #180,
California USA 94040
Notion Press Media Pvt Ltd,
#7, Red Cross Road,
Egmore, Chennai, Tamil Nadu 600008

PROLOGUE

Drug discovery and development is a complex and challenging process that involves a wide range of scientific disciplines and regulatory considerations. In this book, we aim to provide a comprehensive overview of the essential topics related to drug discovery and development, with a particular focus on the care, handling, and breeding techniques of laboratory animals, toxicity testing, and screening methods for pharmacological activity.

This book is designed for M.Pharm Pharmacology and B.Pharm students, as well as anyone involved in drug discovery and development. The first topic covered in this book is the care, handling, and breeding techniques of laboratory animals. The readers are provided with an understanding of how to handle and breed laboratory animals, along with alternative methods to animal studies. The ethical considerations related to animal experimentation are also discussed in detail.

The second topic of the book is toxicity testing. The readers are provided with an understanding of OECD guidelines and the determination of LD50. Acute, sub-acute, and chronic toxicity studies are discussed in detail, and the importance of careful observation and data analysis in toxicity testing is emphasized.

The third topic of the book is dedicated to the organization of screening for pharmacological activity of new substances, with a particular emphasis on the evaluation of antipsychotics, antiepileptics, and antidepressants. The readers are provided with an understanding of the importance of preclinical studies in drug development and the role of screening methods in identifying potential drug candidates.

Finally, the book covers screening methods for anti-diabetic, antiulcer, CHF, and anti-hypertensive drugs, as well as screening methods for anti-inflammatory, analgesics, and antipyretic drugs.

The readers are provided with an overview of the methods used to evaluate the pharmacological activity of these drugs, including in vitro and in vivo assays.

Overall, this book is a valuable resource for anyone involved in drug discovery and development, providing a comprehensive overview of the essential topics related to pharmacology.

I

Care, Handling and Breeding Techniques of Laboratory Animals

The care and handling of laboratory animals is a crucial aspect of biomedical research. These animals play a vital role in the advancement of medical knowledge and the development of new treatments for human diseases. As such, it is imperative that they are treated with the utmost care and respect.

The first principle of laboratory animal care is the provision of appropriate housing and environment. This involves creating a physical and social environment that meets the specific needs of each species of animal used in research. This is essential for promoting their physical and psychological well-being, and for ensuring that the results of experiments conducted on these animals are reliable and meaningful.

Appropriate housing for laboratory animals may include single or group housing, depending on the species and the type of research being conducted. The housing should be clean, spacious, and well-ventilated, with temperature, humidity, and lighting controlled to meet the specific needs of each species. Adequate bedding, toys, and other enrichment items should also be provided to promote the animals' physical and psychological well-being.

The social environment of laboratory animals is also important. Some species are naturally social and require the presence of other animals for their well-being, while others are solitary and do better when housed alone. The social structure of the animals should be taken into consideration when designing their housing and environment.

Here are a few examples to illustrate this:

Rats: Rats are social animals and thrive when housed with other rats. They like to play and groom each other, and can become lonely and depressed when they are housed alone for long periods of time.

Monkeys: Monkeys are also social animals, and live in groups in the wild. They need to interact with other monkeys to learn important social skills and behaviors. When monkeys are housed alone, they can become depressed and develop behavioral problems.

Hamsters: Hamsters, on the other hand, are naturally solitary animals and do better when housed alone. They can become stressed and aggressive if they are forced to share their living space with other hamsters.

Mice: Mice are social animals, but they also have a territorial side. When mice are housed in small groups, they may become aggressive and establish hierarchies, which can lead to stress and fighting.

The social structure of laboratory animals should be taken into consideration when designing their housing and environment. Providing appropriate social interaction and living conditions can help improve the well-being of the animals, while neglecting their social needs can lead to stress, depression, and other health problems.

Adequate nutrition and veterinary care are critical components of laboratory animal care. Proper nutrition is essential for maintaining the health and well-being of the animals, and for ensuring that the results of experiments are reliable and meaningful. A balanced diet that meets the specific nutritional needs of each species should be provided, and the animals should have access to fresh water at all times.

Regular veterinary care is also important for the health and well-being of laboratory animals. This may include routine check-ups, vaccinations, and treatments for any health problems that may arise. In addition, veterinary care should be provided in a manner that minimizes the stress and discomfort experienced by the animals.

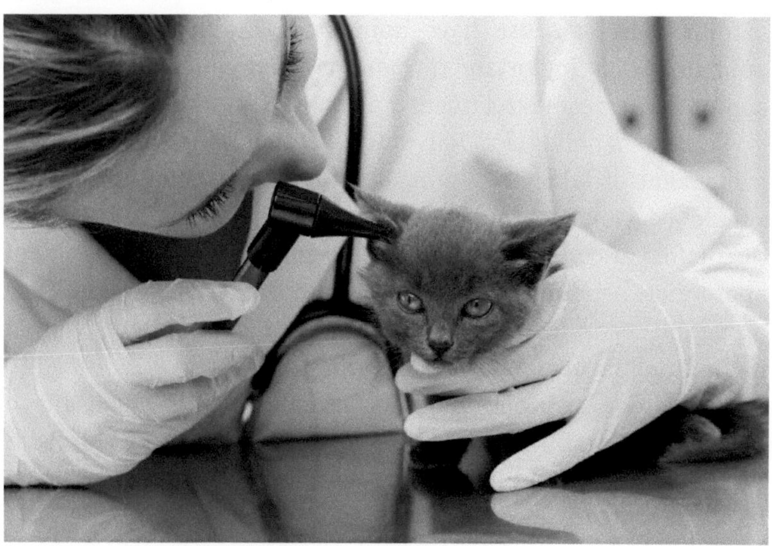

ROUTINE CHECK-UPS

In some cases, the use of specific diets or interventions may be necessary for research purposes. In these cases, it is important to ensure that the animals receive the necessary care and support to minimize any negative impact on their health and well-being.

Here are a few examples:

High-fat diets: In some research studies, high-fat diets may be used to study obesity or other metabolic disorders. However, these diets can also increase the risk of health problems like liver disease, so it's important to monitor the animals closely and provide appropriate care and treatment if any health issues arise.

Invasive surgeries: Some research studies may require invasive surgeries to collect tissue samples or implant devices. While these procedures can be necessary for the research, they can also be stressful and painful for the animals. It's important to provide appropriate pain management and post-surgical care to minimize the impact on the animals' well-being.

Genetic modifications: In some cases, genetic modifications may be used to study specific traits or diseases. However, these modifications can also have unintended health effects on the animals, so it's important to monitor them closely and provide appropriate care and treatment if any health issues arise.

Proper handling of laboratory animals is an essential component of laboratory animal care. The handling of animals should be conducted in a manner that minimizes stress and discomfort, and maximizes their well-being. This includes the use of appropriate handling techniques and equipment, such as gloves and proper lifting devices, as well as training for all personnel involved in the handling of animals.

In addition to proper handling techniques, it is important to minimize the number of times that animals are handled. This helps to reduce stress and discomfort, and minimizes the potential for injury or harm to the animals.

The use of anesthetic or analgesic agents may also be necessary for certain procedures or during certain experiments. In these cases, it is important to use the appropriate agents, and to monitor the animals closely to ensure their well-being.

The use of pain relief and anesthesia during procedures is a crucial aspect of laboratory animal care. The application of pain relief and anesthesia helps to minimize the stress, discomfort, and pain experienced by the animals during procedures or experiments. This not only helps to improve their welfare, but also helps to ensure that the results of the procedures or experiments are not biased by the animals' distress.

Pain relief and anesthesia should be used whenever necessary, and the appropriate agents and techniques should be selected based on the specific needs of each species and procedure. In addition, the use of pain relief and anesthesia should be monitored closely to ensure that the animals are receiving adequate protection from pain and discomfort.

In some cases, the use of pain relief and anesthesia may not be possible, due to the nature of the procedure or the specific requirements of the experiment. In these cases, every effort should be made to minimize the distress experienced by the animals, and to ensure that the results of the procedures or experiments are not biased by the animals' distress.

Here are a few examples of how pain relief and anesthesia should be used when working with laboratory animals:

Surgeries: Any invasive procedure, such as surgery, should be performed with appropriate pain relief and anesthesia to minimize pain and discomfort. For example, when performing a surgery on a rodent, anesthesia may be administered via injection or inhalation to ensure the animal is fully asleep and doesn't feel any pain during the procedure.

Injections: Injections can be painful for animals, so it's important to use appropriate pain relief when possible. This may include using a topical anesthetic or administering a pain-relieving drug prior to the injection to minimize discomfort.

Chronic conditions: Animals with chronic conditions, such as arthritis or cancer, may require ongoing pain relief to manage their symptoms. In these cases, it's important to use the appropriate pain-relieving drugs and monitor the animals closely to ensure that they are receiving adequate pain relief.

In addition to practical considerations, the ethical treatment of laboratory animals is of utmost importance. The use of animals in research and experimentation raises complex ethical questions, and it is essential that the well-being of the animals is considered at all times.

The ethical treatment of laboratory animals requires a consideration of the potential benefits and harm to the animals, and a commitment to minimizing harm and maximizing benefit. This includes the use of appropriate housing, nutrition, veterinary care, handling techniques, and pain relief and anesthesia, as well as the design of experiments and procedures that minimize harm to the animals.

There are several alternatives to using live animals in research, and it's important to explore these options whenever possible. Here are a few examples:

Computer models: In some cases, computer models can be used to simulate biological processes and test the effects of drugs or other interventions. This can help reduce the need for animal testing and provide more accurate results.

In vitro testing: In vitro testing involves studying cells or tissues in a laboratory setting rather than using live animals. This can be used to test the toxicity or effectiveness of drugs or other substances.

Human trials: In some cases, it may be possible to conduct clinical trials on human volunteers instead of using animals. This can be a more ethical and effective way to test the safety and effectiveness of new treatments.

Various types of laboratory animals commonly used

As a research tool, laboratory animals play a crucial role in advancing our understanding of biology and medicine. A wide range of species is used in laboratory settings, each with their own unique characteristics and advantages.

Most common types of laboratory animals used in scientific research.

Albino Mouse

Rodents: Rodents, including mice and rats, are the most commonly used laboratory animals. They are small, inexpensive, and easily bred and maintained in large numbers. Rodents are also highly adaptable, and can be genetically modified to suit specific research needs. Additionally, mice and rats are physiologically and anatomically similar to humans, making them valuable models for the study of human diseases.

Rabbit

Rabbits: Rabbits are often used in laboratory research due to their large size and relative ease of handling. They are frequently used in studies of vision and eye function, and in the development of new drugs and treatments for a range of conditions.

Non-human Primates: Non-human primates, including monkeys and apes, are widely used in laboratory research due to their close biological and behavioral similarities to humans. These species are often used in studies of the nervous system, including neuroscience and drug development. However, their use raises ethical and practical considerations, as they are more complex and expensive to maintain than other laboratory animals.

Fish: Fish are widely used in laboratory research due to their ease of maintenance and versatility as research models. They are frequently used in studies of genetics, physiology, and developmental biology. Zebrafish, in particular, are widely used due to their transparent embryos and rapid development, making them ideal for the study of early developmental processes.

ZEBRA FISH

Pigs: Pigs are often used in laboratory research due to their similarities to humans in terms of anatomy and physiology. They are frequently used in studies of cardiovascular and respiratory function, and in the development of new treatments for human diseases.

Guinea Pigs-Despite its name, the guinea pig (Cavia porcellus) is not actually a pig, but is a species of rodent. The name is likely due to its superficial resemblance to a small pig or a young domesticated pig. Guinea pigs are commonly used in medical research, particularly in studies of the respiratory, cardiovascular, and nervous systems.

Beagles are a popular breed of dog used in preclinical drug development due to their small size and their docile and friendly nature. Beagles are social animals and are easy to train, which makes them an ideal model for behavioral studies. They are also well-suited for non-invasive procedures such as blood collection and imaging, making them an attractive animal model for longitudinal studies.

Dogs: Dogs are often used in laboratory research due to their close similarities to humans in terms of anatomy and behavior. They are frequently used in studies of cardiovascular and respiratory function, as well as in the development of new treatments for human diseases.

Beagles are a commonly used animal model in experimentation for a variety of reasons. Their medium size and docile temperament make them relatively easy to handle and work with, which is a desirable trait for researchers. In addition, Beagles have a relatively uniform genetic makeup, making them a useful model for studying the effects of drugs and other interventions. they are also a commonly bred and readily available breed, which can make them a convenient choice for animal experimentation. They have certain physiological and anatomical similarities to humans, which can make them a useful model for studying certain diseases and conditions

A wide range of species is used in laboratory research, each with their own unique characteristics and advantages. Rodents, rabbits, non-human primates, fish, pigs, and dogs are among the most common types of laboratory animals used in scientific research. By understanding the specific strengths and limitations of each species, researchers can choose the best model for their particular study, and contribute to the advancement of our understanding of biology and medicine.

II

Breeding Techniques

Breeding methods used in laboratory animal research.

Laboratory animal breeding refers to the controlled reproduction of animals for scientific research purposes. This involves using various methods to produce a large number of genetically uniform animals with specific characteristics. Breeding animals in the laboratory is essential for ensuring the consistent quality of research results and for reducing the number of animals needed for experiments.

The importance of laboratory animal breeding cannot be overstated, as it is the foundation of many areas of research, including biomedical, pharmaceutical, and behavioral research. It also plays a critical role in drug discovery, vaccine development, and the study of disease mechanisms. Therefore, it is essential to have a good understanding of the different breeding methods used in laboratory animal research.

Natural Breeding Methods

Natural breeding methods refer to the use of natural reproductive processes to breed animals for scientific research. This includes allowing animals to mate naturally and reproduce in a controlled environment. Natural breeding methods have several advantages, including being cost-effective, easy to manage, and reducing stress and potential health risks for the animals. However, they also have disadvantages, such as limited control over the genetic makeup of the offspring and the potential for uncontrolled mating.

Natural breeding methods can be classified based on the level of intervention by the researcher. These include pure natural breeding, which involves allowing animals to mate without any human intervention, and semi-natural breeding, which involves some level of intervention, such as pairing selected animals for mating.

Commonly used natural breeding methods in laboratory animal research include pairing of males and females in separate cages, housing animals in large groups to encourage mating, and the use of timed breeding protocols to synchronize estrus cycles. These methods are frequently used in the breeding of rodents, rabbits, and some larger species, such as dogs and non-human primates.

Advantages of natural breeding methods

Natural breeding methods are a common way of producing animals for research, and they offer several advantages. One advantage is that they are less costly compared to assisted breeding methods, as they do not require sophisticated equipment or specialized knowledge. Natural breeding methods are also less invasive and less stressful for the animals, which can result in healthier offspring. However, natural breeding methods may have some disadvantages, such as the difficulty of controlling the timing of breeding, which can result in variations in the age and size of the offspring. The genetics of the breeding animals may also be less controlled, which can lead to greater genetic variability in the offspring. Therefore, researchers must carefully consider the pros and cons of natural breeding methods before selecting the appropriate breeding method for their research.

Classification of natural breeding methods

Natural breeding methods can be classified into two categories: random breeding and selective breeding.

Random breeding: In this method, animals are allowed to mate randomly without any specific selection criteria. The genetic makeup of the offspring is determined by chance, and there is no control over the traits that are inherited. This method is often used to maintain genetic diversity in large populations and to produce experimental animals that have a heterogeneous genetic background.

Selective breeding: In this method, animals are selected based on specific traits that are desired for the research purpose. Breeding pairs are chosen based on their individual traits, and the offspring with the desired traits are selectively bred to produce the next generation. This method is used to develop animal models with specific genetic traits that are relevant to the research being conducted. Selective breeding can also be used to improve the performance of animal models over time, such as increasing resistance to disease or improving behavioral traits.

Commonly used natural breeding methods in laboratory animal research

Some examples of commonly used natural breeding methods in laboratory animal research include pairing male and female animals in the same cage, using harem breeding where one male is housed with multiple females, and using colony breeding where multiple males and females are housed together in a larger space. In addition, natural breeding methods may involve monitoring the estrus cycle of female animals and introducing males during the appropriate time for mating. These methods can be used to breed a variety of laboratory animal species, including mice, rats, rabbits, and guinea pigs, among others. However, it is important to note that natural breeding methods may not be suitable for all species, and other methods such as assisted reproductive techniques may be necessary in some cases.

Assisted Breeding Methods

Definition of assisted breeding methods

Assisted breeding methods refer to the use of technologies and techniques to manipulate the reproductive processes of laboratory animals. These methods are used to enhance breeding efficiency and control genetic traits in laboratory animals. Assisted breeding methods include a variety of techniques such as artificial insemination, in vitro fertilization, embryo transfer, and cloning. These techniques can be used in a variety of laboratory animal species, including rodents, rabbits, pigs, and non-human primates.

Advantages and disadvantages of assisted breeding methods

Assisted breeding methods in laboratory animal research have several advantages, including the ability to control the breeding process and manipulate genetic material. These methods can also increase the efficiency of breeding and produce a higher yield of offspring. In addition, assisted breeding methods can help to reduce the risk of disease transmission and improve the genetic quality of the animals.

However, there are also several disadvantages associated with assisted breeding methods. For example, these methods may be expensive and require specialized equipment and expertise. They may also be associated with increased stress for the animals, which can have negative effects on their health and welfare. Additionally, some assisted breeding methods may involve the use of hormones or other drugs that could have potential side effects or health risks for the animals. Overall, it is important to carefully consider the advantages and disadvantages of assisted breeding methods before deciding which methods to use in laboratory animal research.

Classification of assisted breeding methods

Assisted breeding methods in laboratory animals can be classified into several categories based on the techniques used. Some common classification categories include:

In-vitro fertilization (IVF): In this method, the oocytes and sperm are collected from the animals, fertilized outside the body, and then implanted back into the female for further development.

Artificial insemination (AI): In this method, semen is collected from the male and introduced into the reproductive tract of the female using various techniques such as vaginal, intrauterine or intracervical insemination.

Embryo transfer (ET): This method involves the transfer of embryos from a donor female to a recipient female that has been hormonally prepared to receive the embryos.

Gamete and embryo cryopreservation: This method involves the freezing of oocytes, sperm, or embryos to store them for future use or shipment.

Transgenic animal production: This method involves the insertion of foreign genetic material into the genome of an animal, resulting in the production of transgenic animals.

Cloning: This method involves the creation of a genetically identical animal by replacing the nucleus of an egg cell with the nucleus of a donor cell.

Each of these methods has its advantages and disadvantages and can be used in specific situations depending on the research goals and the species of the animal involved.

Conventional breeding methods

Conventional breeding methods are the oldest and most natural form of animal breeding. These methods rely on the natural breeding behaviors of animals and typically involve pairing a male and female animal of the same species to produce offspring. In laboratory animal research, conventional breeding methods are often used to establish breeding colonies and maintain genetically homogenous populations. These methods can be used to produce large numbers of offspring with relatively little intervention, making them a cost-effective and efficient way to produce research animals.

Advantages and disadvantages of conventional breeding methods

Conventional breeding methods, also known as traditional breeding methods, involve natural mating between male and female animals to produce offspring. Some of the advantages of conventional breeding methods include:

Cost-effective: Conventional breeding methods are relatively low-cost and do not require sophisticated technology or equipment.

Genetic diversity: Natural mating allows for greater genetic diversity, which can be important in maintaining genetic variability in a breeding population.

Similar to natural conditions: Conventional breeding methods mimic natural breeding conditions, which can result in animals that are better adapted to their environment.

However, there are also some disadvantages to conventional breeding methods:

Limited control over genetics: With natural mating, it is not possible to control which genes are passed on to offspring, which can limit the ability to create animals with specific genetic traits.

Low efficiency: The success rate of conventional breeding methods can be relatively low, particularly when compared to more advanced assisted reproductive technologies.

Risk of disease transmission: Conventional breeding methods require close contact between animals, which can increase the risk of disease transmission between animals.

Classification of conventional breeding methods

it is based on the mating system used. Some commonly used conventional breeding methods in laboratory animal research include:

Inbreeding is a method of breeding in which individuals that are closely related, such as siblings or first cousins, are mated. This method is used to establish inbred strains of animals that are genetically uniform and homozygous for a particular set of genes. Inbred strains are often used in research because they provide a controlled genetic background for the study of specific traits. There are several different types of inbreeding, each with its own strengths and limitations.

Full-Sib Inbreeding: Full-sib inbreeding is a method of inbreeding in which siblings are mated. This method is used to produce offspring that are genetically uniform and homozygous for a specific set of genes. Full-sib inbreeding can be used to establish inbred strains, or to produce offspring that are homozygous for a specific set of genes for use in further experiments.

Half-Sib Inbreeding: Half-sib inbreeding is a method of inbreeding in which half-siblings are mated. This method is used to produce offspring that are genetically uniform and homozygous for a specific set of genes. Half-sib inbreeding can be used to establish inbred strains, or to produce offspring that are homozygous for a specific set of genes for use in further experiments.

Parent-Offspring Inbreeding: Parent-offspring inbreeding is a method of inbreeding in which parents are mated with their offspring. This method is used to produce offspring that are genetically uniform and homozygous for a specific set of genes. Parent-offspring inbreeding can be used to establish inbred strains, or to produce offspring that are homozygous for a specific set of genes for use in further experiments.

Backcross Inbreeding: Backcross inbreeding is a method of inbreeding in which an individual is mated with one of its parents or grandparents. This method is used to introduce a specific set of genes into an inbred strain, or to produce offspring that are homozygous for a specific set of genes for use in further experiments.

Outbreeding, also known as crossbreeding, is a method of breeding in which individuals from different genetic backgrounds are mated. This method is used to produce offspring that are genetically diverse, heterozygous, and exhibit a range of traits that are characteristic of the parent populations. Outbreeding is commonly used in agriculture and animal husbandry to produce offspring with improved traits, such as increased growth rate, improved meat quality, or increased resistance to disease. There are several different types of outbreeding, each with its own strengths and limitations.

Crossbreeding: Crossbreeding is a method of outbreeding in which individuals from two different breeds or populations are mated. This method is used to produce offspring that have a combination of traits from both parents, and is commonly used in agriculture and animal husbandry to produce offspring with improved traits.

Hybrid Breeding: This involves mating animals from different species or subspecies to create a hybrid offspring with desired traits. This method is used to create animals with specific genetic traits that are not found in either parent species.

Hybrid Vigor: Hybrid vigor, also known as heterosis, is a phenomenon that occurs when offspring produced by outbreeding have improved fitness and performance compared to their parents. Hybrid vigor is thought to be a result of the combination of different alleles from the parent populations, which leads to a more diverse and adaptable genotype.

Advanced Breeding Methods

Definition of advanced breeding methods

Advanced breeding methods refer to the use of assisted reproductive technologies (ART) to manipulate the genetics of laboratory animals, including techniques such as in vitro fertilization, embryo transfer, and genetic modification. These methods are used to overcome specific breeding challenges, such as infertility or genetic disorders, and to improve the efficiency and precision of breeding programs.

While natural breeding methods rely on the natural reproductive process of animals, advanced breeding methods are designed to provide more control over the genetic makeup of the offspring. However, these methods also come with ethical considerations and may involve complex procedures that require specialized expertise and equipment.

Advantages and disadvantages of advanced breeding methods

Increased efficiency: Advanced breeding methods can produce a large number of offspring from a limited number of animals. This can reduce the number of animals needed for breeding and can save time and resources.

Increased control: Advanced breeding methods allow researchers to control the genetic makeup of the animals being bred. This can help to ensure that the animals have specific traits or characteristics needed for research purposes.

Increased precision: Advanced breeding methods can be used to create animals with precise genetic alterations, such as knockouts or transgenics. This can help to model specific human diseases and disorders, and can aid in the development of new treatments and therapies.

However, there are also some potential disadvantages to using advanced breeding methods in laboratory animal research, including:

Technical expertise: Advanced breeding methods may require specialized technical expertise, which can be costly and time-consuming to develop.

Cost: Advanced breeding methods may be more expensive than natural breeding methods, and may require specialized equipment or facilities.

Ethical considerations: Advanced breeding methods, such as genetic engineering, can raise ethical concerns about the welfare of the animals being bred, and about the potential risks and uncertainties associated with these technologies.

Classification of advanced breeding methods

Advanced breeding methods can be classified into several categories based on the specific techniques used. Some common categories include:

Genetic engineering methods: This involves the direct manipulation of an animal's genetic material to produce specific traits or characteristics. Techniques used include gene editing, gene transfer, and gene knockout.

Assisted reproductive technologies: This involves the use of techniques such as in vitro fertilization, embryo transfer, and gamete intrafallopian transfer to increase the efficiency of breeding programs.

Cloning and transgenesis: This involves the use of cloning and transgenesis technologies to produce genetically identical animals or to introduce new genetic material into an animal's genome.

Cryopreservation: This involves the freezing and long-term storage of genetic material, such as sperm or embryos, for future use in breeding programs.

Embryonic stem cell technologies: This involves the use of embryonic stem cells to generate new tissues or organs for transplantation, or to study disease processes.

Each of these categories includes specific methods and techniques that are used in laboratory animal research to produce animals with specific traits or to study disease processes.

Examples of commonly used advanced breeding methods in laboratory animal research

Examples of commonly used advanced breeding methods in laboratory animal research include:

In vitro fertilization (IVF): In this method, eggs are surgically removed from the female animal and fertilized with sperm in a laboratory. Once fertilized, the embryos are then implanted into the female's uterus.

Embryo transfer: In this method, embryos from a donor female animal are surgically removed and transferred to the uterus of a recipient female animal.

Transgenic animal production: Transgenic animals are genetically modified to carry specific genes that are of interest to researchers. This can be done through several methods, including gene editing techniques such as CRISPR-Cas9 or by introducing foreign DNA into the animal's genome.

Cloning: Cloning involves creating a genetic copy of an animal. This can be done by transferring the genetic material from a somatic cell of the donor animal into an egg cell from which the nucleus has been removed. The egg is then stimulated to divide and implanted into a surrogate mother.

Cryopreservation: This involves freezing and storing sperm, eggs, or embryos for future use in breeding or research. This method is useful for preserving the genetic material of valuable animals or for maintaining genetic diversity within a species.

Emerging Breeding Technologies

Examples of emerging breeding technologies that are currently being developed or tested in laboratory animal research include gene editing techniques such as CRISPR-Cas9, in vitro gametogenesis (IVG), and somatic cell nuclear transfer (SCNT)

These technologies are designed to enhance the efficiency, precision, and speed of breeding programs, while also improving animal welfare and reducing the need for animal experimentation.

One potential benefit of emerging breeding technologies is that they can help to reduce the number of animals needed for research. For example, some of these technologies can be used to select animals with specific traits or genetic markers, reducing the need for breeding large numbers of animals to obtain the desired traits. Some emerging technologies can reduce the time and resources needed for breeding, such as by increasing the speed of embryo development or enabling the production of multiple litters from a single female.

However, there are also potential drawbacks to these emerging technologies. For example, there may be ethical concerns around gene editing, particularly if it involves modifying traits that are not related to disease.Some of these technologies may be complex and require specialized equipment and expertise, which may limit their widespread adoption.

While emerging breeding technologies hold great promise for the field of laboratory animal research, it is important to carefully consider both the potential benefits and drawbacks of these methods before implementing them.

Choosing the appropriate breeding method

Choosing the appropriate breeding method is an important consideration in laboratory animal research. There are several factors to consider when selecting a breeding method, including the type of animal model, the research question being addressed, and the resources available. In addition, ethical considerations such as animal welfare and the potential for genetic variation must be taken into account.

When selecting a breeding method, it is important to consider the specific needs of the animal model being used. Some animal models may require more specialized breeding methods to maintain their genetic integrity and to ensure that they remain an accurate representation of the human disease or condition being studied.

The research question being addressed can also impact the choice of breeding method. For example, if the research question involves the study of a particular gene or mutation, it may be necessary to use a breeding method that facilitates the introduction of specific genetic modifications.

Ethical considerations must also be taken into account when selecting a breeding method. Animal welfare must always be a top priority, and efforts should be made to minimize any potential harm or distress caused to the animals during the breeding process. In addition, the potential for genetic variation and its impact on research outcomes should also be considered.

III

Regulations for Laboratory animals

The use of animals in scientific research, education, and testing has been a long-standing tradition in the scientific community. However, the ethical treatment of laboratory animals has become a growing concern in recent years, leading to the implementation of various regulations that aim to ensure the humane and ethical treatment of animals used in these settings. The purpose of these regulations is to balance the needs of scientific research with the welfare of animals, promote transparency and accountability in animal research, and ensure that ethical considerations are taken into account when conducting animal studies.

Laboratory animal regulations refer to the laws, guidelines, and ethical principles that govern the use of animals in scientific research. These regulations vary in coverage and provisions by country, but generally apply to all institutions that use animals in scientific research, testing, and education, and cover issues such as housing, feeding, veterinary care, and the use of alternatives to animal testing. Key provisions of the regulations may include requirements for proper housing, care, and treatment of animals, the use of humane methods of euthanasia, training for researchers and animal care staff, institutional animal care committees, reporting of animal welfare incidents, minimizing pain and distress in animals, and the provision of annual reports on the use of animals in research.

The evolution of animal testing in laboratory settings can be traced back to ancient times, but it was not until the latter half of the 20th century that animal welfare legislation and regulations were introduced to address concerns about the humane treatment of animals used in research. Over the years, the focus has shifted towards minimizing the suffering of animals and ensuring ethical and responsible conduct in animal research. However, the controversy surrounding the use of animals in scientific research continues to be a debated issue, with animal welfare advocates calling for alternative methods that do not involve live animals.

Laboratory animal regulations play a crucial role in ensuring the humane and ethical treatment of animals used in scientific research, testing, and education. These regulations aim to balance the needs of scientific research with the welfare of animals, promote transparency and accountability, and ensure that ethical considerations are taken into account when conducting animal studies. The evolution of animal testing in laboratory settings highlights the ongoing need for regulation and oversight to ensure the humane treatment of animals in these settings.

The development of animal welfare legislation and regulations has been a critical aspect of promoting the humane treatment of animals. The first animal welfare legislation was introduced in the United Kingdom in 1876, with the Cruelty to Animals Act. The act was followed by the Animal Welfare Act (AWA) in the United States in 1966, which established minimum standards of care for animals used in research. Over the years, several countries have introduced animal welfare legislation and regulations with a focus on ensuring the humane treatment of animals and promoting alternatives to animal testing.

The AWA is the primary federal law that regulates the treatment of animals in research, exhibitions, transport, and by dealers in the

United States. The act sets minimum standards for the care and treatment of animals, which includes proper housing, feeding, and veterinary care, protection from pain and distress, and minimizing animal suffering. The act also requires that research facilities be inspected at least once a year by the United States Department of Agriculture (USDA) to ensure compliance with the act's provisions.

The key provisions of the AWA include minimum standards of care, inspections, humane treatment of animals, license and registration, and enforcement. The minimum standards of care include provisions for temperature, humidity, lighting, and ventilation, as well as requirements for food, water, and waste disposal. The act requires facilities to be licensed or registered with the USDA and provides for enforcement through the imposition of penalties and fines for violations.

The development of animal welfare legislation and regulations has been an ongoing process aimed at improving the welfare of animals used in research and other purposes. The AWA is a crucial piece of legislation that provides important protections for animals used in research, exhibitions, transport, and by dealers. The act helps to ensure that these animals are treated humanely and with appropriate care, and serves as a model for other countries to follow in their efforts to promote animal welfare.

The Guide for the Care and Use of Laboratory Animals is a widely recognized and respected set of guidelines for the ethical treatment of animals used in scientific research, education, and testing. The guide was first published in 1963 by the National Academy of Sciences and is now in its eighth edition (2011). The purpose of the guide is to provide recommendations for the humane treatment of animals used in these settings and to ensure that they are treated with appropriate care.

The guide covers a range of topics, including housing and care, use of anesthesia and pain management, euthanasia, and ethical considerations. It requires that institutions establish an Institutional Animal Care and Use Committee (IACUC) to review and approve protocols and monitor the treatment of animals.

Good Laboratory Practice (GLP) regulations are another important resource for ensuring the quality and integrity of laboratory studies. These regulations apply to all non-clinical laboratory studies that support applications for research or marketing permits for products, such as drugs and chemicals. GLP regulations were first established by the US Food and Drug Administration (FDA) in 1978 and are now adopted by regulatory agencies around the world.

The key provisions of GLP regulations include the establishment of a quality assurance program, the creation of standard operating procedures (SOPs), personnel training, maintenance of complete and accurate study records, and preparation of a final study report. GLP regulations are designed to ensure that laboratory studies are conducted in a consistent, reliable, and reproducible manner and that the results are credible and can be relied upon by regulatory agencies.

Thus, both the Guide for the Care and Use of Laboratory Animals and Good Laboratory Practice (GLP) regulations play a critical role in ensuring that laboratory animals are treated humanely and with appropriate care, and that laboratory studies are conducted in a consistent and reliable manner. These guidelines and regulations are essential resources for researchers, educators, and institutions that use animals in their work, and they help to promote the ethical treatment of animals and the integrity of laboratory research.

In addition to these regulations, the Health Research Extension Act requires that institutions receiving federal funding for animal research establish an IACUC to oversee the treatment of animals used in research. The Public Health Service Policy on Humane Care and Use of Laboratory Animals further requires that institutions receiving federal funding for animal research comply with the Guide for the Care and Use of Laboratory Animals and adhere to specific standards for the treatment of laboratory animals.

Outside the United States, similar regulations have been established to ensure the ethical treatment of laboratory animals. For example, the European Convention for the Protection of

Vertebrate Animals Used for Experimental and Other Scientific Purposes, enforced by the Council of Europe, sets standards for the ethical treatment of laboratory animals in Europe. In Canada, the Canadian Council on Animal Care (CCAC) is responsible for setting and enforcing standards for the ethical treatment of animals used in research, teaching, and testing. Similarly, the Australian Code for the Care and Use of Animals for Scientific Purposes sets standards for the ethical treatment of laboratory animals in Australia.

The use of laboratory animals is subject to numerous regulations designed to ensure the ethical treatment of these animals. These regulations help to ensure that animals used in research, education, and testing are treated humanely and with appropriate care. While the regulations may vary slightly from country to country, they all share the common goal of promoting the responsible and ethical use of laboratory animals.

Indian regulations

The Prevention of Cruelty to Animals (PCA) Act, 1960, along with its subsequent amendments, governs the ethical treatment of laboratory animals in India. The Act provides for the prevention of cruelty to animals, including those used for scientific purposes. It requires the establishment of Animal Ethics Committees (AECs) in institutions conducting animal experimentation to oversee the treatment of laboratory animals and ensure that the ethical treatment of animals is upheld and that experiments are conducted in accordance with the guidelines set forth by the government. The PCA Act requires that animals used in scientific experimentation be provided with adequate care, housing, and feeding and that they are maintained in suitable conditions and not subjected to unnecessary suffering or injury.

CPCSEA Guidelines:

The Committee for the Purpose of Control and Supervision of Experiments on Animals (CPCSEA) is a statutory body established by the Government of India under the PCA Act. The CPCSEA is responsible for the administration and enforcement of the provisions of the PCA Act with respect to the use of animals in scientific experimentation. It is responsible for approving animal experiments, monitoring animal experimentation, promoting animal welfare, and educating the public about the ethical treatment of animals used in scientific experimentation.

The CPCSEA operates under the aegis of the Ministry of Social Justice and Empowerment and has the authority to inspect animal facilities, approve animal use protocols, and enforce animal welfare regulations.

The CPCSEA has developed a set of guidelines, known as the CPCSEA Guidelines, to provide guidance on the ethical use of animals in science. These guidelines set forth specific requirements for the care, housing, and management of laboratory animals, as well as the approval and conduct of experiments involving animals. The CPCSEA Guidelines encourage the use of alternatives to animal testing where available and appropriate and require that researchers consider non-animal alternatives before using animals in experiments. In addition, the CPCSEA Guidelines require that personnel involved in animal experimentation be trained in the ethical treatment of animals and be certified by the AEC.

India has robust regulations in place to ensure the ethical treatment of laboratory animals. The PCA Act and CPCSEA provide a comprehensive framework for the treatment of animals used in scientific experimentation, including the establishment of AECs, the care and management of laboratory animals, the permitting of animal experimentation, and the promotion of animal welfare. The CPCSEA Guidelines provide additional guidance and requirements for the ethical use of animals in science, including the use of alternatives to animal testing and the training and certification of personnel.

Guidelines for Animal Care and Management

Requirements of Animal Facility for Small Animal Housing as per CPCSEA

It is important to note that the CPCSEA (Committee for the Purpose of Control and Supervision of Experiments on Animals) has specific guidelines for the housing and care of animals used for scientific and experimental purposes. The design and operation of animal facilities must meet these standards in order to ensure the welfare of the animals and the validity of scientific results. It is the responsibility of facility

Introduction

The CPCSEA, or the Committee for the Purpose of Control and Supervision of Experiments on Animals, is a statutory body established by the government of India in order to regulate the use of animals in scientific and experimental procedures.

Importance of CPCSEA in Animal Welfare

The CPCSEA plays a crucial role in ensuring the welfare of animals used in scientific and experimental procedures. Through its regulations and oversight, the CPCSEA helps to prevent animal suffering, promote the ethical use of animals in research, and advance the scientific validity of results obtained from animal studies. The CPCSEA's efforts to promote animal welfare are guided by the principles of the "3 Rs": Replacement, Reduction, and Refinement. This means that alternatives to the use of animals should be pursued where possible, the number of animals used should be minimized, and the procedures performed on animals should be refined to minimize

Design and Layout of Animal Facility

Physical Space Requirements

The physical space requirements for a small animal housing facility must be designed to meet the specific needs of the animals being housed. This includes adequate space for movement, resting, and socialization. It is important to ensure that the animal housing units are well-ventilated, free from overcrowding and provide a clean and safe environment.

Lighting and Ventilation Requirements

Proper lighting is essential for the well-being of animals in a small animal housing facility. Adequate natural or artificial light should be provided to support the animals' circadian rhythm and prevent stress. The lighting should be regulated to provide a consistent light-dark cycle.

Ventilation is also critical to maintain the health and welfare of the animals. Adequate ventilation should be provided to ensure the exchange of fresh air, prevent the buildup of toxic gases and reduce the risk of infection. The ventilation system should be designed to minimize noise and prevent drafts.

Equipment and Furniture Requirements

The equipment and furniture used in a small animal housing facility should be safe, durable, and appropriate for the species being housed. This includes items such as cages, bedding, feeders, and water bottles. The cages should be designed to provide adequate space for the animals to move, rest and perform natural behaviors. It is important to ensure that all equipment and furniture is regularly cleaned and maintained to prevent the spread of disease.

Staff and Training

Qualifications and Duties of Animal Care Staff

The qualifications and duties of animal care staff in a small animal housing facility are critical to the health and welfare of the animals. Staff should be knowledgeable in animal biology, behavior, and husbandry practices. Additionally, they should be trained in the safe handling and care of the animals, as well as the proper use of equipment and facilities. It is important that staff is familiar with local and national regulations and guidelines, including CPCSEA regulations.

Importance of Regular Training and Education Regular training and education of animal care staff is essential to maintain high standards of animal welfare and ensure compliance with CPCSEA regulations. This includes training in the recognition of signs of illness and stress in animals, as well as the proper administration of veterinary care. Ongoing training and education helps to keep staff up-to-date on the latest research and advancements in animal care, and helps to maintain a high level of expertise among staff. In addition, regular training and education helps to ensure that all staff members are following consistent procedures and protocols, leading to improved animal welfare and reduced risk of errors or accidents.

Animal Care and Management

Feeding and Water Requirements

The feeding and water requirements for the animals in a small animal housing facility are crucial for their health and welfare. A balanced and nutritious diet should be provided to meet the specific nutritional needs of the species being housed. Feed and water should be available in a clean and easily accessible manner at all times, and the food and water containers should be regularly cleaned and disinfected to prevent contamination.

Sanitation and Hygiene Requirements

Sanitation and hygiene are important factors in maintaining the health of the animals in a small animal housing facility. This includes regular cleaning and disinfecting of the animal housing units, equipment, and facilities, as well as proper waste management practices. Personal hygiene is also important, and staff should follow appropriate infection control procedures to reduce the risk of disease transmission.

Health Monitoring and Veterinary Care

Regular health monitoring of the animals in a small animal housing facility is essential to detect and address any health issues in a timely manner. This includes routine physical examinations, monitoring for signs of illness or stress, and regular veterinary check-ups. The facility should have a designated veterinarian who is responsible for providing veterinary care and overseeing the health of the animals. Any medical treatments or procedures should be performed by a qualified veterinarian or veterinary technician, and all animals should be treated with compassion and respect.

Record Keeping

Importance of Maintaining Accurate Records

Accurate record keeping is essential in a small animal housing facility to ensure the health and welfare of the animals, as well as to meet regulatory requirements. This includes tracking the animals' health status, feed and water consumption, and veterinary treatments. Records should be kept on all aspects of animal care, including housing conditions, feeding and watering schedules, and veterinary treatments.

Types of Records to be Kept

- Animal identification and census records
- Health records, including veterinary treatments and vaccination histories
- Feed and water consumption records
- Environmental conditions, such as temperature and humidity
- Sanitation and cleaning records
- Training records for staff

Mortality and disposal records Accurate and comprehensive record keeping helps to ensure the health and welfare of the animals, supports scientific research, and assists with regulatory compliance.

Guidelines for Animal Research and Teaching Activities

Animal research and teaching activities have been an integral part of scientific advancement for centuries. However, the ethical treatment of animals in research and teaching settings has been a topic of concern for many years. In order to ensure that animals are treated humanely and ethically, it is important to follow established guidelines for animal research and teaching activities. One such set of guidelines is provided by the Committee for the Purpose of Control and Supervision of Experiments on Animals (CPCSEA), which is a statutory body established under the Ministry of Environment, Forest and Climate Change, Government of India.

The CPCSEA is responsible for overseeing the use of animals in research and teaching activities in India. The CPCSEA regulations are designed to ensure that animals are used ethically, responsibly and with respect for their welfare. The guidelines provide detailed information on the use of animals in research, including the types of animal experiments that are acceptable, the procedures that must be followed and the conditions that must be met. These guidelines are based on the principle of minimizing animal suffering and ensuring that animals are used only when there is no alternative.

One of the key aspects of the CPCSEA guidelines is the requirement for prior approval from an Institutional Animal Ethics Committee (IAEC) before any animal research or teaching activity can take place. The IAEC is a group of experts from various fields, including animal welfare, veterinary medicine and science, who are responsible for reviewing animal research proposals and monitoring ongoing animal research studies. The IAEC is also responsible for ensuring that animal research is conducted in accordance with CPCSEA regulations and guidelines.

The CPCSEA guidelines also emphasize the importance of following the 3Rs principle of animal research: Replacement, Reduction and Refinement. This principle emphasizes the need to replace the use of animals with alternative methods where possible, to reduce the number of animals used in research and to refine the methods used to minimize animal suffering. The CPCSEA guidelines also provide detailed information on the physical and environmental conditions that must be met for the housing and care of animals in research and teaching settings.

In addition, the CPCSEA guidelines emphasize the importance of training and education for animal care staff and researchers. Animal care staff must be trained in the proper techniques for handling and caring for animals and must be knowledgeable about the CPCSEA regulations and guidelines. Researchers must also be trained in the ethical and responsible use of animals in research and must be aware of the CPCSEA regulations and guidelines.

The CPCSEA guidelines are essential for ensuring that animal research and teaching activities are conducted ethically and responsibly. The guidelines provide clear and detailed information on the use of animals in research, including the types of animal experiments that are acceptable, the procedures that must be followed and the conditions that must be met. By following these guidelines, we can ensure that animal welfare is protected and that the validity and reliability of research results are not compromised.

In conclusion, the CPCSEA guidelines for animal research and teaching activities provide an important framework for ensuring the ethical treatment of animals in research and teaching settings. By following these guidelines, we can ensure that animals are used ethically, responsibly and with respect for their welfare, and that animal research and teaching activities are conducted in a manner that is consistent with the principles of minimizing animal suffering and ensuring animal welfare.InstituionalAnimalEthics Committee

Institutional Animal Ethics Committee (IAEC)

An Institutional Animal Ethics Committee (IAEC) is a committee that is established to oversee the ethical aspects of animal research and teaching activities within a specific institution. The IAEC is responsible for ensuring that animal research is conducted in a humane and ethical manner, in accordance with national and international animal welfare regulations.

Importance of IAEC in Animal Welfare

The establishment of an IAEC is crucial in promoting the welfare of animals used in research and teaching activities. The IAEC is responsible for reviewing animal research proposals, monitoring ongoing animal research studies, and ensuring that appropriate animal care and management practices are in place. This helps to ensure that animals are used in a manner that is both ethical and responsible, and that their welfare is protected at all times.

Overview of the Role and Responsibilities of IAEC

- Reviewing and approving animal research proposals
- Monitoring the conduct of ongoing animal research studies
- Ensuring that animal care and management practices are in compliance with national and international animal welfare regulations
- Reviewing and updating ethical policies and guidelines for animal research
- Promoting the welfare of animals used in research and teaching activities
- Advising researchers and institutions on ethical and responsible animal research practices. IAECs play a vital role in promoting animal welfare and ensuring ethical and responsible animal research practices. By fulfilling these responsibilities, IAECs help to ensure that animal research is conducted in a manner that is both scientifically rigorous and ethically sound.

Composition of IAEC

Membership Criteria

The membership of an IAEC should include individuals with diverse backgrounds and expertise, including scientists, veterinarians, animal welfare experts, ethicists, and representatives from the general public. This diversity of perspectives and expertise helps to ensure that the IAEC is well-equipped to review animal research proposals and monitor ongoing studies from a variety of angles.

Roles and Responsibilities of IAEC Members

IAEC members are responsible for reviewing animal research proposals, monitoring ongoing animal research studies, and ensuring that appropriate animal care and management practices are in place. They may also provide advice to researchers and institutions on ethical and responsible animal research practices, and review and update ethical policies and guidelines for animal research.

Frequency of IAEC Meetings

The frequency of IAEC meetings will depend on the volume of animal research proposals being reviewed, as well as the level of monitoring required for ongoing animal research studies. Typically, IAECs meet on a regular basis, such as once a month or every quarter, to review animal research proposals and monitor ongoing studies. These meetings provide an opportunity for IAEC members to discuss and make decisions regarding the use of animals in research and teaching activities.

Functions of IAEC

Review of Animal Research Proposals

One of the primary functions of the IAEC is to review animal research proposals. This involves evaluating the scientific merit and ethical considerations of the proposed study, and ensuring that the study design and methods will result in minimal harm to the animals used. The IAEC may also provide advice to researchers on how to improve the study design or methods to reduce harm to animals.

Monitoring of Ongoing Animal Research Studies

Another important function of the IAEC is to monitor ongoing animal research studies. This involves regularly reviewing the study protocols, conducting site visits to the animal facilities, and evaluating the care and management of animals. The IAEC may also make recommendations for improvements to the study design or methods, or for changes to the animal care and management practices, in order to minimize harm to the animals used.

Oversight of Animal Care and Management Practices

The IAEC also has a responsibility to ensure that animal care and management practices are in compliance with national and international animal welfare regulations. This may involve reviewing animal care policies and procedures, conducting regular evaluations of the animal facilities, and ensuring that appropriate training and education programs are in place for animal care staff. The IAEC may also make recommendations for changes to animal care and management practices in order to improve animal welfare.

The functions of the IAEC are to review animal research proposals, monitor ongoing animal research studies, and oversee animal care and management practices. Through these functions, the IAEC plays a critical role in promoting animal welfare and ensuring ethical and responsible animal research practices.

Approval Process for Animal Research Studies

Review Criteria for Animal Research Proposals

The IAEC uses specific criteria to review animal research proposals, which may include the scientific merit and ethical considerations of the study design and methods. The IAEC may also evaluate the potential impact of the study on the animals used, including the severity of any harm that may be inflicted, and the measures in place to minimize harm. The IAEC may also consider the benefits of the study, including the potential for advancing knowledge and improving human and animal health.

Importance of Considering Alternatives to the Use of Animals

The IAEC recognizes the importance of considering alternatives to the use of animals in research and teaching activities. This may include the use of in vitro methods, computer models, and other non-animal techniques that can replace, reduce, or refine the use of animals in research. The IAEC may also require researchers to provide a detailed evaluation of alternative methods, and to demonstrate why the use of animals is necessary for their study.

Consideration of the 3Rs in Animal Research

The IAEC also considers the principles of the 3Rs (Replacement, Reduction, and Refinement) in its review of animal research proposals. The 3Rs are a framework for promoting ethical and responsible animal research practices, and encourage researchers to consider alternative methods, reduce the number of animals used, and refine the methods used in order to minimize harm to animals. The IAEC may require researchers to demonstrate how they have applied the 3Rs in their study design and methods, and to provide evidence of their efforts to minimize harm to animals.

In conclusion, the approval process for animal research studies involves a comprehensive evaluation of the scientific merit, ethical considerations, and potential impact on the animals used. The IAEC recognizes the importance of considering alternatives to the use of animals, and of applying the principles of the 3Rs in order to promote ethical and responsible animal research practices.

Ethical Considerations in Animal Research

Consideration of the Welfare of the Animals

The IAEC recognizes the importance of ensuring the welfare of animals used in research and teaching activities. This includes ensuring that animals are housed in appropriate facilities, are provided with adequate food and water, and receive appropriate veterinary care. The IAEC may also consider the social and environmental needs of the animals, and may require researchers to provide detailed information about their housing and management practices.

Importance of Minimizing Animal Suffering

The IAEC also places a strong emphasis on minimizing animal suffering in research and teaching activities. This may include evaluating the severity of any harm that may be inflicted on the animals, and the measures in place to minimize harm. The IAEC may also require researchers to provide evidence of their efforts to minimize animal suffering, and to demonstrate their knowledge of pain and distress management techniques.

Compliance with National and International Animal Welfare Regulations

The IAEC is committed to ensuring that animal research and teaching activities are conducted in compliance with national and international animal welfare regulations. This may include ensuring that researchers comply with the guidelines of the CPCSEA, the Animals (Scientific Procedures) Act 1986 (UK), the European Convention for the Protection of Vertebrate Animals Used for Experimental and Other Scientific Purposes, and other relevant regulations. The IAEC may also require researchers to provide evidence of their compliance with these regulations, and to demonstrate their commitment to animal welfare.

In conclusion, the IAEC recognizes the importance of ethical considerations in animal research and teaching activities. This includes ensuring the welfare of the animals, minimizing animal suffering, and compliance with national and international animal welfare regulations. The IAEC is committed to promoting ethical and responsible animal research practices, and to ensuring that animal research and teaching activities are conducted in a manner that protects the welfare of the animals used.

IV

The Committee for the Purpose of Control and Supervision of Experiments on Animals (CPCSEA)

Note: In a letter dated January 6, 2023, the Member Secretary of CPCSEA announced that the Committee for the Purpose of Control and Supervision of Experiments on Animals (CPCSEA) will henceforth be referred to as the Committee for Control and Supervision of Experiments on Animals (CCSEA).Hence readers must note this change.

The Committee for the Purpose of Control and Supervision of Experiments on Animals (CPCSEA) is a statutory body established by the Government of India under the PCA Act. The CPCSEA is responsible for the administration and enforcement of the provisions of the PCA Act with respect to the use of animals in scientific experimentation. It is responsible for approving animal experiments, monitoring animal experimentation, promoting animal welfare, and educating the public about the ethical treatment of animals used in scientific experimentation.

The CPCSEA operates under the aegis of the Ministry of Social Justice and Empowerment and has the authority to inspect animal facilities, approve animal use protocols, and enforce animal welfare regulations.

The CPCSEA has developed a set of guidelines, known as the CPCSEA Guidelines, to provide guidance on the ethical use of animals in science. These guidelines set forth specific requirements for the care, housing, and management of laboratory animals, as well as the approval and conduct of experiments involving animals. The CPCSEA Guidelines encourage the use of alternatives to animal testing where available and appropriate and require that researchers consider non-animal alternatives before using animals in experiments. In addition, the CPCSEA Guidelines require that personnel involved in animal experimentation be trained in the ethical treatment of animals and be certified by the AEC.

India has robust regulations in place to ensure the ethical treatment of laboratory animals. The PCA Act and CPCSEA provide a comprehensive framework for the treatment of animals used in scientific experimentation, including the establishment of AECs, the care and management of laboratory animals, the permitting of animal experimentation, and the promotion of animal welfare. The CPCSEA Guidelines provide additional guidance and requirements for the ethical use of animals in science, including the use of alternatives to animal testing and the training and certification of personnel.

Guidelines for Animal Care and Management

Requirements of Animal Facility for Small Animal Housing as per CPCSEA

It is important to note that the CPCSEA (Committee for the Purpose of Control and Supervision of Experiments on Animals) has specific guidelines for the housing and care of animals used for scientific and experimental purposes. The design and operation of animal facilities must meet these standards in order to ensure the welfare of the animals and the validity of scientific results. It is the responsibility of facility

Introduction

The CPCSEA, or the Committee for the Purpose of Control and Supervision of Experiments on Animals, is a statutory body established by the government of India in order to regulate the use of animals in scientific and experimental procedures.

Importance of CPCSEA in Animal Welfare

The CPCSEA plays a crucial role in ensuring the welfare of animals used in scientific and experimental procedures. Through its regulations and oversight, the CPCSEA helps to prevent animal suffering, promote the ethical use of animals in research, and advance the scientific validity of results obtained from animal studies. The CPCSEA's efforts to promote animal welfare are guided by the principles of the "3 Rs": Replacement, Reduction, and Refinement. This means that alternatives to the use of animals should be pursued where possible, the number of animals used should be minimized, and the procedures performed on animals should be refined to minimize

Design and Layout of Animal Facility

Physical Space Requirements

The physical space requirements for a small animal housing facility must be designed to meet the specific needs of the animals being housed. This includes adequate space for movement, resting, and socialization. It is important to ensure that the animal housing units are well-ventilated, free from overcrowding and provide a clean and safe environment.

Lighting and Ventilation Requirements

Proper lighting is essential for the well-being of animals in a small animal housing facility. Adequate natural or artificial light should be provided to support the animals' circadian rhythm and prevent stress. The lighting should be regulated to provide a consistent light-dark cycle.

Ventilation is also critical to maintain the health and welfare of the animals. Adequate ventilation should be provided to ensure the exchange of fresh air, prevent the buildup of toxic gases and reduce the risk of infection. The ventilation system should be designed to minimize noise and prevent drafts.

Equipment and Furniture Requirements

The equipment and furniture used in a small animal housing facility should be safe, durable, and appropriate for the species being housed. This includes items such as cages, bedding, feeders, and water bottles. The cages should be designed to provide adequate space for the animals to move, rest and perform natural behaviors. It is important to ensure that all equipment and furniture is regularly cleaned and maintained to prevent the spread of disease.

Staff and Training

Qualifications and Duties of Animal Care Staff

The qualifications and duties of animal care staff in a small animal housing facility are critical to the health and welfare of the animals. Staff should be knowledgeable in animal biology, behavior, and husbandry practices. Additionally, they should be trained in the safe handling and care of the animals, as well as the proper use of equipment and facilities. It is important that staff is familiar with local and national regulations and guidelines, including CPCSEA regulations.

Importance of Regular Training and Education Regular training and education of animal care staff is essential to maintain high standards of animal welfare and ensure compliance with CPCSEA regulations. This includes training in the recognition of signs of illness and stress in animals, as well as the proper administration of veterinary care. Ongoing training and education helps to keep staff up-to-date on the latest research and advancements in animal care, and helps to maintain a high level of expertise among staff. In addition, regular training and education helps to ensure that all staff members are following consistent procedures and protocols, leading to improved animal welfare and reduced risk of errors or accidents.

Animal Care and Management

Feeding and Water Requirements

The feeding and water requirements for the animals in a small animal housing facility are crucial for their health and welfare. A balanced and nutritious diet should be provided to meet the specific nutritional needs of the species being housed. Feed and water should be available in a clean and easily accessible manner at all times, and the food and water containers should be regularly cleaned and disinfected to prevent contamination.

Sanitation and Hygiene Requirements

Sanitation and hygiene are important factors in maintaining the health of the animals in a small animal housing facility. This includes regular cleaning and disinfecting of the animal housing units, equipment, and facilities, as well as proper waste management practices. Personal hygiene is also important, and staff should follow appropriate infection control procedures to reduce the risk of disease transmission.

Health Monitoring and Veterinary Care

Regular health monitoring of the animals in a small animal housing facility is essential to detect and address any health issues in a timely manner. This includes routine physical examinations, monitoring for signs of illness or stress, and regular veterinary check-ups. The facility should have a designated veterinarian who is responsible for providing veterinary care and overseeing the health of the animals. Any medical treatments or procedures should be performed by a qualified veterinarian or veterinary technician, and all animals should be treated with compassion and respect.

Record Keeping

Importance of Maintaining Accurate Records

Accurate record keeping is essential in a small animal housing facility to ensure the health and welfare of the animals, as well as to meet regulatory requirements. This includes tracking the animals' health status, feed and water consumption, and veterinary treatments. Records should be kept on all aspects of animal care, including housing conditions, feeding and watering schedules, and veterinary treatments.

Types of Records to be Kept The types of records that should be kept in a small animal housing facility

Animal identification and census records

Health records, including veterinary treatments and vaccination histories

Feed and water consumption records

Environmental conditions, such as temperature and humidity

Sanitation and cleaning records

Training records for staff

Mortality and disposal records Accurate and comprehensive record keeping helps to ensure the health and welfare of the animals, supports scientific research, and assists with regulatory compliance.

Guidelines for Animal Research and Teaching Activities

Animal research and teaching activities have been an integral part of scientific advancement for centuries. However, the ethical treatment of animals in research and teaching settings has been a topic of concern for many years. In order to ensure that animals are treated humanely and ethically, it is important to follow established guidelines for animal research and teaching activities. One such set of guidelines is provided by the Committee for the Purpose of Control and Supervision of Experiments on Animals (CPCSEA), which is a statutory body established under the Ministry of Environment, Forest and Climate Change, Government of India.

The CPCSEA is responsible for overseeing the use of animals in research and teaching activities in India. The CPCSEA regulations are designed to ensure that animals are used ethically, responsibly and with respect for their welfare. The guidelines provide detailed information on the use of animals in research, including the types of animal experiments that are acceptable, the procedures that must be followed and the conditions that must be met. These guidelines are based on the principle of minimizing animal suffering and ensuring that animals are used only when there is no alternative.

One of the key aspects of the CPCSEA guidelines is the requirement for prior approval from an Institutional Animal Ethics Committee (IAEC) before any animal research or teaching activity can take place. The IAEC is a group of experts from various fields, including animal welfare, veterinary medicine and science, who are responsible for reviewing animal research proposals and monitoring ongoing animal research studies. The IAEC is also responsible for ensuring that animal research is conducted in accordance with CPCSEA regulations and guidelines.

The CPCSEA guidelines also emphasize the importance of following the 3Rs principle of animal research: Replacement, Reduction and Refinement. This principle emphasizes the need to replace the use of animals with alternative methods where possible, to reduce the number of animals used in research and to refine the methods used to minimize animal suffering. The CPCSEA guidelines also provide detailed information on the physical and environmental conditions that must be met for the housing and care of animals in research and teaching settings.

In addition, the CPCSEA guidelines emphasize the importance of training and education for animal care staff and researchers. Animal care staff must be trained in the proper techniques for handling and caring for animals and must be knowledgeable about the CPCSEA regulations and guidelines. Researchers must also be trained in the ethical and responsible use of animals in research and must be aware of the CPCSEA regulations and guidelines.

The CPCSEA guidelines are essential for ensuring that animal research and teaching activities are conducted ethically and responsibly. The guidelines provide clear and detailed information on the use of animals in research, including the types of animal experiments that are acceptable, the procedures that must be followed and the conditions that must be met. By following these guidelines, we can ensure that animal welfare is protected and that the validity and reliability of research results are not compromised.

In conclusion, the CPCSEA guidelines for animal research and teaching activities provide an important framework for ensuring the ethical treatment of animals in research and teaching settings. By following these guidelines, we can ensure that animals are used ethically, responsibly and with respect for their welfare, and that animal research and teaching activities are conducted in a manner that is consistent with the principles of minimizing animal suffering and ensuring animal welfare.InstituionalAnimalEthics Committee

V

Institutional Animal Ethics Committee

An Institutional Animal Ethics Committee (IAEC) is a committee that is established to oversee the ethical aspects of animal research and teaching activities within a specific institution. The IAEC is responsible for ensuring that animal research is conducted in a humane and ethical manner, in accordance with national and international animal welfare regulations.

Importance of IAEC in Animal Welfare

The establishment of an IAEC is crucial in promoting the welfare of animals used in research and teaching activities. The IAEC is responsible for reviewing animal research proposals, monitoring ongoing animal research studies, and ensuring that appropriate animal care and management practices are in place. This helps to ensure that animals are used in a manner that is both ethical and responsible, and that their welfare is protected at all times.

Role and Responsibilities of IAEC

1. Reviewing and approving animal research proposals

2. Monitoring the conduct of ongoing animal research studies
3. Ensuring that animal care and management practices are in compliance with national and international animal welfare regulations
4. Reviewing and updating ethical policies and guidelines for animal research
5. Promoting the welfare of animals used in research and teaching activities
6. Advising researchers and institutions on ethical and responsible animal research practices
7. IAECs play a vital role in promoting animal welfare and ensuring ethical and responsible animal research practices.

By fulfilling these responsibilities, IAECs help to ensure that animal research is conducted in a manner that is both scientifically rigorous and ethically sound.

Composition of IAEC

Membership Criteria

The membership of an IAEC should include individuals with diverse backgrounds and expertise, including scientists, veterinarians, animal welfare experts, ethicists, and representatives from the general public. This diversity of perspectives and expertise helps to ensure that the IAEC is well-equipped to review animal research proposals and monitor ongoing studies from a variety of angles.

Roles and Responsibilities of IAEC Members

IAEC members are responsible for reviewing animal research proposals, monitoring ongoing animal research studies, and ensuring that appropriate animal care and management practices are in place. They may also provide advice to researchers and institutions on ethical and responsible animal research practices, and review and update ethical policies and guidelines for animal research.

Frequency of IAEC Meetings

The frequency of IAEC meetings will depend on the volume of animal research proposals being reviewed, as well as the level of monitoring required for ongoing animal research studies. Typically, IAECs meet on a regular basis, such as once a month or every quarter, to review animal research proposals and monitor ongoing studies. These meetings provide an opportunity for IAEC members to discuss and make decisions regarding the use of animals in research and teaching activities.

Functions of IAEC

Review of Animal Research Proposals

One of the primary functions of the IAEC is to review animal research proposals. This involves evaluating the scientific merit and ethical considerations of the proposed study, and ensuring that the study design and methods will result in minimal harm to the animals used. The IAEC may also provide advice to researchers on how to improve the study design or methods to reduce harm to animals.

Monitoring of Ongoing Animal Research Studies

Another important function of the IAEC is to monitor ongoing animal research studies. This involves regularly reviewing the study protocols, conducting site visits to the animal facilities, and evaluating the care and management of animals. The IAEC may also make recommendations for improvements to the study design or methods, or for changes to the animal care and management practices, in order to minimize harm to the animals used.

Oversight of Animal Care and Management Practices

The IAEC also has a responsibility to ensure that animal care and management practices are in compliance with national and international animal welfare regulations. This may involve reviewing animal care policies and procedures, conducting regular evaluations of the animal facilities, and ensuring that appropriate training and education programs are in place for animal care staff. The IAEC may also make recommendations for changes to animal care and management practices in order to improve animal welfare.

The functions of the IAEC are to review animal research proposals, monitor ongoing animal research studies, and oversee animal care and management practices. Through these functions, the IAEC plays a critical role in promoting animal welfare and ensuring ethical and responsible animal research practices.

Approval Process for Animal Research Studies

Review Criteria for Animal Research Proposals

The IAEC uses specific criteria to review animal research proposals, which may include the scientific merit and ethical considerations of the study design and methods. The IAEC may also evaluate the potential impact of the study on the animals used, including the severity of any harm that may be inflicted, and the measures in place to minimize harm. The IAEC may also consider the benefits of the study, including the potential for advancing knowledge and improving human and animal health.

Importance of Considering Alternatives to the Use of Animals

The IAEC recognizes the importance of considering alternatives to the use of animals in research and teaching activities. This may include the use of in vitro methods, computer models, and other non-animal techniques that can replace, reduce, or refine the use of animals in research. The IAEC may also require researchers to provide a detailed evaluation of alternative methods, and to demonstrate why the use of animals is necessary for their study.

Consideration of the 3Rs in Animal Research

The IAEC also considers the principles of the 3Rs (Replacement, Reduction, and Refinement) in its review of animal research proposals. The 3Rs are a framework for promoting ethical and responsible animal research practices, and encourage researchers to consider alternative methods, reduce the number of animals used, and refine the methods used in order to minimize harm to animals. The IAEC may require researchers to demonstrate how they have applied the 3Rs in their study design and methods, and to provide evidence of their efforts to minimize harm to animals.

In conclusion, the approval process for animal research studies involves a comprehensive evaluation of the scientific merit, ethical considerations, and potential impact on the animals used. The IAEC recognizes the importance of considering alternatives to the use of animals, and of applying the principles of the 3Rs in order to promote ethical and responsible animal research practices.

Ethical Considerations in Animal Research

Consideration of the Welfare of the Animals

The IAEC recognizes the importance of ensuring the welfare of animals used in research and teaching activities. This includes ensuring that animals are housed in appropriate facilities, are provided with adequate food and water, and receive appropriate veterinary care. The IAEC may also consider the social and environmental needs of the animals, and may require researchers to provide detailed information about their housing and management practices.

Importance of Minimizing Animal Suffering

The IAEC also places a strong emphasis on minimizing animal suffering in research and teaching activities. This may include evaluating the severity of any harm that may be inflicted on the animals, and the measures in place to minimize harm. The IAEC may also require researchers to provide evidence of their efforts to minimize animal suffering, and to demonstrate their knowledge of pain and distress management techniques.

VI
Alternative to animal studies

Animal studies have been an essential part of scientific research for many years, and they have contributed significantly to the advancement of scientific knowledge. However, with the advancement of technology, there has been an increasing need to find alternative methods that are more humane, efficient, and cost-effective.

The use of animals in research can be traced back to the early days of scientific discovery, and it has been used to study a wide range of topics, including biology, medicine, and psychology. Despite the valuable contributions of animal studies to scientific knowledge, there are many ethical concerns associated with the use of animals in research. Animal studies are often associated with pain, suffering, and death, which raises ethical questions about the use of animals for scientific purposes.

Furthermore, there are many scientific limitations associated with the use of animals in research. For instance, animals often do not accurately represent human biology, and the results obtained from animal studies do not always translate to humans. As such, there is a growing need to find alternative methods that are more efficient, accurate, and humane.

There are several alternative methods to animal studies that can provide a more efficient, cost-effective, and humane approach to scientific research.

Invitro methods
computer simulations and modeling
Organoids and tissue engineering
Imaging and post-mortem studies
Microdosing and human studies
Epidemiological studies
3 R Principles

Issues with Animal Studies

Animal studies are often associated with ethical concerns. Many people believe that using animals in research is unethical and that it is wrong to cause pain, suffering, and death to animals in the name of science. Furthermore, animals used in research may be subjected to stressful and unnatural living conditions that further contribute to their suffering. Animal welfare advocates argue that animals have the right to be treated with respect and dignity and that using them in research violates their rights.

There are scientific limitations associated with the use of animals in research. One of the key criticisms is that animals often do not accurately represent human biology, and the results obtained from animal studies do not always translate to humans. For example, studies on drugs or diseases may show promising results in animals but fail to work in humans. As a result, some critics argue that animal studies may be misleading and do not provide accurate information about human biology.

There are economic and practical issues associated with animal studies. Animal studies can be costly and time-consuming, and they may not always provide the most efficient use of resources. Furthermore, alternative methods to animal studies, such as in vitro methods and computer simulations, are often more cost-effective and efficient.

Types of Alternatives to Animal Studies:

In vitro methods

In vitro methods are alternative methods that make use of cells, tissues or organs in a controlled laboratory environment, outside of a live animal. This type of alternative is gaining popularity due to advancements in technology, which has allowed the creation of more sophisticated and accurate models in the laboratory. Examples of in vitro methods are cell culture, organ-on-a-chip, and microfluidic systems. In vitro methods offer several advantages over animal studies, such as greater control over environmental conditions, the ability to conduct large-scale screenings and experiments, and reduced ethical and welfare concerns. However, there are also limitations to in vitro methods, such as the absence of a complete and accurate representation of in vivo processes and the difficulty in extrapolating results from in vitro studies to the whole animal.

Computer simulations and mathematical models

Computer simulations and mathematical models are alternatives to animal studies that utilize computer software and mathematical equations to model biological processes and simulate the effects of interventions. This method allows researchers to study complex biological systems and predict the outcomes of treatments without the use of live animals. However, there are also limitations to these methods, such as the need for accurate and complete data on biological processes, the limitations of current technology, and the difficulty in extrapolating results from simulations to real-life situations.

Microdosing studies

Microdosing studies are alternatives to animal studies that involve the administration of very small amounts of a substance to human volunteers to gather early safety and pharmacokinetic data. This method provides relevant data for human use and reduces ethical and welfare concerns associated with animal studies.

Human studies: Human studies, such as clinical trials, epidemiological studies, and observational studies, involve human volunteers and provide an alternative to animal studies by gathering data directly from human subjects. These methods have the advantage of providing data that is directly relevant to human biology and disease processes. However, there are also limitations to human studies, such as the need for large numbers of volunteers, the difficulties in controlling extraneous variables, and the ethical and legal considerations associated with human subjects research.

High-throughput screening: High-throughput screening involves the use of automated systems to screen large numbers of compounds or treatments for potential efficacy and toxicity. This method allows for efficient testing and reduces the use of live animals in scientific research.

Organoids and Tissue Engineering:

Organoids are three-dimensional (3D) structures that are generated from stem cells and designed to mimic the structure and function of specific organs. Organoids offer a unique opportunity to study disease development, drug responses, and toxicology in a human context. Furthermore, organoids can be used for personalized medicine, where a patient's own cells can be used to generate organoids for disease modeling and drug testing.

Tissue engineering is a field of research that involves the creation of artificial tissues and organs through the use of scaffolds, cells, and biologically active molecules. Tissue engineering offers a promising solution for organ transplantation, as it provides an opportunity to create functional tissues and organs that can be transplanted into patients without the need for immunosuppression.

Imaging and post-mortem studies

Imaging and post-mortem studies are alternatives to animal studies that involve the use of imaging technologies and post-mortem examinations to study human anatomy and disease processes. These methods provide a deeper understanding of human anatomy, disease progression, and treatment outcomes, without the use of live animals. Imaging technologies, such as MRI and CT scans, provide non-invasive images of the human body. Post-mortem studies involve the examination of human tissues and organs after death and provide valuable information about anatomy, disease progression, and treatment outcomes. However, there are also limitations to these methods, such as the need for adequate numbers of human subjects and the difficulties in extrapolating results from these studies to thegeneral population, and the potential ethical concerns regarding the manipulation of variables in these studies.

Epidemiological studies

Epidemiological studies are an alternative to animal studies because they provide a way to study disease in human populations without using animals. In the past, animal studies were used to identify risk factors and potential causes of disease, but it has become increasingly clear that animal studies do not always provide accurate information about human biology. In contrast, epidemiological studies directly investigate human populations and can provide more accurate information about the distribution and causes of diseases in humans.

Epidemiological studies are essential for identifying the risk factors associated with disease development and progression. This information is critical for developing effective prevention and treatment strategies for human diseases. By identifying the risk factors associated with disease, epidemiological studies can help guide public health policies and interventions that promote the health and well-being of human populations.

Epidemiological studies are a valuable tool for understanding disease in human populations and provide an alternative to animal studies. By using epidemiological studies, researchers can gain a better understanding of disease development and progression in humans, without the ethical concerns and scientific limitations associated with animal studies.

Replacement, Reduction, Refinement (3Rs) Principles:

The 3Rs principles were developed to promote the ethical and humane use of animals in research. These principles encourage researchers to use alternatives to animal studies when possible, and to minimize the number of animals used in research. In this lecture, we will discuss the 3Rs principles and their importance in animal research.

Replacement:

The replacement principle of the 3Rs encourages researchers to use non-animal methods when possible. This can include the use of cell cultures, computer models, and other in vitro methods. By using non-animal methods, researchers can reduce the number of animals used in research and minimize the ethical concerns associated with animal studies.

Reduction:

The reduction principle of the 3Rs encourages researchers to minimize the number of animals used in research. This can include using statistical methods to reduce sample sizes, sharing data and samples between researchers, and optimizing study designs to reduce the number of animals needed for research. By reducing the number of animals used in research, researchers can minimize the ethical concerns associated with animal studies and reduce the cost and time associated with animal research.

Refinement:

The refinement principle of the 3Rs encourages researchers to improve the welfare of animals used in research. This can include providing animals with better living conditions, minimizing pain and distress, and using anesthesia and analgesia to reduce pain and discomfort. By improving the welfare of animals used in research, researchers can reduce the ethical concerns associated with animal studies and improve the scientific validity of their research.

The 3Rs principles are essential for promoting the ethical and humane use of animals in research. By encouraging the use of alternatives to animal studies when possible, minimizing the number of animals used in research, and improving the welfare of animals used in research, the 3Rs principles provide a framework for reducing the ethical concerns and scientific limitations associated with animal studies. The 3Rs principles are widely recognized as a key component of responsible animal research and are essential for promoting the welfare of animals and the advancement of scientific knowledge.

Advantages of Alternatives to Animal Studies

Improved Accuracy and Relevance:

Alternatives to animal studies can offer improved accuracy and relevance compared to traditional animal-based methods. For example, the use of in vitro methods such as organoids or tissue engineering can provide more precise and relevant data than animal studies. This can help researchers to better understand biological mechanisms and make more accurate predictions about human responses to drugs or other interventions.

Increased Efficiency and Speed:

Alternatives to animal studies can also be more efficient and faster than traditional animal-based methods. For example, computer models can simulate complex biological systems and predict drug interactions, potentially reducing the need for lengthy and expensive animal studies.

Cost Savings:

Using alternatives to animal studies can also be cost-effective. Traditional animal-based methods can be expensive and time-consuming, requiring significant resources and infrastructure to maintain. In contrast, alternatives to animal studies can often be conducted with fewer resources, reducing the cost and time associated with research.

Reduction in Animal Suffering

Finally, using alternatives to animal studies can help to reduce the amount of animal suffering involved in research. Animal studies can be painful, stressful, and even deadly for animals. By using alternatives to animal studies, researchers can minimize the ethical concerns associated with animal studies and reduce the harm caused to animals.

Challenges and Limitations of Alternatives to Animal Studies

While alternatives to animal studies offer many advantages, there are also several challenges and limitations associated with these methods. Some of the key challenges and limitations include:

Technical Challenges

Alternatives to animal studies often involve complex and technically demanding methods. For example, the use of organoids or tissue engineering may require specialized equipment and expertise. This can be a significant challenge for researchers who may not have access to the necessary resources or technical expertise.

Regulatory Hurdles

Alternatives to animal studies may also face regulatory hurdles. For example, regulatory agencies may require additional validation studies or may be hesitant to accept new methods that have not been extensively tested. This can create additional barriers for researchers seeking to use alternatives to animal studies.

Funding Issues

The development and validation of alternatives to animal studies can also be expensive. Researchers may struggle to secure funding to support the development of these methods, particularly if they are competing with established animal-based methods for limited research funding.

Lack of Standardization and Validation

Finally, alternatives to animal studies may lack standardization and validation. This can make it difficult for researchers to compare results across different studies or to validate new methods. Without standardized methods and validation criteria, it can be challenging to ensure that alternatives to animal studies are producing accurate and reliable results.

The Role of Stakeholders in Promoting Alternatives to Animal Studies

The use of alternatives to animal studies is a complex and multidisciplinary issue that involves a range of stakeholders. Some of the key stakeholders and their roles in promoting alternatives include:

Researchers and Academia

Researchers and academic institutions play a crucial role in promoting the use of alternatives to animal studies. By developing and validating new methods, and by publishing research that demonstrates the utility and validity of alternatives, researchers can help to shift the scientific community towards the use of non-animal methods.

Industry and Regulatory Agencies

Industry and regulatory agencies are also key stakeholders in the development and adoption of alternatives to animal studies. Industry has a vested interest in ensuring that new products are safe and effective, and regulatory agencies are responsible for ensuring that products are safe for human use. By working with researchers to develop and validate new methods, and by accepting and approving the use of alternatives in product development and safety testing, industry and regulatory agencies can help to drive the adoption of alternatives.

Government and Policy Makers

Government and policy makers also have an important role to play in promoting the use of alternatives to animal studies. By providing funding and support for research, and by setting policies and regulations that encourage the use of non-animal methods, government and policy makers can help to create an environment that is conducive to the development and adoption of alternatives.

Animal Welfare Organizations and Advocacy Groups

Finally, animal welfare organizations and advocacy groups are also important stakeholders in the promotion of alternatives to animal studies. By raising awareness about the ethical concerns associated with animal studies, and by advocating for the use of non-animal methods, these groups can help to drive change in the scientific community and society as a whole.

VII

Toxicity test -The Organization for Economic Cooperation and Development Guidelines

Toxicity testing refers to the process of evaluating the potential harmful effects of chemical substances or drugs on living organisms, including humans, animals, and the environment. Toxicity testing is an essential step in drug development to ensure the safety of drugs before they are approved for use in humans or animals. The testing can also help to identify potential environmental risks associated with the use of chemicals in various settings.

Importance of toxicity testing in drug development and regulatory approval

Toxicity testing is a critical aspect of drug development and regulatory approval. It is necessary to determine the safety of a drug candidate before it is administered to humans or animals. The testing is carried out to identify any potential toxic effects of the drug, such as organ damage, teratogenicity, and carcinogenicity, among others. The results of toxicity testing can also inform decisions regarding dosing and administration schedules for the drug.

Overview of OECD and its role in setting guidelines for toxicity testing

The Organization for Economic Cooperation and Development (OECD) is an international organization comprising 38 member countries. The OECD's mission is to promote policies that will improve the economic and social well-being of people around the world. The OECD also provides a forum for member countries to work together to develop and promote best practices in a wide range of policy areas, including health and the environment.

One of the areas in which the OECD has been particularly active is the development of guidelines for toxicity testing. The organization has established a system for the mutual acceptance of data (MAD) for chemicals, which enables regulatory authorities to accept data generated in other countries for use in chemical safety assessments. The MAD system is based on the use of harmonized OECD test guidelines for the testing of chemicals and the development of standardized test methods. These guidelines cover a wide range of topics, from acute toxicity testing to carcinogenicity and reproductive toxicity testing. The OECD test guidelines are regularly updated to reflect new scientific knowledge and to ensure that they remain relevant to current regulatory needs.

The OECD plays a crucial role in setting guidelines for toxicity testing, which are used by regulatory authorities worldwide to assess the safety of chemicals and drugs. These guidelines help to ensure that toxicity testing is conducted in a standardized and scientifically sound manner, and that the results of toxicity testing are accepted across different jurisdictions, thereby promoting global harmonization in chemical safety assessment.

OECD Guidelines for Toxicity Testing

Purpose and Scope

The OECD Guidelines for the Testing of Chemicals provide a framework for the design and conduct of toxicity studies, to ensure that the resulting data is reliable, relevant and can be used for regulatory purposes. The guidelines cover a wide range of substances, including chemicals, pesticides, and drugs, and are applicable to both laboratory and field studies.

The purpose of the guidelines is to provide a standardized approach to toxicity testing, which allows the results of studies to be compared across different laboratories and regions. This helps to ensure that the safety of humans, animals and the environment can be evaluated using consistent and reliable data.

The scope of the guidelines covers a range of areas, including acute toxicity testing, repeated dose toxicity testing, carcinogenicity testing, reproductive and developmental toxicity testing, and environmental toxicity testing. The guidelines also cover the use of alternative test methods, such as in vitro and computational methods, which can reduce the need for animal testing.

The guidelines are regularly updated to reflect advances in science and technology, and to incorporate new test methods that can improve the accuracy and relevance of toxicity testing. The most recent update, in 2021, includes revisions to the sections on skin sensitization, endocrine disruption, and developmental neurotoxicity testing.

The OECD Guidelines for Toxicity Testing provide a comprehensive and internationally recognized framework for the design and conduct of toxicity studies, which is essential for the safety assessment of chemicals, drugs and other substances.

Types of toxicity testing guidelines developed by OECD

Acute toxicity testing: This type of testing determines the harmful effects of a single exposure to a substance, usually within 24 hours. OECD guidelines recommend the use of at least two different animal species to assess acute toxicity, and to determine the lethal dose (LD50) of the substance.

Repeated dose toxicity testing: This type of testing evaluates the harmful effects of a substance after repeated exposure over a period of time. The guidelines provide recommendations on the duration of the study, the frequency of dosing, and the number of animals to be used.

Genotoxicity testing: This type of testing examines the ability of a substance to cause damage to genetic material. The OECD guidelines provide recommendations on the types of assays to be used, such as the Ames test, the micronucleus assay, and the comet assay.

Carcinogenicity testing: This type of testing assesses the potential of a substance to cause cancer. OECD guidelines recommend the use of at least two different animal species for carcinogenicity testing, and the use of a long-term study design.

Reproductive toxicity testing: This type of testing assesses the potential of a substance to cause harm to the reproductive system. The guidelines provide recommendations on the types of studies to be conducted, such as fertility and early embryonic development, and the duration of the study.

Key principles and features of OECD guidelines

Test methods: The guidelines provide detailed descriptions of the test methods to be used for each type of toxicity testing. These methods have been standardized to ensure that results are comparable across different studies and laboratories.

Study design: The guidelines provide recommendations on the study design, including the number of animals to be used, the duration of the study, and the frequency and amount of exposure to the substance.

Quality control and assurance: The guidelines emphasize the importance of quality control and assurance measures to ensure the accuracy and reliability of the study results.

Reporting requirements: The guidelines provide detailed instructions on the information to be included in study reports, such as the description of the test substance, the study design, and the results of the study.

Ethics and animal welfare considerations: The guidelines also include recommendations on the ethical use of animals in toxicity testing, including the principles of the 3Rs (replacement, reduction, and refinement) and the importance of minimizing animal suffering.

VIII

Determination of Lethal Dose 50

Definition of LD50

The LD50 is the dose of a substance that is lethal to 50% of a group of test animals. It is a widely used measure of acute toxicity, providing a quantitative estimate of the potential harm of a substance.

Importance of determining LD50

The LD50 (Lethal Dose 50) value is a critical parameter in toxicology that is used to evaluate the safety of various substances, including drugs, chemicals, and environmental pollutants. The LD50 value is defined as the dose of a substance that causes death in 50% of the animals (usually rodents) tested. The LD50 value is expressed in terms of milligrams of substance per kilogram of body weight (mg/kg) and is typically determined through animal testing.

The determination of LD50 is essential in the assessment of the toxicity of a substance. The LD50 value serves as an indicator of the potency of the substance and its potential for causing harm. It is used to classify substances according to their toxicity and to set safe exposure limits. For example, substances with low LD50 values are considered to be highly toxic, while those with high LD50 values are considered to be less toxic.

The LD50 value is also used to compare the toxicity of different substances. When two or more substances are tested using the same animal model, the LD50 values can be compared to determine which substance is more toxic. This information can be used to identify potential hazards and to prioritize testing of substances for regulatory purposes.

The LD50 value is also important in the development and testing of new drugs. Before a new drug can be approved for use in humans, it must undergo extensive testing to evaluate its safety and efficacy. One of the tests performed during drug development is the determination of LD50 in animal models. This information is used to establish a safe starting dose for human clinical trials.

The determination of LD50 is a crucial step in evaluating the safety of various substances, including drugs, chemicals, and environmental pollutants. The LD50 value is used to classify substances according to their toxicity, to set safe exposure limits, and to compare the toxicity of different substances. The LD50 value is also important in the development and testing of new drugs, where it is used to establish a safe starting dose for human clinical trials.

Historical background and development of LD50 testing

The LD50 (Lethal Dose 50%) test was first introduced in the late 1920s as a way to evaluate the acute toxicity of chemical substances. The test was developed by J.W. Trevan, a British pharmacologist, who suggested using the ratio of the minimum lethal dose to the maximum non-lethal dose as a measure of toxicity. This ratio became known as the therapeutic index.

In the 1940s, the LD50 test gained wider use as a standard method for assessing the toxicity of chemicals, drugs, and other substances. The test involved administering a range of doses of the substance to a group of animals and observing the dose at which 50% of the animals died within a specified period of time. The LD50 value was then calculated by extrapolating the dose-response curve.

However, with the growing awareness of animal welfare concerns, the use of the LD50 test has become more controversial. In many countries, there are regulations that require alternative methods to be used whenever possible. Nonetheless, the LD50 test remains a standard method for evaluating the acute toxicity of chemicals and drugs. It is also used in the classification and labeling of chemicals, as well as in the risk assessment of environmental pollutants.

LD50 testing procedures

LD50 testing is performed to determine the lethal dose of a substance in a test population. The test is typically conducted on animals, and the dose is gradually increased until 50% of the animals in the test population die. The LD50 value is then calculated based on the dose at which this occurs.

The LD50 testing procedure typically involves the following steps:

Animal selection: The test population is selected based on the requirements of the study. The animals must be healthy and free from any pre-existing conditions that could affect the results.

Dose selection: A range of doses of the test substance is selected based on previous information about the substance and its toxicity. Typically, a range of doses is tested, starting at low doses and increasing gradually until the LD50 is reached.

Administration of test substance: The test substance is administered to the animals in the test population. This can be done by injection, oral ingestion, or inhalation, depending on the substance being tested and the requirements of the study.

Observation and recording of effects: The animals are closely observed for a set period after the test substance has been administered. Any adverse effects or symptoms are recorded and monitored throughout the study.

Calculation of LD50: The LD50 value is calculated based on the dose of the substance that causes 50% of the animals in the test population to die.

Statistical analysis: Statistical analysis is performed to determine the variability of the results and to ensure that the results are reliable and reproducible.

Reporting of results: The results of the LD50 testing are reported, along with any relevant data and observations. The results are typically used to classify the substance according to its toxicity and to determine safe exposure limits.

It is important to note that LD50 testing has ethical and practical limitations, and alternative methods of toxicity testing are being developed and used where possible. These alternative methods include in vitro testing, computer modeling, and other non-animal testing methods.

Experimental design

Experimental design is an important aspect of LD50 testing as it can influence the accuracy and reliability of the results obtained. The following are some key considerations in designing an LD50 test:

Selection of test animals: The choice of test animals depends on the specific requirements of the test. The most commonly used animals include mice, rats, rabbits, and guinea pigs. The selected animal should be healthy, free from infections, and of the appropriate age and weight.

Dose selection: The starting dose for LD50 testing is usually based on prior knowledge of the substance or on data from preliminary toxicity studies. The dose range should be broad enough to produce a range of responses, but not so wide as to produce deaths at the lowest dose or no deaths at the highest dose.

Route of administration: The route of administration should be chosen based on the intended use of the substance. The most common routes of administration are oral, dermal, and inhalation. The route of administration can affect the toxicity of the substance.

Number of animals: The number of animals used should be sufficient to produce statistically significant results. The number of animals required depends on the variability of the response, the level of statistical significance desired, and the ethical considerations involved in animal testing.

Observation period: The observation period should be long enough to detect delayed toxic effects. The length of the observation period depends on the half-life of the substance and the route of administration. Typically, the observation period ranges from 24 hours to 14 days.

Control groups: Control groups are used to establish a baseline response to the vehicle or diluent used in the test. The control group should be treated identically to the test groups, except that it should receive the vehicle or diluent only.

Data analysis: The data obtained from LD50 testing is usually analyzed using statistical methods. The results are expressed as the LD50 value, which is the dose that causes 50% mortality in the test animals.

A well-designed LD50 test should provide reliable and reproducible results that can be used to determine the toxicity of a substance and to set safe exposure limits.

Dose-response curve determination

After the LD50 test has been performed, the data is used to plot a dose-response curve. This curve shows the relationship between the dose or concentration of the substance and the percentage of animals that die as a result of exposure to that dose. The curve typically follows a sigmoidal shape, with a steep slope at low doses, a plateau region at intermediate doses, and a shallow slope at high doses.

The determination of the dose-response curve is important because it provides additional information beyond just the LD50 value. For example, the slope of the curve can indicate the steepness of the toxic response, which may have implications for the severity of the toxic effects in humans. The curve can also help determine the threshold dose for toxic effects and the maximum tolerated dose.

The dose-response curve is typically generated by testing a range of doses or concentrations of the substance, with each dose group consisting of at least five animals. The data is then plotted on a graph, with the x-axis representing the dose or concentration and the y-axis representing the percentage of animals that die. A curve is then fitted to the data using mathematical models such as the probit or logit method. The point on the curve where 50% of the animals die is the LD50 value.

It is important to note that the LD50 value and the shape of the dose-response curve can vary depending on the species, sex, and age of the animals used in the test, as well as the route of exposure and the duration of the study. Therefore, it is important to carefully consider these factors when designing and interpreting LD50 studies.

Calculation of LD50

After the dose-response curve has been plotted, the LD50 value can be calculated. The LD50 is the dose of a substance that is lethal to 50% of the test population. The LD50 can be calculated using different methods, depending on the experimental design and the dose-response curve.

Graphical method: The LD50 can be estimated graphically by plotting the dose-response curve and drawing a line at 50% mortality. The point on the curve where the line intersects the curve represents the LD50.

Probit analysis: Probit analysis is a statistical method used to determine the LD50. In probit analysis, the dose-response data is transformed into probits, which are units of standard deviation from the mean. A probit plot is then generated, which is a graph of the probit values versus the log dose. The LD50 is calculated from the intercept of the probit plot with the dose axis.

Karber's method: Karber's method is a quick and simple method for calculating the LD50. In this method, the doses are arranged in ascending order, and the number of animals dying at each dose is recorded. The cumulative percentage mortality is calculated for each dose, and the dose that produces 50% mortality is estimated by interpolation.

Once the LD50 value has been calculated, it can be used to classify the substance according to its toxicity and to set safe exposure limits. The lower the LD50 value, the more toxic the substance is considered to be. The LD50 value can also be used to compare the toxicity of different substances and to identify potential hazards. However, it is important to note that the LD50 value is only one measure of toxicity and should be interpreted in the context of other toxicity data and the intended use of the substance.

Confidence limits and significance of LD50

After calculating the LD50 value, it is important to determine the confidence limits and significance of the value. Confidence limits refer to the range of doses within which the true LD50 is likely to fall with a certain level of probability. The most commonly used level of probability is 95%.

There are several statistical methods that can be used to determine confidence limits, such as the Spearman-Karber method and the probit analysis method. These methods take into account the number of animals tested, the number of deaths observed, and the dose-response relationship.

The significance of the LD50 value can also be determined using statistical tests. One commonly used test is the Fisher's exact test, which compares the number of deaths observed in each dose group with the number of deaths expected based on the LD50 value. If the observed number of deaths differs significantly from the expected number, the LD50 value may not be accurate.

It is important to note that the LD50 value should not be used as the sole determinant of toxicity, as it only provides information on acute toxicity and does not take into account other factors such as chronic exposure and individual susceptibility. Therefore, other tests such as repeated dose toxicity testing and genotoxicity testing should also be conducted to fully evaluate the safety of a substance.

Factors Affecting LD50

LD50 testing can be influenced by a variety of factors, including species variability. Different animal species have different susceptibilities to toxic substances, which can lead to variations in LD50 values. For example, rats are generally more sensitive to certain toxins than mice, while guinea pigs are more sensitive to others than rats. Therefore, it is important to select the appropriate animal species for LD50 testing, depending on the substance being tested.

Age and sex

Age and sex can also affect the results of LD50 testing. Young animals are generally more sensitive to toxic substances than adult animals, and males and females may also differ in their susceptibility. Therefore, it is important to use animals of the appropriate age and sex for LD50 testing.

Route of administration

The route of administration can also affect LD50 values. Different routes of administration can result in different rates of absorption, distribution, metabolism, and excretion of the substance being tested. For example, oral administration may result in slower absorption and lower LD50 values than intravenous administration, which may result in more rapid absorption and higher LD50 values.

Formulation and purity of the substance

The formulation and purity of the substance being tested can also affect LD50 values. Impurities or contaminants in the substance may affect its toxicity, leading to variations in LD50 values. Similarly, different formulations of the substance may have different toxicity profiles, leading to differences in LD50 values.

Environmental factors

Environmental factors, such as temperature, humidity, and lighting conditions, can also affect the results of LD50 testing. These factors can influence the animal's metabolism, immune function, and other physiological processes, which may affect its susceptibility to toxic substances. Therefore, it is important to control for these environmental factors during LD50 testing.

Absorption, distribution, metabolism, and excretion (ADME)

ADME are important factors that can affect the toxicity of a substance and, consequently, the LD50 value. Absorption refers to the uptake of a substance into the body, distribution is the movement of a substance to different organs and tissues, metabolism is the process of breaking down a substance in the body, and excretion is the elimination of a substance from the body. Differences in ADME between species can result in varying toxicity levels and LD50 values. For example, a substance that is rapidly metabolized and eliminated in one species may have a higher LD50 value than in another species where it is not metabolized or eliminated as quickly.

Interactions with other chemicals

The toxicity of a substance can be affected by interactions with other chemicals, either increasing or decreasing its toxicity. This can complicate the determination of LD50 values when a substance is tested in combination with other chemicals. In addition, pre-existing medical conditions, age, sex, and genetic differences can also influence the toxicity of a substance and its LD50 value.

Ethical and regulatory considerations

Ethical and regulatory considerations are an important aspect of LD50 testing. Animal testing is a controversial issue, and many organizations and individuals are opposed to the use of animals in research. As such, there are strict regulations and guidelines in place that govern the use of animals in research.

In many countries, animal research is regulated by government agencies, such as the US National Institutes of Health (NIH) and the European Union's European Medicines Agency (EMA). These agencies have established guidelines that researchers must follow in order to ensure that animal testing is conducted in a humane and ethical manner. These guidelines address issues such as animal welfare, pain and distress, and the use of anesthesia and analgesia.

Many organizations have developed ethical standards for animal testing. For example, the International Council for Laboratory Animal Science (ICLAS) has developed a set of principles for the care and use of laboratory animals. These principles emphasize the importance of animal welfare, the reduction of animal use, and the use of alternative methods when possible.

When conducting LD50 testing, researchers must take into account both regulatory and ethical considerations. They must ensure that the animals are treated humanely and that their pain and distress are minimized. They must also ensure that the testing is conducted in accordance with regulatory guidelines and that the results are reliable and accurate.

To address these concerns, researchers may use alternative testing methods when possible, such as computer modeling or in vitro testing. They may also use animals that are specifically bred for research purposes and have been carefully selected to minimize pain and distress.

IX

Acute Toxicity Testing

Acute toxicity studies are a critical step in the preclinical development of drugs and other substances. These studies are conducted to evaluate the potential for adverse effects of a substance after a single or short-term exposure. The objective of these studies is to identify the acute toxicity profile of the substance and determine the appropriate safety precautions to minimize the risks to human health.

Acute toxicity testing is typically performed using animal models, including rats, mice, rabbits, and non-human primates. The test animals are exposed to various doses of the substance, and the effects on their behavior, physiology, and survival are monitored.

The results of acute toxicity studies are used to determine the dose at which the substance causes toxic effects and to establish the potential target organs. These data are used to develop safety guidelines and establish the safe exposure limits for the substance. In addition, the results of acute toxicity studies are used to identify potential hazards associated with the substance and to inform risk assessments.

Acute toxicity studies play a critical role in ensuring the safety of drugs and other substances for human use. These studies provide essential information for regulatory agencies and industry professionals to evaluate the safety of new substances and make informed decisions about their use.

Experimental design

The experimental design for acute toxicity studies may vary depending on the specific test substance and the intended use of the substance. However, there are some general guidelines that should be followed to ensure the reliability and relevance of the data generated.

The first step in designing an acute toxicity study is to determine the appropriate animal species and strain to be used. This choice is based on various factors such as the intended use of the substance, the expected target organ(s), and the availability of animal models. Commonly used animal species in acute toxicity studies include rats, mice, rabbits, and guinea pigs.

The next step is to determine the route of administration of the test substance. The route of administration can affect the absorption, distribution, metabolism, and excretion of the substance and can influence the toxic effects observed. Common routes of administration in acute toxicity studies include oral, dermal, inhalation, and intravenous.

The dose selection is a critical component of experimental design in acute toxicity studies. The dose should be high enough to elicit toxic effects but not so high as to cause immediate death. The selection of the dose should be based on the available information on the substance, including previous toxicity studies, and on the regulatory requirements for the intended use of the substance.

After administration of the test substance, the animals are observed for clinical signs of toxicity such as changes in behavior, respiratory rate, and body weight. The observation period may vary depending on the substance and the route of administration, but typically ranges from a few hours to several days.

During the observation period, the animals are subjected to a range of tests, including hematological and biochemical analysis, gross and microscopic examination of tissues, and organ weight measurements. These tests can provide information on the potential target organ(s) and the extent of the toxic effects observed.

The experimental design for acute toxicity studies should be carefully planned to ensure that the data generated are reliable, relevant, and useful for the evaluation of the safety of the test substance.

Dose selection

To determine the dose selection for acute toxicity studies, several factors should be considered, including the substance's route of administration, chemical and physical properties, intended use, and target population. The initial dose level is usually based on previous data from similar substances or studies, or on estimated human exposure levels.

The doses tested should cover a broad range and should include a high dose that causes severe toxicity and a low dose that does not cause any adverse effects. The spacing of doses is also important, and a logarithmic scale is often used to ensure that the doses are evenly distributed.

For oral administration, the dose is usually expressed in mg/kg of body weight. For other routes of administration, such as inhalation or injection, the dose may be expressed in mg/m3 or mg/kg, respectively. The dose may also be adjusted based on the animal species and strain used in the study, as different species may have different sensitivities to the substance.

In general, the dose selection for acute toxicity studies should ensure that the study provides sufficient information to identify the dose-response relationship, estimate the potential risk to humans, and inform regulatory decision-making.

Endpoints

In addition to mortality and LD50 values, other endpoints can be used to assess the adverse effects of the test substance. Clinical signs of toxicity, such as changes in behavior, respiratory rate, and body weight, are closely monitored and recorded throughout the study. Blood samples may be collected to assess hematological and biochemical parameters, providing insight into the effects of the test substance on organ systems such as the liver, kidneys, and blood cells.

Gross and microscopic examination of tissues can also provide valuable information on the target organs affected by the test substance. Organ weight measurements can help identify changes in organ size and function, which may indicate toxicity. Other endpoints, such as histopathological examination, can provide detailed information on tissue damage and help identify the mechanism of toxicity.

It is essential to select appropriate endpoints based on the test substance's known toxicity and potential target organs. The selection of endpoints should be carefully considered to ensure that they provide a comprehensive assessment of the substance's acute toxicity.

Methods

Acute toxicity testing can be performed using a variety of methods, including both in vitro (test-tube) and in vivo (animal) tests. In vitro tests involve the use of isolated cells, tissues, or organs to determine the toxicity of a substance. In vivo tests involve the administration of a substance to live animals, usually rodents such as mice or rats, to determine the effects of the substance on the whole organism. Rodent tests are the most commonly used type of in vivo test for evaluating acute toxicity. Non-rodent tests, such as those involving fish, birds, or dogs, are sometimes used to supplement or confirm the results of rodent tests.

In vitro tests, also known as test-tube or cell culture tests, are laboratory procedures that use isolated cells, tissues, or organs to evaluate the toxicity of a substance. These tests can be divided into two main categories: cell-based assays and biochemical assays. Cell-based assays involve the exposure of live cells to the test substance, and are used to evaluate a variety of toxic effects, including cell death, changes in cell proliferation, and alterations in gene expression. Biochemical assays are used to evaluate the effects of a substance on specific biochemical pathways or enzymes. In vitro tests have several advantages, including the ability to perform high-throughput screening and investigate the effects of substances at the cellular and molecular level. However, in vitro tests also have limitations, including the inability to accurately reflect the complex interactions that occur in a living organism and the difficulty in extrapolating results to predict the toxicity of a substance in a living organism.

In vivo tests, also known as animal tests, are laboratory procedures that use live animals, typically rodents, to evaluate the toxicity of a substance. In vivo tests can be divided into two main categories: acute toxicity tests and chronic toxicity tests. Acute toxicity tests are performed by administering a single dose of the substance to the animal and observing the effects over a defined period of time. Chronic toxicity tests are performed by administering repeated doses of the substance to the animal over a longer period of time, typically several months to a year. In vivo tests provide information about the effects of a substance on a whole organism and take into account the interplay between different physiological processes and organ systems.

Both in vitro and in vivo tests are essential tools in the evaluation of substance toxicity. The results of these tests are crucial for making informed decisions about the safety of these substances for human and environmental health. In vitro tests complement in vivo studies by providing additional information about the toxic effects of a substance, while in vivo tests provide the most reliable method for evaluating acute toxicity by providing information about the effects of the substance on multiple organ systems.

Regulatory considerations

Regulatory agencies such as the United States Food and Drug Administration (FDA) and the European Medicines Agency (EMA) require acute toxicity studies to be conducted as part of the preclinical safety assessment of new drugs. These studies are usually performed in compliance with the guidelines set forth by the ICH. The ICH guideline S1A outlines the basic requirements for acute toxicity testing in non-clinical drug development.

According to the ICH guidelines, the objective of acute toxicity testing is to provide information on the potential hazards of a substance and to aid in the selection of safe starting doses for subsequent studies. The guidelines specify that acute toxicity studies should be conducted in at least two species, typically rodents such as rats and mice, and that both sexes should be tested. The guidelines also recommend that a range of doses be tested, with at least three dose levels, including a high dose that causes severe toxicity and a low dose that does not cause any observable toxicity.

In addition to the ICH guidelines, other regulatory bodies, such as the Environmental Protection Agency (EPA) in the United States, have their own guidelines for acute toxicity testing. These guidelines provide specific requirements for testing different classes of substances, such as pesticides or industrial chemicals.

Regulatory authorities require acute toxicity studies to ensure that new drugs are safe for use in humans and to establish safe starting doses for subsequent studies.

Limitations and Criticisms of Acute Toxicity Tests

Despite its importance, acute toxicity testing has several limitations and criticisms that have been raised over the years. The use of animals in toxicity testing has been criticized due to the limitations of extrapolating the results of animal studies to humans. Species differences in anatomy, physiology, and metabolism can affect the results of toxicity tests, leading to unreliable predictions of human toxicity. The use of animals in toxicity testing also raises ethical concerns, as animals are subjected to procedures that can cause pain, suffering, and death. In addition, acute toxicity tests may not accurately predict the long-term toxic effects of a substance, particularly for chronic or low-dose exposures, or the toxicity of mixtures of substances or substances in combination with other environmental stressors.

Acute toxicity tests play a crucial role in evaluating the safety of products for human and environmental health. The regulatory requirements for these tests vary depending on the type of product and the jurisdiction in which it is marketed. Despite its importance, acute toxicity testing has several limitations and criticisms, including the limitations of extrapolating the results of animal studies to humans, ethical concerns, and limitations in predicting human toxicity. The development of alternative testing methods and the refinement of existing methods is ongoing and may help to overcome some of the limitations and criticisms of acute toxicity tests in the future.

It is essential to follow the guidelines set forth by regulatory authorities such as the International Conference on Harmonisation to ensure that the studies are conducted in a standardized and consistent manner. By conducting well-designed and well-executed acute toxicity studies, researchers can better understand the potential risks associated with a substance and ensure that it is safe for clinical use.

X

Sub Acute Toxicity Studies

Subacute toxicity refers to the toxic effects that may occur after repeated exposure to a substance over a short period of time, typically ranging from a few days to several weeks. Subacute toxicity testing is a critical component in the assessment of the long-term safety of a substance and can provide valuable information for risk assessment and safety evaluation. This is because it can identify adverse effects that may not have been detected in acute toxicity tests, which are designed to evaluate the immediate harmful effects of a substance after a single or short-term exposure.

Purpose: The purpose of subacute toxicity studies is to identify the target organs and potential toxic effects of a substance that may occur after repeated exposure. The studies also help in determining the no observed adverse effect level (NOAEL), which is the highest dose at which no adverse effects are observed in the animals.

Experimental design

In subacute toxicity studies, the experimental design is critical for obtaining reliable and accurate results. The design should take into consideration the substance being tested, the animal species, the route of administration, the dose levels, and the duration of exposure. The test substance is usually administered daily or weekly, and the dose levels are selected based on previous acute toxicity studies, pharmacological and toxicological data, and regulatory requirements.

The animals used in subacute toxicity studies are usually rodents such as rats or mice, but other species such as rabbits, dogs, or primates may be used depending on the study objectives and regulatory requirements. The route of administration can be oral, dermal, inhalation, or intravenous, depending on the intended use of the substance.

During the study, the animals are observed for clinical signs of toxicity such as changes in behavior, respiratory rate, and body weight. Other assessments include hematological and biochemical analysis, gross and microscopic examination of tissues, and organ weight measurements. These assessments can provide information about the potential toxic effects of the substance on various organs and systems, such as the liver, kidney, nervous system, and immune system.

The experimental design should also include appropriate control groups, such as a vehicle control group and a positive control group, to ensure that any observed effects are due to the test substance and not to other factors. The number of animals per group should also be determined based on statistical considerations, such as the power of the study and the expected variability of the data.

The experimental design of subacute toxicity studies should be scientifically sound, well-controlled, and meet regulatory requirements to ensure the safety of the test substance.

Dose selection

In subacute toxicity studies, dose selection is critical and should be based on the available information on the substance's toxicity. Generally, a range of doses is tested to identify the dose-response relationship and to determine the no-observed-adverse-effect level (NOAEL) and the lowest-observed-adverse-effect level (LOAEL).

The NOAEL is the highest dose that does not cause any adverse effects, while the LOAEL is the lowest dose at which adverse effects are observed. These values provide important information for setting exposure limits and determining safe levels of the substance for human use.

The doses used in subacute toxicity studies should reflect the expected human exposure levels. The highest dose should not exceed the maximum tolerated dose (MTD), which is the highest dose that does not cause severe toxicity, as determined in the acute toxicity studies.

It is also important to consider the route of administration, as the toxicokinetics of the substance may differ depending on the route of exposure. The chosen dose levels should reflect the intended route of administration in humans, whether it be oral, inhalation, or dermal.

Endpoints

Endpoints in subacute toxicity studies are similar to those in acute toxicity studies, but they are assessed over a longer period of time. The primary endpoints are typically mortality, clinical signs of toxicity, body weight changes, and organ damage. In addition, subacute toxicity studies may also include assessments of reproductive and developmental effects, neurotoxicity, and immunotoxicity, depending on the nature of the test substance and its intended use. The choice of endpoints depends on the regulatory requirements and the specific objectives of the study. It is important to note that some endpoints may require additional testing beyond the subacute toxicity study, such as reproductive toxicity studies or developmental toxicity studies.

Regulatory considerations

Subacute toxicity studies are required by regulatory authorities worldwide before a new drug can be approved for clinical use. The International Conference on Harmonisation of Technical Requirements for Registration of Pharmaceuticals for Human Use (ICH) provides guidelines on the design, conduct, and reporting of subacute toxicity studies.

In general, subacute toxicity studies are required to provide data on the potential adverse effects of a substance after repeated exposure. The regulatory authorities may also require additional studies, such as subchronic and chronic toxicity studies, to evaluate the potential risks associated with long-term exposure to the substance. The data generated from these studies are used to determine the safety profile of the substance and to establish safe exposure limits for humans.

It is important to note that regulatory requirements may vary depending on the country or region. Therefore, it is essential to consult the relevant regulatory guidance documents to ensure compliance with the specific requirements.

Factors affecting subacute toxicity studies

There are several factors that can affect the outcome of subacute toxicity studies, including:

Dose selection: The dose selection for subacute toxicity studies should take into account the available information on the substance's toxicity and the expected human exposure levels. It is essential to determine the no observed adverse effect level (NOAEL) and the lowest observed adverse effect level (LOAEL) to identify the dose-response relationship.

Duration of exposure: The duration of exposure should be appropriate for the intended use of the substance. It is important to note that longer exposure periods may increase the likelihood of observing toxic effects.

Route of administration: The route of administration should be relevant to the intended use of the substance. For example, if the substance is intended for oral use, it should be administered orally.

Species selection: The selection of animal species should be based on the intended use of the substance and the availability of suitable models. It is essential to consider the similarities and differences between the animal species and humans in terms of anatomy, physiology, and metabolism.

Interactions with other chemicals: Substances may interact with other chemicals present in the environment, food, or drugs, which can affect their toxicity. Therefore, it is important to consider potential interactions with other chemicals during subacute toxicity studies.

Gender and age: Gender and age can also affect the outcome of subacute toxicity studies. Therefore, it is essential to consider these factors when selecting animal models.

Nutritional status: The nutritional status of the animals can also affect the outcome of subacute toxicity studies. It is important to ensure that the animals receive a balanced diet and appropriate nutritional support throughout the study.

Environmental factors: Environmental factors, such as temperature, humidity, and lighting, can affect the outcome of subacute toxicity studies. It is essential to control these factors to ensure the validity of the study.

Evaluation of toxicity in subacute toxicity studies

It involves several techniques, including physical examination, blood and urine analysis, organ weight measurement, and histopathological examination. Physical examination involves observing the study subjects for any adverse effects such as changes in appearance, behavior, or movement. Blood and urine analysis can provide information about the effects of the substance on various organ systems, including the liver, kidneys, and heart.

Organ weight measurement and histopathological examination can provide additional information about the effects of the substance on specific organ systems.

Subacute toxicity studies play a crucial role in preclinical safety evaluation of a substance, especially for identifying potential toxic effects that may occur after repeated exposure. The experimental design, dose selection, and endpoints in these studies should be carefully considered to ensure that the results obtained are scientifically valid and meet regulatory requirements. In addition, various factors such as species, gender, age, and route of administration can affect the outcome of the study and should be taken into account during the study design and interpretation of results. Overall, subacute toxicity studies are an essential tool in evaluating the safety of a substance before it can be tested in clinical trials or approved for use in humans.

XI

Chronic Toxicity Studies

Chronic toxicity studies are preclinical safety evaluations that are conducted to determine the potential toxic effects of a test substance after repeated exposure over an extended period of time. Chronic toxicity studies are typically conducted over several months to several years, depending on the regulatory requirements and the nature of the substance being tested.

Chronic toxicity studies are crucial in drug development as they provide information on the long-term effects of a substance that may not be apparent in acute or subacute toxicity studies. Chronic toxicity studies are also important for evaluating the potential risks associated with occupational and environmental exposure to chemicals.

Importance of Chronic Toxicity Studies in Drug Development

Chronic toxicity studies are essential in drug development as they provide critical information on the potential long-term effects of a drug that may not be observed in short-term studies. Chronic toxicity studies help to identify potential target organs for toxicity, establish dose-response relationships, and determine the No Observed Adverse Effect Level (NOAEL), which is the highest dose at which no significant adverse effects are observed.

The data generated from chronic toxicity studies are used to inform the design of clinical trials and to set safe exposure limits for humans. The results of chronic toxicity studies also provide valuable information for risk assessment and regulatory decision-making.

Comparison with Acute and Subacute Toxicity Studies

Acute toxicity studies involve the administration of a single dose of a substance to animals and the observation of adverse effects over a short period. Subacute toxicity studies involve repeated exposure to a substance over a period of 28 to 90 days.

In contrast, chronic toxicity studies involve repeated exposure to a substance over a more extended period, typically several months to several years. Chronic toxicity studies are designed to identify potential adverse effects that may occur as a result of long-term exposure.

While acute and sub -acute toxicity studies provide valuable information on the immediate effects of a substance, chronic toxicity studies are crucial in assessing the potential long-term effects of exposure. These studies are especially important for substances that may be used over an extended period, such as drugs used to treat chronic conditions like diabetes or hypertension.

Chronic toxicity studies involve administering the test substance to animals for a prolonged period, usually 6 months to 2 years, depending on the regulatory requirements. The animals are monitored for signs of toxicity, and various tests are performed, including clinical observations, body weight measurements, hematology, and clinical chemistry evaluations. Additionally, the animals are subjected to gross and microscopic examination of tissues, including organs that are likely to be affected by the substance under investigation.

The information obtained from chronic toxicity studies is crucial in determining the safety of a substance and its potential long-term effects on human health. Regulatory authorities require chronic toxicity studies for drugs and other substances that are expected to be used over extended periods. The International Council for Harmonisation of Technical Requirements for Pharmaceuticals for Human Use (ICH) provides guidelines on the design, conduct, and reporting of chronic toxicity studies.

Experimental design for chronic toxicity studies

Duration of the study: Chronic toxicity studies are designed to evaluate the effects of long-term exposure, which typically involves repeated administration of the test substance over several months to several years. The duration of the study depends on the regulatory requirements, the type of substance being tested, and the intended duration of use.

Species selection: The species selected for the study should be relevant to the intended use of the substance and have similar physiological and metabolic characteristics to humans. Commonly used species include rodents, dogs, and non-human primates.

Dose selection: Dose selection for chronic toxicity studies is based on the maximum tolerated dose (MTD) from previous studies or on a range of doses that covers a wide range of exposure levels. The highest dose should produce some adverse effects without causing severe toxicity or mortality.

Number of animals: The number of animals used in chronic toxicity studies is determined by statistical power calculations based on the expected variability and effect size. Typically, a minimum of 50 animals per group is recommended to ensure sufficient statistical power.

Route of administration: The route of administration should be relevant to the intended use of the substance, and different routes may produce different toxic effects. The most common routes of administration for chronic toxicity studies include oral, inhalation, and dermal exposure.

Control groups: Chronic toxicity studies require the use of control groups, including vehicle control (animals receiving the vehicle without the test substance) and untreated control (animals receiving no treatment). The use of positive control (animals receiving a known toxic substance) may also be necessary to validate the study results.

Endpoints

Chronic toxicity studies have a broader range of endpoints compared to acute and subacute studies. These studies aim to identify potential adverse effects that may occur as a result of long-term exposure. The following are some of the commonly used endpoints in chronic toxicity studies:

Clinical signs of toxicity: Animals are observed for any clinical signs of toxicity such as changes in behavior, appearance, and body weight.

Mortality: The number of deaths occurring during the course of the study is recorded and analyzed.

Hematological and biochemical parameters: Blood samples are collected periodically during the study to evaluate changes in hematological and biochemical parameters, including red blood cell count, white blood cell count, liver enzymes, and kidney function.

Gross and microscopic examination of tissues: At the end of the study, animals are euthanized, and their tissues are examined for any abnormalities or lesions.

Organ weight measurements: The weight of organs such as liver, kidney, and spleen are measured and compared to control animals to evaluate any changes in organ size and function.

The choice of endpoints depends on the specific characteristics of the test substance, the expected route of exposure, and the target organs for toxicity. These endpoints are carefully evaluated to ensure that the study is scientifically valid and meets regulatory requirements.

Interpretation of Results

Chronic toxicity studies produce a large amount of data, which needs to be interpreted carefully. The following points should be considered when interpreting the results:

Dose-response relationship: Chronic toxicity studies are designed to identify the dose-response relationship, which can help to determine the maximum tolerated dose, the no observed adverse effect level (NOAEL), and the lowest observed adverse effect level (LOAEL). The NOAEL is the highest dose that does not cause any adverse effects, while the LOAEL is the lowest dose at which adverse effects are observed.

Identification of target organs: Chronic toxicity studies can help to identify the target organs that are affected by the substance. The identification of target organs can provide insights into the mechanism of toxicity and aid in the development of therapeutic interventions.

Assessment of carcinogenicity and mutagenicity: Chronic toxicity studies can provide valuable information on the potential carcinogenic and mutagenic effects of a substance. The identification of such effects can lead to regulatory action to protect public health.

Extrapolation to human risk assessment: Chronic toxicity studies can be used to extrapolate the findings to humans and estimate the potential risks associated with long-term exposure to the substance. This information is critical in the risk assessment of new drugs and other substances.

Chronic toxicity studies are essential in drug development and regulatory approval. The careful design and interpretation of these studies can provide valuable insights into the potential adverse effects of a substance and aid in the development of safe and effective drugs.

Factors affecting chronic toxicity studies

Species variability: Different species may react differently to a particular substance due to variations in metabolism, physiology, and susceptibility to toxicity. Therefore, the selection of an appropriate animal model is critical for the accuracy and relevance of the results.

Age and sex: Age and sex can affect the toxicity of a substance, as young or elderly animals may be more vulnerable to certain toxic effects. Sex differences in metabolism, hormonal balance, and susceptibility to toxicity should also be considered.

Nutritional and environmental factors: The nutritional and environmental status of animals can affect their response to a toxic substance. For example, malnourished or stressed animals may be more susceptible to toxicity.

Interactions with other chemicals: Exposure to multiple chemicals can lead to additive, synergistic, or antagonistic effects on toxicity. Therefore, potential interactions with other substances should be considered in the design and interpretation of chronic toxicity studies.

These factors should be taken into account when designing and conducting chronic toxicity studies to ensure the reliability and relevance of the results.

Evaluation of Toxicity

Physical examination, blood and urine analysis, organ weight measurement, and histopathological examination are all methods used to evaluate the toxicity of a substance in chronic toxicity studies. Physical examination assesses any changes in appearance, behavior, or overall health, while blood and urine analysis can provide information about changes in organ function, blood chemistry, or hormone levels. Organ weight measurement helps to identify changes in organ size or function, while histopathological examination examines tissues under a microscope to identify changes in cell structure or function.

Ethical considerations

The use of animals in chronic toxicity studies raises ethical concerns, and researchers must follow guidelines and regulations to ensure that the studies are conducted ethically. One important principle is the 3Rs principle: replacement, reduction, and refinement. Replacement involves finding alternatives to animal testing, while reduction involves minimizing the number of animals used in studies. Refinement involves improving the experimental design and minimizing any potential harm or distress to the animals.

Additionally, animal welfare considerations must be taken into account, including proper housing, feeding, and care of the animals during the study. The animals must be treated humanely and given appropriate medical treatment if needed. It is also important to minimize any pain or distress caused by the administration of the test substance. Ethical considerations are important not only from a moral perspective but also because adherence to ethical guidelines is necessary for regulatory approval of the study results.

Chronic toxicity studies are an essential part of the drug development process as they provide valuable information on the potential adverse effects of long-term exposure to a substance. Careful experimental design, including dose selection, species selection, and endpoint evaluation, is necessary for the study to be scientifically valid and meet regulatory requirements. Additionally, ethical considerations regarding animal welfare must be taken into account during the study. The 3Rs principle of replacement, reduction, and refinement can help to minimize the use of animals and optimize their welfare. Finally, advances in in vitro and in silico methods for toxicity testing have the potential to reduce the need for animal testing and improve the predictivity of safety evaluations.

XII

Screening of Pharmacological Activity of New substances

The process of drug discovery, which involves the identification and development of new compounds that have potential therapeutic benefits. However, before these compounds can be tested in humans, they must first be screened for pharmacological activity to determine their safety, efficacy, and potential side effects.

This is where the organization of screening comes in. The screening process involves a series of tests and evaluations to determine a compound's pharmacological properties, and to identify any potential safety or toxicity issues. This process can be quite involved, and can require a variety of specialized techniques and technologies.

In this Chapter, we will explore the organization of screening for pharmacological activity of new substances, including the different stages of the screening process, the various techniques and technologies used in screening, and the challenges and opportunities associated with this process.

By the end of this chapter, you should have a better understanding of the complex process of drug discovery and development, and the crucial role that screening for pharmacological activity plays in this process.

Definition of drug discovery and development

Drug discovery is a complex process that involves the identification of new chemical compounds that have the potential to be developed into therapeutic agents for treating diseases.

The goal of drug discovery is to find new compounds that can be used to treat diseases that currently have no effective treatments, or to develop more effective treatments for diseases that currently have limited options.

The process of drug discovery often involves a wide range of scientific disciplines, including chemistry, biology, pharmacology, and toxicology, among others.

Once promising compounds are identified, the process of drug development begins. This involves optimizing the pharmacological properties of the compound to create a safe and effective drug.

Drug development is a highly regulated process, with strict guidelines and regulations that must be followed to ensure the safety and efficacy of the final product.

The process of drug discovery and development can be time-consuming and expensive, often taking several years and millions of dollars to complete.

However, the potential benefits of discovering and developing new drugs are immense, as they can improve the quality of life for millions of people around the world.

Importance of screening for pharmacological activity

The process of drug discovery and development is a long and expensive process.

Screening for pharmacological activity is one of the earliest steps in this process, and plays a crucial role in identifying potential drug candidates.

The goal of pharmacological screening is to identify compounds that have a specific biological effect, such as inhibiting the activity of a disease-causing enzyme or receptor, or promoting the activity of a beneficial pathway.

Without effective screening methods, the discovery of new drugs would be largely based on trial and error, which is not only time-consuming, but also expensive.

Screening allows for the identification of promising candidates, which can then be optimized and developed into safe and effective drugs.

Methods of pharmacological screening

There are a variety of methods used for pharmacological screening, including in vitro and in vivo assays.

In vitro assays involve testing compounds in laboratory settings, such as in test tubes or petri dishes, to determine their biological activity.

In vivo assays involve testing compounds in living organisms to determine their pharmacokinetic and pharmacodynamic properties.

Both in vitro and in vivo assays have their own advantages and disadvantages, and the choice of screening method depends on the specific goals of the study.

Challenges in pharmacological screening

Despite the importance of pharmacological screening, there are a number of challenges that researchers must face.

One of the biggest challenges is the sheer number of compounds that must be screened.

To overcome this challenge, high-throughput screening methods have been developed, which allow for the rapid testing of large numbers of compounds.

Another challenge is the development of screening assays that accurately reflect the complex biological systems in which drugs will eventually be used.

Moreover, it can be difficult to translate the results of in vitro and in vivo screening assays to human clinical trials, which highlights the need for robust preclinical testing.

Importance of screening for pharmacological activity

The process of drug discovery and development is a long and expensive process.

Screening for pharmacological activity is one of the earliest steps in this process, and plays a crucial role in identifying potential drug candidates.

The goal of pharmacological screening is to identify compounds that have a specific biological effect, such as inhibiting the activity of a disease-causing enzyme or receptor, or promoting the activity of a beneficial pathway.

Without effective screening methods, the discovery of new drugs would be largely based on trial and error, which is not only time-consuming, but also expensive.

Screening allows for the identification of promising candidates, which can then be optimized and developed into safe and effective drugs.

In Vitro Screening

In vitro screening is a crucial step in the drug discovery and development process. This method involves testing the effect of a drug candidate on isolated cells or biological systems, such as enzymes, tissues, or organs. In vitro screening is often used to identify compounds that interact with specific targets or pathways, such as receptor binding or enzyme inhibition.

High-throughput screening (HTS) is a technique that can be used in in vitro screening.High-throughput screening (HTS) refers to the use of automated systems and robotics to test large numbers of compounds in a short amount of time. HTS methods use automation and robotics to quickly test large numbers of compounds against specific biological targets or pathways. This method is essential for drug discovery and development, as it allows for the efficient identification of potential drug candidates from large libraries of compounds.

For example, a common approach in HTS is to use microtiter plates, which are small plastic plates with multiple wells. Each well can contain a different compound, and automated systems can rapidly test the compounds against a target. The results can be analyzed using specialized software.

There are different high-throughput screening methods, such as cell-based assays, biochemical assays, and phenotypic assays. Cell-based assays involve the use of cultured cells to test the effect of compounds on specific cellular pathways or functions. Biochemical assays measure the activity of specific enzymes or proteins that are involved in disease processes. Phenotypic assays involve the testing of compounds on whole organisms, such as zebrafish or fruit flies, to evaluate their effect on specific phenotypes or disease models.

Advantages of high-throughput screening methods include their speed and efficiency in screening large numbers of compounds, their ability to detect both known and novel drug targets, and the availability of standardized assays that can be replicated across different laboratories. These methods also allow for the identification of lead compounds that can be optimized for further development.

However, there are also limitations to high-throughput screening methods. These include the potential for false positives or false negatives, as well as the lack of information on the mechanism of action of identified compounds. In addition, high-throughput screening methods may not accurately predict the safety and efficacy of compounds in vivo, and may miss compounds that have complex or multi-target effects.

Overall, high-throughput screening methods are a valuable tool in drug discovery and development, but must be used in conjunction with other screening methods and validated in animal models to ensure the safety and efficacy of identified compounds.

One of the major advantages of in vitro screening is its speed and cost-effectiveness. It is much faster and less expensive than in vivo screening, as it does not require the use of living organisms. In vitro assays are highly automated, which allows for the testing of large numbers of compounds in a short period of time. Additionally, in vitro screening provides valuable information on the mechanism of action of the drug candidate, allowing researchers to optimize the compound for further testing.

In vivo Screening

In vivo screening is a critical stage in the drug discovery and development process, where the safety and efficacy of promising compounds are evaluated in living organisms. This stage is typically slower and more expensive than in vitro screening, but it is essential for identifying compounds that have the potential to be developed into safe and effective drugs.

The primary goal of in vivo screening is to evaluate the pharmacokinetic properties of compounds, which refers to how the body absorbs, distributes, metabolizes, and eliminates them. This information is crucial for determining the appropriate dosage and administration of a drug.

In vivo screening involves testing compounds in different animal models, such as mice, rats, dogs, or non-human primates, to assess their safety and efficacy. Animal models are chosen based on their relevance to the human disease being studied and the availability of the model. For example, mice are commonly used in cancer research, while rats are often used in cardiovascular disease research.

During in vivo screening, researchers evaluate the safety of compounds by monitoring for any adverse effects or toxicities. They also assess the efficacy of compounds by measuring their ability to produce the desired therapeutic effect. This may involve measuring changes in disease biomarkers, evaluating the reduction in disease symptoms, or assessing the overall survival of the animal.

In vivo screening is a complex and time-consuming process that requires careful planning and execution. Ethical considerations must also be taken into account when working with animal models. However, this stage is essential for identifying compounds that have the potential to be developed into safe and effective drugs that can improve human health.

Advantages and disadvantages of animal models in drug screening

Animal models have been an essential tool in drug screening and development for many decades. While they have many advantages, they also have their limitations and drawbacks.

On the one hand, animal models provide a means to study the effects of potential drugs in a whole organism, which is more complex than studying individual cells or tissues. Animal models can also be used to study diseases in a more complete way, as they allow researchers to observe the development of disease and track its progression over time. In addition, animal models allow for the evaluation of complex interactions between multiple organ systems, which is impossible to simulate in vitro.

However, the use of animal models also comes with some significant drawbacks. One of the major concerns is the ethical considerations and animal welfare. The use of animals in research raises important ethical issues, and many people question the validity and ethical acceptability of animal experimentation. In addition, animal models are often expensive to maintain, and their use can be time-consuming and technically challenging. Furthermore, animal models are not always predictive of human outcomes, meaning that a drug that is effective in an animal model may not be effective in humans, leading to expensive failures in later phases of drug development.

It is also important to note that different species of animals may respond differently to the same drug, and that the results obtained in animal models may not be generalizable to other species, including humans. This highlights the importance of carefully considering the selection of animal models in drug screening, and being aware of the limitations of animal models in drug development.

While animal models have been an essential tool in drug screening and development for many years, their use comes with important ethical considerations, technical challenges, and limitations in terms of predicting human outcomes. Nonetheless, animal models remain an important tool for understanding the complex biological processes underlying human disease and drug responses.

Future of animal models in drug screening

The future of animal models in drug screening is an important and evolving topic. While there are many ethical and technical challenges associated with animal models, they will likely continue to be used in the foreseeable future due to the important role they play in the development of new drugs.

One area of focus in the future will be improving the predictive power of animal models for human outcomes. This will likely involve the development of more complex animal models that more closely resemble human disease and physiology, as well as the incorporation of new technologies such as humanized animal models and organ-on-a-chip systems.

Another area of focus will be the reduction of the number of animals used in research. This will involve the development of more efficient and effective animal models, as well as the use of in vitro and in silico methods to complement animal models.

There will also be a continued focus on ensuring that the use of animal models in research is ethical and transparent, and that animal welfare is a top priority. This will involve the development of more humane and less invasive methods for animal experimentation, as well as greater transparency in animal research practices.

The future of animal models in drug screening will likely involve a continued balancing of the benefits and drawbacks of animal models, as well as ongoing efforts to improve the ethical, technical, and predictive aspects of animal research.

Commonly used animal models in drug screening

- **Rodent models**
- **Non-human primate models**
- **Canine models**
- **Porcine models**
- **Zebrafish models**

Rodent models

Rodents, particularly mice and rats, are widely used in drug screening due to their relatively low cost, ease of handling, and short reproductive cycle. You could discuss the various types of rodent models that are commonly used, such as transgenic mice or spontaneously hypertensive rats, and their applications in drug screening.Rodents, particularly mice and rats, are widely used in drug screening due to their relatively low cost, ease of handling, and short reproductive cycle.

Transgenic rodent models: Transgenic mice and rats have been genetically engineered to express specific genes or mutations associated with human diseases, allowing researchers to study the underlying biology and test potential drugs. You could discuss the development and applications of various transgenic rodent models, such as Alzheimer's disease or cancer models.

Spontaneous rodent models: Some rodent models of disease occur naturally, without genetic engineering. For example, spontaneously hypertensive rats have been used as a model for hypertension and cardiovascular disease. You could discuss the advantages and limitations of spontaneous rodent models, as well as the challenges in identifying and characterizing these models.

Knockout rodent models: Knockout mice and rats have been engineered to lack specific genes, allowing researchers to study the function of those genes and their potential involvement in disease. You could discuss the development and applications of knockout rodent models, as well as the advantages and limitations of these models.

Xenograft rodent models: Xenograft models involve transplanting human cancer cells or tissue into immunodeficient mice, allowing researchers to study the behavior of human tumors in a more controlled environment. You could discuss the development and applications of various xenograft rodent models, as well as the challenges in modeling human cancer in mice.

Behavioral rodent models: Rodents are also commonly used to study behavioral and neurological disorders, such as anxiety, depression, or addiction. You could discuss the development and applications of various behavioral rodent models, as well as the challenges in translating these models to human behavior.

Transgenic rodent models

Transgenic rodent models have been an important tool in drug discovery and development, allowing researchers to study the underlying biology of human diseases and test potential drugs. These models involve genetically engineering mice or rats to express specific genes or mutations associated with a particular disease, such as Alzheimer's or cancer.

One example of a **transgenic rodent model** is the **Tg2576 mouse**, which overexpresses the human amyloid precursor protein (APP) gene and is widely used as a model for Alzheimer's disease. This model displays a progressive accumulation of amyloid plaques in the brain, similar to what is seen in human patients with the disease. Researchers can use this model to test potential drugs that target the accumulation of amyloid plaques.

Another example of a transgenic rodent model is the **TRAMP (transgenic adenocarcinoma of the mouse prostate) model**, which is used to study prostate cancer. This model involves the overexpression of the SV40 T antigen in the prostate gland, leading to the development of prostate cancer in the mice. Researchers can use this model to study the mechanisms of prostate cancer and test potential drugs for treating the disease.

Transgenic rodent models have provided valuable insights into the biology of human diseases and have been instrumental in the development of new drugs for treating these diseases.

Spontaneous rodent models

Spontaneous rodent models are animal models of human diseases that occur naturally, without genetic manipulation. These models are often used in preclinical drug screening because they closely resemble the pathology of human diseases. One example of a spontaneous rodent model is the spontaneously hypertensive rat, which has been used as a model for hypertension and cardiovascular disease.

One advantage of using spontaneous rodent models is that they reflect the complexity and heterogeneity of human diseases, providing a more accurate representation of the disease than genetically engineered models. Additionally, spontaneous rodent models are often more accessible and affordable than transgenic models.

However, there are also limitations to using spontaneous rodent models. The genetic variability of these models can make them more difficult to standardize and replicate, which can affect the reproducibility of experimental results. Furthermore, the natural occurrence of these models can make it more challenging to identify and characterize their disease phenotype and underlying pathology.

Despite these limitations, spontaneous rodent models remain a valuable tool in drug screening and the study of human diseases. To overcome the challenges of using these models, researchers must carefully characterize the model, optimize experimental conditions, and validate results to ensure the reliability and reproducibility of the findings.

Knockout rodent models

Knockout rodent models have been developed to study the function of specific genes and their role in disease. In these models, a specific gene is targeted and disrupted or "knocked out" in a mouse or rat, resulting in a loss of function of that gene. This allows researchers to study the consequences of that loss of function and the potential role of the gene in disease.

Knockout rodent models have been used extensively in drug discovery and development, particularly in the study of genetic diseases. For example, mouse models lacking the cystic fibrosis transmembrane conductance regulator (CFTR) gene have been used to study the mechanisms of cystic fibrosis and to test potential therapies.

One advantage of knockout rodent models is that they can provide valuable insights into the function of specific genes and their potential role in disease. They can also be used to validate potential drug targets and test the efficacy of drugs targeting those targets.

However, there are also limitations to knockout rodent models. For example, the loss of function of a single gene may not accurately reflect the complex interactions between genes and environmental factors that contribute to many diseases. In addition, the results of knockout rodent models may not always be directly applicable to humans.

Knockout rodent models are a valuable tool in drug discovery and development, but they must be used in conjunction with other models and approaches to fully understand the complexities of disease and develop effective therapies.

Xenograft rodent models

Xenograft rodent models are an important tool in cancer research as they allow for the study of human tumors in a more controlled environment. These models involve transplanting human cancer cells or tissue into immunodeficient mice, which lack the ability to reject the foreign cells.Xenograft rodent models are an important tool in cancer research as they allow for the study of human tumors in a more controlled environment. These models involve transplanting human cancer cells or tissue into immunodeficient mice, which lack the ability to reject the foreign cells.

The development of xenograft models involves selecting appropriate cancer cell lines, optimizing transplant conditions, and monitoring tumor growth and progression. Xenograft models can be established using a variety of cancer types, including breast, lung, and prostate cancer.

One advantage of xenograft models is that they allow for the study of human tumors in a more controlled environment, as opposed to studying tumors in human patients, which can be complicated by factors such as individual variation and treatment history. Xenograft models can also be used to test the efficacy of potential cancer drugs and to study the mechanisms of drug resistance.

However, there are also limitations to xenograft models. The immune system plays an important role in cancer development and response to treatment, and the lack of a functional immune system in immunodeficient mice can limit the relevance of xenograft models to human disease. In addition, the use of mouse stromal cells to support the transplanted human cancer cells can also introduce potential confounding factors.

Xenograft rodent models are a valuable tool in cancer research, but their limitations must be carefully considered and addressed to ensure the relevance and translatability of the findings to human disease.

Behavioral rodent models

Behavioral rodent models are a commonly used type of animal model for studying behavioral and neurological disorders, such as anxiety, depression, or addiction. These models are particularly useful because they allow researchers to observe and measure changes in behavior in response to different treatments or interventions.

There are a wide variety of behavioral rodent models that have been developed for different disorders. For example, the forced swim test is a commonly used model for studying depression in rodents, while the elevated plus maze is a model for studying anxiety. The conditioned place preference test is a model for studying addiction, in which rodents learn to associate a particular environment with a drug or other rewarding stimulus.

Behavioral rodent models are typically created by inducing a particular behavioral state in the rodents, either through genetic manipulation, environmental manipulation, or drug treatment. Researchers can then observe and measure changes in behavior, such as changes in locomotor activity, social interaction, or learning and memory.

One of the challenges of using behavioral rodent models is that rodents are not humans, and so it can be difficult to translate the results of these studies to human behavior. Additionally, there is often significant individual variation within groups of rodents, which can make it difficult to draw clear conclusions from the data.

Despite these challenges, behavioral rodent models remain a valuable tool for understanding the underlying biology of behavioral and neurological disorders, and for testing potential treatments or interventions.

Anxiety models: Anxiety is a complex disorder that is difficult to model in rodents, but several behavioral tests have been developed to measure different aspects of anxiety-like behavior, such as the elevated plus maze or the open field test.

Depression models: Like anxiety, depression is a complex disorder that is difficult to model in rodents, but several behavioral tests have been developed to measure different aspects of depression-like behavior, such as the forced swim test or the tail suspension test.

Addiction models: Addiction is a complex disorder that involves multiple brain regions and neurotransmitter systems. Several behavioral tests have been developed to model different aspects of addiction, such as drug self-administration or conditioned place preference.

Cognitive models: Rodents are also commonly used to study cognitive disorders, such as Alzheimer's disease or schizophrenia. Several behavioral tests have been developed to measure different aspects of cognition, such as the Morris water maze or the novel object recognition test.

Social behavior models: Rodents are social animals and display a wide range of social behaviors, such as aggression, mating, or maternal behavior. Several behavioral tests have been developed to measure different aspects of social behavior, such as the resident-intruder test or the maternal separation test.

Anxiety models

Elevated plus maze: The elevated plus maze is a widely used test for anxiety-like behavior in rodents. The maze consists of two open arms and two closed arms, and the amount of time spent in the open arms is used as a measure of anxiety-like behavior. You could discuss the advantages and limitations of this test, as well as how it has been used to screen potential anxiolytic drugs.

Open field test: The open field test is another commonly used test for anxiety-like behavior in rodents. The test measures the amount of time spent in the center of an open field arena, which is considered to be a measure of anxiety-like behavior. You could discuss the advantages and limitations of this test, as well as how it has been used to screen potential anxiolytic drugs.

Light/dark box: The light/dark box is a test that measures the willingness of a rodent to explore a brightly lit open area in the presence of a dark enclosed area. The test measures the amount of time spent in the brightly lit area and the number of transitions between the two areas. You could discuss the advantages and limitations of this test, as well as how it has been used to screen potential anxiolytic drugs.

Social interaction test: The social interaction test measures the amount of time a rodent spends interacting with another rodent, which is thought to be a measure of social anxiety. The test can be modified to include a non-social object as a control. You could discuss the advantages and limitations of this test, as well as how it has been used to screen potential anxiolytic drugs.

Novelty-induced hypophagia: The novelty-induced hypophagia test measures the suppression of feeding behavior in the presence of a novel stimulus, which is thought to be a measure of anxiety-like behavior. The test can be modified to include water deprivation as a motivation for the animal to drink from a novel water source. You could discuss the advantages and limitations of this test, as well as how it has been used to screen potential anxiolytic drugs.

Non-human primate models

Non-human primate models refer to the use of non-human primates, such as monkeys and apes, in scientific research to study human diseases, biology, behavior, and cognition. Non-human primate models are considered essential for many areas of research, including neuroscience, infectious diseases, reproductive biology, drug development, and toxicology.

There are several advantages to using non-human primates as models for human research. One of the primary advantages is their close genetic and physiological similarity to humans. Non-human primates share a high degree of genetic and biological similarity to humans, making them valuable models for studying human diseases and drug development. Additionally, their larger size compared to rodents allows for more detailed studies of anatomical and physiological features.

Non-human primates are also useful in studies of complex cognitive and behavioral functions, such as language and social behavior, which cannot be easily modeled in other animals. These studies can provide insights into human evolution and behavior, as well as potential treatments for neurological disorders.

However, the use of non-human primates in research also raises ethical concerns, and the high cost of their maintenance and care can limit their use. Additionally, the availability of non-human primates can be limited, and they are susceptible to many of the same diseases that affect humans.

There are several types of non-human primate models, including macaques, baboons, and chimpanzees. Macaques are the most commonly used non-human primate model in research due to their genetic and physiological similarity to humans, as well as their availability and relatively low cost.

Non-human primate models have been used in a variety of research areas, including studies of infectious diseases, such as HIV and Zika virus, neurodegenerative diseases, such as Alzheimer's disease, and drug development for conditions like cancer and diabetes.

Non-human primate models provide a valuable tool for studying human diseases and biology, as well as complex cognitive and behavioral functions. While the use of non-human primates in research raises ethical concerns and can be expensive, their close genetic and physiological similarity to humans make them essential models for many areas of research.

Non-human primates (NHPs) are widely used as animal models for human diseases and biomedical research due to their similarities to humans in physiology, anatomy, and behavior. There are several types of NHP models used in biomedical research, including:

Macaques: Macaques are the most commonly used NHP model in biomedical research. They are genetically and physiologically similar to humans, making them useful for studying a wide range of diseases, including infectious diseases, cancer, and neurological disorders. They are also commonly used in vaccine development and testing.

Marmosets: Marmosets are small NHPs that are becoming increasingly popular in biomedical research. They have a short lifespan, reproduce quickly, and are less expensive to maintain than other NHPs. Marmosets are commonly used to study infectious diseases, neuroscience, and regenerative medicine.

Chimpanzees: Chimpanzees are the closest genetic relatives to humans and have been used in biomedical research for many years. However, due to ethical concerns, the use of chimpanzees in research is now highly restricted and limited to specific situations where there are no other suitable animal models.

Tarsiers: Tarsiers are small nocturnal primates that are native to Southeast Asia. They have unique features, such as large eyes and long hind legs, which make them useful for studying vision and locomotion. They are also used to study the evolution of primate behavior and social structure.

Gibbons: Gibbons are small apes that are known for their unique arm-swinging locomotion. They are used in research to study primate behavior and evolution, as well as to model human neurological disorders.

Each NHP model has its unique advantages and limitations in research, and the choice of model depends on the specific research question and the disease being studied.

Macaques

Macaques are one of the most commonly used non-human primate models in biomedical research. They are a type of Old World monkey that belong to the genus Macaca and are native to various parts of Asia, including China, India, and Indonesia.

Macaques have a high degree of genetic similarity to humans, making them valuable models for studying diseases that affect humans. They are particularly useful for studying infectious diseases such as HIV, as they can be infected with simian immunodeficiency virus (SIV), a virus closely related to HIV.

Macaques have also been used to study neurological disorders such as Parkinson's disease and Alzheimer's disease, as well as reproductive and developmental biology. They are social animals and can be housed in groups, making them suitable for studying social behavior and group dynamics.

One of the major advantages of using macaques as a model is their similarity to humans in terms of physiology, anatomy, and behavior. This makes it easier to extrapolate findings from macaque studies to humans. Macaques also have a relatively long lifespan, allowing for the study of chronic diseases and long-term effects of interventions.

However, the use of macaques in research is controversial, as many people consider it unethical to use primates for biomedical research. Macaque studies can also be costly and time-consuming, as the animals require specialized care and facilities. Additionally, there are concerns about the variability between individual animals and the potential for confounding factors to affect study results.

Marmosets

Marmosets are small non-human primates that are increasingly being used as a model for biomedical research due to their unique biological and behavioral characteristics. One of the advantages of using marmosets as animal models is their cognitive abilities, which are more complex than those of rodents but less complex than those of larger primates, such as macaques and baboons.

Marmosets have a relatively large brain for their body size and exhibit complex social behaviors, such as vocal communication and cooperative parenting. These features make them a valuable model for studying various neurological and cognitive functions. For instance, researchers have used marmoset models to study neural mechanisms underlying vocal communication, including the role of different brain regions and neurotransmitters in vocal production and perception.

Another example of how marmosets have been utilized in research is in the field of visual perception. Marmosets have excellent color vision and are capable of discriminating between colors that appear identical to humans. As a result, they are useful models for studying the neural mechanisms of color vision and have been employed in studies exploring color vision-related disorders, such as color blindness.

Marmosets are also emerging as models for infectious diseases, such as Zika virus and COVID-19, due to their susceptibility to these pathogens and similarities to humans in immune responses. The use of marmosets in infectious disease research could aid in the development of vaccines and therapeutics for these diseases.

The unique biological and cognitive characteristics of marmosets make them a promising animal model for studying various aspects of human health and disease.

Chimpanzees

Chimpanzees are a type of non-human primate commonly used in biomedical research, particularly in the study of infectious diseases and vaccine development. They share more than 98% of their DNA with humans and have similar physiological and immune systems, making them a valuable model for studying human diseases and potential treatments.

One of the advantages of chimpanzee models is their susceptibility to certain infectious diseases that affect humans, such as hepatitis C virus (HCV) and malaria. This allows researchers to study the disease mechanisms and test potential treatments in a closely related species. For example, the development of effective HCV treatments was largely based on studies in chimpanzees.

However, the use of chimpanzees in research has been controversial due to ethical concerns and the fact that they are an endangered species. In 2013, the US National Institutes of Health (NIH) announced that it would retire most of its chimpanzee research colony and significantly limit the use of chimpanzees in research. Currently, the use of chimpanzees in biomedical research is highly regulated and requires approval from multiple ethical committees.

Tarsiers

Tarsiers are small, nocturnal primates found in Southeast Asia. They are unique among primates for their large eyes, which are fixed in their skulls and cannot be moved. Tarsiers have been used in research to study visual processing and neurophysiology, as well as their unique adaptations to nocturnal life. However, their use in research is more limited due to their protected status and difficulty in captivity.

Gibbons

Gibbons are a type of small ape that belong to the family Hylobatidae. They are native to the rainforests of Southeast Asia, and are known for their long arms and ability to move rapidly through the trees.

Gibbons have been used in research as a non-human primate model, although they are less commonly used than other primate species such as macaques or chimpanzees. One advantage of using gibbons in research is their close genetic relationship to humans - they share over 98% of their DNA with humans.

Gibbons have been studied in the context of comparative genomics, as well as in research on vocal communication and language evolution. Their unique vocalizations have been the subject of extensive research, as they provide insights into the neural and anatomical basis of language and communication in primates. Gibbons have also been studied in the context of conservation biology, as they are endangered in the wild due to habitat loss and hunting.

Baboons

Baboons are a type of Old World monkey that are often used as non-human primate models in medical research. They are larger than marmosets and macaques, making them a better model for studying certain physiological processes and disease states that are more similar to humans.

Baboons have been used in a wide range of research studies, including studies on cardiovascular disease, HIV/AIDS, and vaccine development. They are particularly useful in studying the progression and treatment of cardiovascular disease because they are prone to developing atherosclerosis, a condition in which the arteries become clogged with fatty deposits, similar to humans.

Baboons are also used as a model for HIV/AIDS because they can be infected with the simian immunodeficiency virus (SIV), a virus that is closely related to HIV. This allows researchers to study the virus and potential treatments in a model that is more similar to human physiology than rodents.

One disadvantage of using baboons as a model is their size and cost of housing and maintenance. Additionally, there is some controversy around the use of non-human primates in research, with some people arguing that their use is unethical due to their cognitive and emotional capacities.

Canine models are a type of animal model used in biomedical research, particularly in the study of diseases and therapeutics. Dogs share many anatomical and physiological similarities with humans, making them valuable models for understanding disease pathogenesis and developing new treatments. They also have the added advantage of being social animals that live in close proximity to humans, allowing for easier access to study their behavior and environment.

Canine models are used in various stages of drug development, including screening methods, to evaluate the safety and efficacy of potential drugs. In particular, dogs have been used to evaluate the toxicity and pharmacokinetics of compounds, as well as their potential effects on the cardiovascular and nervous systems. Canine models can provide valuable information on the safety and efficacy of a compound before it is tested in humans, and can help identify potential risks and side effects.

In screening methods, canine models can be used in both in vitro and in vivo testing. In vitro screening can involve testing the effects of a compound on isolated canine cells or biological systems, while in vivo screening can involve administering the compound to dogs and monitoring its effects on various physiological systems. Canine models can also be used in behavioral and cognitive testing, particularly for neurological disorders such as epilepsy.

Overall, canine models offer a valuable tool for evaluating the safety and efficacy of potential drugs, and can provide important insights into the potential risks and benefits of new therapies.

Here are some examples of different canine models used in screening methods:

Beagles:

Greyhounds: Greyhounds have been used in medical research due to their unique physiology. They are an athletic breed with a high oxygen-carrying capacity and low body fat, making them useful for studying conditions related to endurance and muscle physiology.

German Shepherds: German Shepherds have been used in drug development research, particularly for studying drug pharmacokinetics and pharmacodynamics. Their size and easy-to-handle nature make them useful for research requiring larger animals.

Labrador Retrievers: Labrador Retrievers have been used in a range of screening methods, including drug development and medical device testing. They are a popular breed due to their friendly disposition and eagerness to please, making them easy to work with in research settings.

Dachshunds: Dachshunds have been used in the study of spinal cord injuries and neurological conditions. Their long, low-slung bodies make them a useful model for spinal cord research, and they are often used to test therapies for spinal cord injuries.

Each breed has its own unique characteristics that make it suitable for specific research purposes. The choice of canine model will depend on the research question, the specific characteristics of the breed, and the availability of appropriate animals.

Porcine models

Porcine models, which involve the use of pigs in biomedical research, have become increasingly popular in recent years. Pigs are anatomically and physiologically similar to humans in many ways, making them a valuable model for a variety of human diseases and conditions. Here are some detailed notes on porcine models:

Anatomy and physiology: Pigs have many similarities to humans in terms of their anatomy and physiology, including the structure and function of their cardiovascular, respiratory, gastrointestinal, and immune systems. Pigs also have a similar body size and shape to humans, which can be beneficial for surgical procedures or other interventions.

Disease models: Porcine models have been used to study a wide range of human diseases, including cardiovascular disease, diabetes, cancer, infectious diseases, and more. One notable example is the use of pig models to study the Zika virus and its impact on fetal development.

Transplantation: Pigs have been used as a source of organs for transplantation into humans due to their anatomical and physiological similarities. Researchers have been working to genetically modify pigs to reduce the risk of organ rejection and increase the success of xenotransplantation.

Toxicology and drug development: Porcine models are also used to study the toxicity and efficacy of potential drugs, as well as to test medical devices and other interventions. They are particularly useful for assessing the safety and efficacy of cardiovascular devices and therapies.

Challenges: While porcine models have many advantages, there are also some challenges to using them in research. For example, pigs are relatively expensive compared to other animal models, and their large size can make housing and handling them difficult. Additionally, there are some anatomical and physiological differences between pigs and humans that must be taken into account when interpreting research findings.

Porcine models are a valuable tool for biomedical research due to their similarities to humans in terms of anatomy and physiology. They have been used to study a wide range of diseases and conditions, as well as for drug development and toxicology testing. However, their use also presents some challenges that must be carefully considered.

Zebrafish models

Zebrafish (Danio rerio) are small, freshwater fish that have become an increasingly popular model organism for biomedical research. Zebrafish have a number of advantages as a model organism, including their small size, rapid development, transparent embryos, and ease of genetic manipulation. Zebrafish are particularly useful for studying early development and disease, including cancer, neurodegenerative disorders, and cardiovascular disease.

Zebrafish have a number of physiological similarities to humans, including a vertebrate body plan, similar organ systems, and conserved genetic pathways. For example, zebrafish have a similar cardiovascular system to humans, with a two-chambered heart and similar blood vessel architecture. Zebrafish also have a similar nervous system to humans, with many conserved genes involved in neural development and function.

Zebrafish are also amenable to high-throughput screening, as they can be easily maintained in large numbers and their transparent embryos allow for rapid screening of potential drugs or genetic manipulations. Zebrafish are also relatively inexpensive to maintain compared to other model organisms, such as mice.

There are several different strains of zebrafish used in research, each with their own advantages and disadvantages. For example, the AB strain is commonly used as a wild-type strain, while the casper strain has been genetically modified to be transparent throughout development. The Tg(fli1a:egfp) strain has green fluorescent protein (GFP) expression in endothelial cells, allowing for visualization of the vasculature, while the Tg(ngn1:GAL4-VP16,UAS:egfp) strain has GFP expression in the nervous system.

Zebrafish models provide a powerful tool for understanding disease mechanisms, screening potential therapeutics, and identifying novel targets for drug development.

ꕥ

In addition to the in vitro and in vivo stages, the screening process can also involve several other steps, such as:

Target identification: In this step, researchers identify a biological target that is involved in a disease process, and which can be targeted by a drug to produce a therapeutic effect.

Compound library generation: This step involves creating a large collection of compounds that can be screened for pharmacological activity. The library can be composed of natural products, synthetic compounds, or a combination of both.

Hit identification: In this step, the screening process identifies a compound that interacts with the biological target, producing a desired effect. These compounds are referred to as hits, and they undergo further optimization to improve their pharmacological properties.

Hit-to-lead optimization: This step involves improving the potency, selectivity, and pharmacokinetic properties of the hit compounds, to enhance their efficacy and safety.

Lead optimization: In this step, researchers further optimize the lead compounds to improve their safety, bioavailability, and pharmacokinetic properties. The goal is to identify a compound that has the desired pharmacological activity and can be developed into a safe and effective drug.

Preclinical studies: Before a drug can be tested in humans, it must undergo preclinical studies to evaluate its safety and efficacy. These studies involve testing the drug in animals to determine its pharmacokinetic properties, toxicity, and potential adverse effects.

Clinical trials: If the preclinical studies are successful, the drug can advance to clinical trials, which involve testing the drug in humans to evaluate its safety and efficacy.

The screening process is a complex and iterative process that requires a multidisciplinary team of researchers with expertise in chemistry, biology, pharmacology, and other areas. The goal is to identify new therapeutic agents that can improve human health, and the process can take several years and cost millions of dollars.

XIII

Anti-Psychotics, Anti Epileptics, Anti Depressants

Antipsychotics

Antipsychotics are medications used to treat various psychotic disorders, such as schizophrenia, bipolar disorder, and major depressive disorder with psychotic features. These medications work by altering the levels of certain neurotransmitters in the brain, particularly dopamine and serotonin.

Screening methods for antipsychotics aim to evaluate the efficacy and safety of potential new drugs for treating psychotic disorders. The screening methods can vary depending on the specific goals of the study, but many of them involve using animal models to observe behavioral changes and other physiological responses to the drug. Commonly used animal models include rodents and non-human primates.

Some of the commonly used screening methods for antipsychotics include behavioral tests, such as the forced swim test and the tail suspension test, which can assess depressive-like symptoms in animals. Other methods involve examining neurotransmitter levels in the brain or conducting histological analyses of brain tissue to observe changes in cellular and molecular markers.

Screening methods for antipsychotics are crucial for the development of new and effective treatments for psychotic disorders, and they play an essential role in advancing our understanding of the neurobiological mechanisms underlying these conditions.

Behavioral Assays:

Behavioral assays are tests that evaluate the effects of new substances on specific behaviors or physiological responses. These assays can be used to assess the antipsychotic activity of new substances and can provide information about the potential therapeutic benefits and adverse effects of treatment. For example, behavioral assays can be used to evaluate the effects of new substances on measures of anxiety, depression, or aggression in animals.

Behavioral assays play a crucial role in the evaluation of antipsychotic activity of new substances. These assays can be performed in both animal models and humans, and can provide valuable information about the potential therapeutic benefits and adverse effects of new substances.

Some of the commonly used behavioral assays for evaluating antipsychotic activity

Elevated Plus Maze (EPM) test

The Elevated Plus Maze is a widely used behavioral test in preclinical research to evaluate anxiety-like behavior in rodents. The test is based on the natural aversion of rodents to open and elevated spaces, which is considered a measure of anxiety-related behavior. The EPM consists of a plus-shaped maze with two opposing open arms and two opposing closed arms, connected by a central platform. The test animal is placed in the center of the maze facing an open arm, and its behavior is recorded. The EPM is a simple, fast, and cost-effective test that requires minimal training and equipment. It is considered a useful tool for evaluating the anxiolytic potential of drugs, as well as for studying the neurobiological mechanisms of anxiety disorders.

This assay is also used to evaluate the effects of new substances on anxiety levels in animals. The test involves placing an animal in an elevated platform with four arms, two of which are enclosed and two of which are open. The amount of time that the animal spends in the enclosed versus open arms can provide information about the animal's level of anxiety and the potential therapeutic benefits of the new substance.

Materials:

Elevated plus maze (made of Plexiglas or similar material)

1. Stopwatch or timer
2. Paper and pencil for recording data
3. Animal handling gloves
4. Animal holding area
5. Lighting source (50 lux)
6. Animals:
7. Adult rats or mice (weighing 200-300 g)

Procedure:

1. The elevated plus maze should be placed in a dimly lit room with a lighting source of 50 lux.
2. The animals should be transported to the experimental room at least 30 minutes prior to testing to acclimate to the new environment.

3. The animals are individually placed on the center of the maze, facing one of the closed arms, and allowed to explore the maze for a specific duration, typically 5 minutes.
4. The time spent on the open and closed arms and the number of entries into each arm are recorded. An entry is defined as all four paws entering the arm.
5. After each animal is tested, the maze should be cleaned with a 70% ethanol solution to remove any potential olfactory cues.
6. The data collected can be analyzed using statistical software to calculate the percentage of time spent on the open arms and the number of entries into each arm.

Values:

- The percentage of time spent on the open arms is calculated as (time spent on open arms / total time in maze) x 100.
- The number of entries into each arm can be recorded and used as an additional measure of anxiety-like behavior.

Note: The values obtained from the EPM should be interpreted in the context of other behavioral tests and the animal's overall behavior to determine anxiety-like behavior.

Porsolt swim test:

The Porsolt swim test, also known as the forced swim test, is a commonly used behavioral test in preclinical research to evaluate the effectiveness of antidepressant drugs. The test is based on the observation that rodents exhibit an immobility response when placed in an inescapable cylinder filled with water, which is thought to represent a state of despair or hopelessness. Antidepressant drugs are known to reduce this immobility response, indicating a potential therapeutic effect.

The Porsolt swim test is considered to be a valuable tool for screening potential antidepressant drugs and evaluating their efficacy in animal models. The test has been widely used in the development of selective serotonin reuptake inhibitors (SSRIs), which are commonly prescribed antidepressant drugs.

While the Porsolt swim test has been criticized for its limited ability to model the complex nature of depression and for its reliance on a single behavioral endpoint, it remains a widely used and accepted test in preclinical research.

Methodology

Introduction: The Porsolt swim test is a widely used behavioral assay to evaluate antidepressant activity in rodents. The test is based on the principle that antidepressant drugs decrease immobility time in a forced swimming situation. The test involves placing a rodent in a large cylinder of water and recording its behavior over a set period of time. The data obtained from this test can provide valuable insights into the efficacy of potential antidepressant drugs.

Materials:

- A large cylinder tank (60 cm height x 30 cm diameter) filled with water (23 ± 1°C) up to a height of 30 cm.
- Stopwatch or timer
- Recording device (video camera or software)

Methodology:

Pre-test adaptation:

The animals are placed in the testing room for at least 30 minutes before the start of the test to allow them to adapt to the environment.

The animals are not allowed to eat or drink for at least 2 hours before the test.

Test procedure:

1. The animals are individually placed in the water-filled cylinder for a single 6-minute session.
2. The test is conducted under dim light conditions to reduce stress in the animals.
3. The behavior of the animal is recorded using a video camera or software for subsequent analysis.
4. The following parameters are recorded during the test:
5. Immobility time: time spent floating without any activity except for movements necessary to keep the head above water
6. Swimming time: time spent actively swimming
7. Climbing time: time spent attempting to escape by climbing the walls of the cylinder

The recorded behavior is analyzed by an observer who is blind to the treatment groups.

Immobility time, swimming time and climbing time are measured using a stopwatch or software.

The data obtained is statistically analyzed using appropriate methods, such as ANOVA or Student's t-test.

Note: The Porsolt swim test is a widely used and validated test for assessing antidepressant activity in rodents. However, it is important to recognize the limitations of the test and use it in conjunction with other assays to fully evaluate the potential of a drug candidate. Care should be taken to ensure the humane treatment of animals and adherence to local animal welfare regulations.

The Apomorphine-induced stereotypy test

It is a commonly used behavioral assay to evaluate the effects of potential antipsychotic drugs on motor stereotypy in animals. Stereotypy refers to repetitive and purposeless movements or behaviors that can be observed in animals with psychotic-like symptoms. The test involves administering the dopamine receptor agonist apomorphine, which induces stereotypic behaviors in rodents. The test can be used to screen potential antipsychotic drugs for their ability to reduce or inhibit apomorphine-induced stereotypy, providing insights into their potential efficacy in treating psychotic symptoms. The test is relatively easy to perform and has good face validity, as it mimics some of the key features of human psychosis.

Methodology

- The test is typically performed on rats or mice that have been previously exposed to psychostimulant drugs.
- Apomorphine, a dopamine receptor agonist, is administered to the animal either subcutaneously or intraperitoneally. The dose of apomorphine is typically 0.05-0.25 mg/kg.
- The animal is observed for a period of 60-90 minutes following apomorphine administration. The frequency and duration of stereotypic behaviors, such as repetitive sniffing, head bobbing, or gnawing, are recorded.
- A stereotypy score is assigned to the animal based on the frequency and duration of stereotypic behaviors. The score is typically on a scale of 0-4, with 0 indicating no stereotypy and 4 indicating intense and continuous stereotypy.
- The test is used to evaluate the efficacy of potential antipsychotic drugs in reducing apomorphine-induced stereotypy. The test drug is administered to the animal before or after apomorphine administration, and the frequency and duration of stereotypic behaviors are recorded and compared to the control group.
- The data obtained from the test are analyzed using statistical methods to determine the significance of the differences between the control group and the experimental group.

It's important to note that the exact methodology can vary depending on the specific experimental conditions and the research question being addressed.

The Conditioned Avoidance Response (CAR) test

The Conditioned Avoidance Response (CAR) test is a preclinical behavioral test that is used to screen the potential antipsychotic effects of new drug candidates. The CAR test is based on the principle that animals will learn to avoid a conditioned stimulus that has been paired with an aversive unconditioned stimulus.

In the CAR test, animals are trained to avoid a specific cue, such as a light or tone, that has been paired with an aversive stimulus, such as a mild electric shock. The animals are then tested for their ability to avoid the cue in the presence of different drugs.

Antipsychotic drugs are known to attenuate the CAR response, meaning that animals are less likely to avoid the cue when they are under the influence of an antipsychotic drug. Therefore, the CAR test can be used as a screening tool to identify potential antipsychotic drug candidates.

The CAR test has been widely used in preclinical research to screen antipsychotic drugs and to better understand the underlying neural mechanisms of schizophrenia and other psychotic disorders. However, it's worth noting that the results from animal tests may not necessarily translate directly to human patients, and additional testing is required before any drug can be approved for clinical use.

Methodology:

Animals: Male rodents (such as rats or mice) are commonly used for this test. The animals are typically housed in individual cages under standard laboratory conditions (temperature, humidity, light/dark cycle, etc.) and are given access to food and water ad libitum.

Apparatus: The CAR test apparatus consists of a conditioning chamber (also known as a shuttle box) that is divided into two compartments separated by a sliding door. One compartment has a grid floor that can deliver a mild electric shock, and the other has a smooth floor. A tone or light stimulus is presented from a speaker or light source that is positioned above the compartment with the smooth floor.

Training: During the training phase, animals are placed in the shuttle box and exposed to a tone or light stimulus that is immediately followed by a mild electric shock (such as 0.3 mA, 1 s duration). The animals are then allowed to move to the other compartment to avoid the shock. This pairing of the stimulus and shock is repeated for a set number of trials (such as 20-30) until the animal learns to associate the stimulus with the shock and reliably avoids it.

Testing: Once the animals have been trained to avoid the stimulus, they are tested for their ability to avoid the stimulus in the presence of different drugs. The animals are typically injected with a test drug or a placebo, and the stimulus is presented again. The number of avoidances (defined as crossing from the compartment with the shock grid to the compartment with the smooth floor) is recorded over a set period of time (such as 3 minutes).

Data analysis: The percentage of successful avoidance responses is calculated for each animal, and the results are compared across different drugs or doses. The data is typically analyzed using statistical software (such as SPSS or GraphPad Prism) to determine if the drug has a significant effect on the CAR response compared to the placebo.

Controls: To ensure that the results are not confounded by factors such as motor impairment or sedation, additional control tests may be performed, such as open-field tests or grip strength tests.

Conditioned suppression test

The Conditioned Suppression Test (CST) is a preclinical behavioral test used to evaluate the potential antipsychotic effects of new drug candidates. The CST is based on the principle that animals can be trained to exhibit a conditioned fear response, and this response can be used to assess the effects of drugs on behavior.

In the CST, animals are trained to associate a particular cue or context (such as a tone or a specific chamber) with an aversive stimulus, such as a mild electric shock or an air puff. Once the animals have learned to associate the cue with the aversive stimulus, they will exhibit a fear response (such as freezing behavior) when the cue is presented.

To evaluate the potential antipsychotic effects of drugs, animals are given a test drug or placebo, and the conditioned fear response is measured in the presence of the cue. Antipsychotic drugs are known to attenuate the conditioned fear response, meaning that animals are less likely to exhibit the fear response when they are under the influence of an antipsychotic drug. Therefore, the CST can be used as a screening tool to identify potential antipsychotic drug candidates.

The CST has been widely used in preclinical research to evaluate the potential antipsychotic effects of new drug candidates and to better understand the underlying neural mechanisms of schizophrenia and other psychotic disorders. However, as with all preclinical testing, the results must be interpreted with caution and additional testing is required before any drug can be approved for clinical use.

Methodology:

Animals: Male rodents (such as rats or mice) are commonly used for this test. The animals are typically housed in individual cages under standard laboratory conditions (temperature, humidity, light/dark cycle, etc.) and are given access to food and water ad libitum.

Apparatus: The CST apparatus consists of a conditioning chamber (such as a fear conditioning chamber) that can deliver a tone or light stimulus and an aversive stimulus (such as a mild electric shock or an air puff). The apparatus is equipped with software to control the delivery of the stimuli and to record the animal's behavior.

Conditioning: During the conditioning phase, animals are placed in the conditioning chamber and exposed to a tone or light stimulus that is immediately followed by an aversive stimulus (such as a mild electric shock or an air puff). This pairing of the stimulus and the aversive stimulus is repeated for a set number of trials (such as 10-15) until the animal learns to associate the stimulus with the aversive stimulus and exhibits a conditioned fear response (such as freezing behavior).

Testing: Once the animals have been conditioned, they are tested for their ability to suppress the conditioned fear response in the presence of different drugs. The animals are typically injected with a test drug or a placebo, and the conditioned stimulus is presented again. The level of conditioned suppression is measured by the proportion of time the animal spends freezing during the presentation of the stimulus. Typically, the duration of the conditioned stimulus is 30 seconds, and the test period is 5 minutes.

Data analysis: The level of conditioned suppression is calculated for each animal, and the results are compared across different drugs or doses. The data is typically analyzed using statistical software (such as SPSS or GraphPad Prism) to determine if the drug has a significant effect on the conditioned suppression response compared to the placebo.

Controls: To ensure that the results are not confounded by factors such as motor impairment or sedation, additional control tests may be performed, such as open-field tests or grip strength tests.

Overall, the CST is a widely used preclinical screening tool for antipsychotic drugs. While this method involves animal testing, it can provide valuable insights into potential therapeutic effects and underlying neural mechanisms. However, as with all preclinical testing, the results must be interpreted with caution and additional testing in humans is required before any drug can be approved for clinical use.

The locomotor activity test

It is a behavioral test used to assess the motor activity of an animal in response to a stimulus. This test is commonly used in preclinical research to evaluate the effects of drugs on locomotion, and to study the underlying mechanisms of disorders such as Parkinson's disease and schizophrenia. In this test, the animal is placed in an open field and its movements are monitored and recorded. The test can provide information on the stimulant or depressant effects of drugs on the central nervous system, as well as their effects on coordination and balance.

The locomotor activity test can be performed in various animal species, including mice, rats, and zebrafish. The test can be conducted in a variety of settings, including an open field, an enclosed chamber, or a maze. The test can be modified to suit the specific needs of the experiment, such as by altering the duration or intensity of the stimulus, or by combining it with other behavioral tests. The locomotor activity test is considered to be a simple, reliable, and valid tool for assessing the effects of drugs on locomotion and behavior.

Methodology

Experimental animals: The Locomotor Activity Test can be conducted in various animal species, including mice, rats, and guinea pigs.

Apparatus: A locomotor activity chamber is required for conducting this test. The chamber should be made of clear Plexiglas and should be equipped with infrared photocells for detecting animal movement. The dimensions of the chamber can vary, but a common size is 40 x 40 x 30 cm.

Habituation: Prior to conducting the experiment, animals should be allowed to habituate to the test environment. This can be done by placing animals in the locomotor activity chamber for 30 minutes to 1 hour each day for 2-3 days before the experiment.

Testing: On the day of the experiment, animals are placed in the locomotor activity chamber and allowed to habituate for 30 minutes. After habituation, the activity of the animal is recorded for a set period of time, usually 30 minutes to 1 hour. The number of infrared photocell beam breaks is used as a measure of locomotor activity.

Drug administration: The Locomotor Activity Test can be used to assess the effects of various drugs on locomotor activity. The drug can be administered either systemically or directly into the brain, depending on the research question being addressed.

Data analysis: The data obtained from the Locomotor Activity Test can be analyzed using various statistical methods, including analysis of variance (ANOVA) and t-tests. The number of beam breaks is often analyzed as a function of time to assess changes in locomotor activity over the course of the experiment.

Controls: Appropriate control groups should be included in the experiment to account for any confounding variables. For example, a group of animals that receive a saline injection or vehicle control should be included to control for the effects of the injection itself.

Overall, the Locomotor Activity Test is a widely used assay for assessing the effects of drugs on animal behavior. The test can be used to evaluate the effects of drugs on locomotor activity and can be applied in various animal models of neurological and psychiatric disorders.

Prepulse inhibition (PPI) test

Prepulse inhibition (PPI) test is a behavioral assay used to assess sensorimotor gating in animals, which involves the ability of an organism to filter out unnecessary or irrelevant stimuli in its environment. In this test, a prepulse sound stimulus is presented before the onset of a startling sound stimulus. The prepulse sound stimulus is typically presented at a lower intensity and is meant to prime the organism and reduce its response to the startling sound stimulus. The PPI test is often used in research related to schizophrenia and other psychiatric disorders, as individuals with these disorders are known to have deficits in sensorimotor gating.

Methodology: The PPI test is typically conducted using rodents such as rats or mice. The animals are placed in a startle chamber, which is a sound-attenuated enclosure with a platform on which the animal sits or stands. The animal is acclimated to the chamber for a period of time before the test begins. During the test, the animal is exposed to a series of acoustic stimuli, including a prepulse stimulus followed by a startling stimulus. The prepulse stimulus is typically presented at a range of intensities (e.g., 74, 78, and 82 dB), and the startling stimulus is presented at a fixed intensity (e.g., 110 dB). The amplitude of the startle response is measured by sensors on the platform, and the level of PPI is calculated as the percentage reduction in the startle response amplitude in the presence of the prepulse stimulus compared to the startle response amplitude in the absence of the prepulse stimulus. The test is conducted under different conditions, such as varying the interstimulus interval (the time between the prepulse and startling stimuli), the intensity and frequency of the stimuli, and the background noise level in the chamber. The PPI test is useful in assessing the effects of drugs or other interventions on sensorimotor gating and in screening potential therapeutics for psychiatric disorders.

The Catalepsy test

It is a behavioral assay used to assess the motor function and neurological disorders in animals, particularly rodents. The test measures the ability of an animal to maintain a static posture for a prolonged period of time. Catalepsy is defined as a state of sustained immobility, where animals appear frozen in place, holding an unusual posture for an extended period.

Methodology:

Experimental animals: The Catalepsy test is commonly used in rats and mice, but can be adapted to other species.

Apparatus: A standard wooden or Perspex platform is required. The size of the platform should be large enough to accommodate the animal and allow for its movement.

Testing: The test can be conducted in two different ways:

a) Bar test: The animal is placed in a cage or on a platform, and a horizontal bar is placed at a height of 3-4 cm above the base of the platform. The animal is then gently placed on the bar, and the duration of the immobility is recorded. A cut-off time of 60 seconds is commonly used.

b) Board test: In this variation, the animal is placed on a flat wooden board or platform, and one or both of its forepaws are gently placed on a raised surface. The duration of the immobility is then recorded.

Data analysis: The duration of the cataleptic state is recorded in seconds and can be used to assess the effects of drugs or experimental treatments on motor function.

Controls: Appropriate control groups should be included in the experiment to account for any confounding variables. For example, a group of animals that receive a saline injection or vehicle control should be included to control for the effects of the injection itself.

The Catalepsy test is a reliable and widely used assay for assessing motor function and neurological disorders in animals. It has been used to study the effects of a wide range of drugs, including antipsychotics, antidepressants, and antiepileptics. The test has also been used in various animal models of neurological and psychiatric disorders, including Parkinson's disease, Huntington's disease, and schizophrenia.

The social interaction test

The social interaction test is a behavioral assay used to assess social behavior in animals, particularly rodents such as mice and rats. The test is often used in research related to autism spectrum disorders, schizophrenia, depression, and anxiety.

Introduction: Social interaction behavior is important for many species, including humans, as it can have an impact on survival and reproduction. In the social interaction test, the time spent interacting with a conspecific animal is measured to assess the level of social behavior in the tested animal.

Methodology:

Animals: The test can be performed in various animal species, but rodents such as mice and rats are commonly used. Both sexes can be used, but typically same-sex animals are used.

Apparatus: A testing arena or chamber is required for conducting the social interaction test. The arena should be large enough to accommodate the animals and should have minimal visual and auditory distractions. A video camera and software for recording and analyzing the behavior are also required.

Habituation: Prior to conducting the experiment, animals should be allowed to habituate to the test environment. This can be done by placing animals in the testing arena for a period of time (usually 30 minutes) on the day before the experiment.

Testing: On the day of the experiment, two animals of the same sex (e.g., test animal and a stranger animal) are placed in the testing arena and allowed to interact for a set period of time (e.g., 10 minutes). The behavior of the animals is recorded using a video camera and later analyzed by a trained observer using specialized software.

Scoring: The behavior of the animals during the test is scored based on several parameters, such as the time spent in social interaction (e.g., sniffing, following, grooming) and the number of aggressive or defensive behaviors.

Controls: Appropriate control groups should be included in the experiment to account for any confounding variables. For example, a group of animals that are isolated from other animals should be included to control for the effects of social isolation.

Data analysis: The data obtained from the social interaction test can be analyzed using various statistical methods, including analysis of variance (ANOVA) and t-tests.

The Forced Swim Test

It is a behavioral test used to assess depressive-like behavior in rodents, specifically to evaluate the efficacy of antidepressant drugs. The test is based on the observation that rodents will exhibit immobility when placed in a container of water, which is interpreted as a state of despair or hopelessness.

Methodology:

Experimental animals: The Forced Swim Test can be conducted in various animal species, including mice, rats, and guinea pigs.

Apparatus: A cylindrical container made of glass or clear Plexiglas is required for the test. The dimensions of the container can vary, but a common size is 30 cm in height and 20 cm in diameter. The container should be filled with water to a depth of 20-25 cm and maintained at a temperature of 23-25°C.

Testing: On the day of the experiment, the animal is placed in the container and allowed to swim for a set period of time, usually 5-10 minutes. The animal's behavior is videotaped or observed by an experimenter who is blind to the treatment condition.

Data analysis: The behavior of the animal during the test is classified into two categories: immobility and mobility. Immobility is defined as the absence of active movements, while mobility is defined as any active movement, including swimming, climbing, or struggling. The duration of immobility is used as a measure of depressive-like behavior, with longer durations of immobility indicating a greater level of despair or hopelessness.

Drug administration: The Forced Swim Test can be used to evaluate the effects of various drugs on depressive-like behavior. The drug can be administered either systemically or directly into the brain, depending on the research question being addressed. Antidepressant drugs are expected to reduce the duration of immobility, while drugs that exacerbate depressive-like behavior are expected to increase the duration of immobility.

Controls: Appropriate control groups should be included in the experiment to account for any confounding variables. For example, a group of animals that receive a saline injection or vehicle control should be included to control for the effects of the injection itself.

The Forced Swim Test is a widely used assay for assessing depressive-like behavior in rodents and for evaluating the efficacy of antidepressant drugs. However, there is ongoing debate about the validity and reliability of the test, and it is recommended that the test be used in combination with other behavioral tests to provide a more comprehensive assessment of depressive-like behavior.

Morris water maze test

The Morris water maze test is a widely used behavioral assay to evaluate spatial learning and memory in rodents. The test requires animals to learn and remember the location of a hidden platform in a pool of water.

Methodology:

Apparatus: The Morris water maze consists of a circular pool filled with opaque water. The pool is divided into four quadrants and is surrounded by visual cues on the walls of the testing room.

Animals: The Morris water maze can be used in various animal species, including rats and mice.

Procedure:

Acquisition phase: During the acquisition phase, animals are trained to locate a hidden platform in the pool. The platform is placed in one of the quadrants of the pool and is submerged beneath the surface of the water. Animals are placed in the pool and allowed to swim until they locate the platform. Once they find the platform, they are allowed to remain on it for a fixed period of time before being removed from the pool. This process is repeated several times over multiple days to assess learning and memory.

Probe trial: After the acquisition phase, a probe trial is conducted to evaluate memory retention. During the probe trial, the platform is removed from the pool, and animals are placed in the water at a location opposite to where the platform was previously located. The time spent in the quadrant where the platform was previously located is measured as an index of spatial memory retention.

Data analysis: The data obtained from the Morris water maze test can be analyzed using various statistical methods, including analysis of variance (ANOVA) and t-tests. The time spent in the quadrant where the platform was previously located is often used as a measure of spatial learning and memory.

Overall, the Morris water maze test is a widely used assay for evaluating spatial learning and memory in rodents. The test can be used to assess the effects of drugs or other interventions on learning and memory and can be applied in various animal models of neurological and psychiatric disorders.

Open field test

The Open Field Test is a widely used behavioral assay for assessing locomotor and exploratory activity in rodents. The test involves placing an animal in a novel, open environment and recording its movements over a set period of time. The open field test is used to study a range of behaviors, including anxiety, exploration, locomotion, and habituation.

Methodology: The Open Field Test can be conducted using various animal species, including mice, rats, and guinea pigs. The test is typically performed in a square or circular arena that is surrounded by walls to prevent the animal from escaping.

The animal is placed in the center of the arena and allowed to explore the environment for a set period of time, usually 5-10 minutes. The movement of the animal is recorded using a video camera, and a computer-based tracking system is used to analyze the animal's movements.

The open field arena is often divided into a central area and a peripheral area, and the time the animal spends in each area is recorded. The total distance traveled by the animal, the velocity of movement, the frequency and duration of rearing (standing on hind legs), and the number of fecal boli are also commonly recorded.

Data obtained from the Open Field Test can be analyzed using various statistical methods, including analysis of variance (ANOVA) and t-tests. Changes in behavior can be analyzed as a function of time, and different aspects of behavior can be analyzed separately, such as locomotion, anxiety-like behavior, and exploration.

Controls: Appropriate control groups should be included in the experiment to account for any confounding variables. For example, a group of animals that receive a saline injection or vehicle control should be included to control for the effects of the injection itself. The Open Field Test is also commonly used in combination with other behavioral assays, such as the Elevated Plus Maze, to provide complementary measures of anxiety-like behavior.

Overall, the Open Field Test is a widely used assay for assessing locomotor and exploratory behavior in rodents, and it can be applied in various animal models of neurological and psychiatric disorders.

Tail suspension test

The Tail Suspension Test is a behavioral test used to evaluate antidepressant-like effects of drugs in rodents. It is based on the observation that animals subjected to a stressful stimulus, such as being suspended by the tail, exhibit immobility, which is considered to be a behavior related to behavioral despair or depression. The test measures the amount of time the animal remains immobile during the test session.

Methodology:

Experimental Animals: The Tail Suspension Test is commonly conducted in mice and rats.

Apparatus: A tail suspension apparatus is required for this test. The apparatus consists of a horizontal bar suspended by a metal frame. The tail of the animal is attached to the horizontal bar using adhesive tape.

Test Procedure: The test is usually performed in a quiet, dimly lit room. The animal is suspended by its tail from the horizontal bar for a set period of time, typically 6 minutes. During this time, the animal's behavior is recorded, and the amount of time the animal remains immobile is measured.

Drug Administration: The Tail Suspension Test can be used to evaluate the effects of various drugs on immobility. The drug can be administered either systemically or directly into the brain, depending on the research question being addressed.

Data Analysis: The amount of time the animal remains immobile is measured using a stopwatch or an automated tracking system. The data obtained from the Tail Suspension Test can be analyzed using various statistical methods, including analysis of variance (ANOVA) and t-tests.

Controls: Appropriate control groups should be included in the experiment to account for any confounding variables. For example, a group of animals that receive a saline injection or vehicle control should be included to control for the effects of the injection itself.

Overall, the Tail Suspension Test is a widely used assay for assessing the effects of drugs on animal behavior related to depression. It is a simple and efficient test that allows for rapid screening of potential antidepressant drugs.

Antipsychotics are a class of drugs used in the treatment of various mental disorders, including schizophrenia and bipolar disorder. There are several screening methods used for evaluating the antipsychotic activity of new drug candidates, including behavioral and molecular assays.

Behavioral assays for antipsychotics include tests for locomotor activity, stereotypy, catalepsy, and other behaviors associated with psychosis in animal models. Molecular assays for antipsychotics include receptor binding assays, signaling pathway assays, and gene expression analysis.

While these assays provide valuable information about the potential efficacy of new antipsychotic drugs, they do not always predict clinical efficacy or adverse effects. Therefore, further testing in preclinical animal models and in human clinical trials is necessary to fully evaluate the safety and efficacy of new antipsychotic drugs.

The screening methods for antipsychotics are an important first step in the drug development process and can provide valuable insights into the potential activity of new drug candidates.

Anti -Epileptics

Screening methods for antiepileptic drugs aim to identify new drugs that can effectively treat seizures with minimal adverse effects. These tests use animal models of epilepsy to assess the ability of a drug to prevent or reduce seizures.

Animal models of epilepsy are used to evaluate the efficacy of new antiepileptic drugs. These models can range from chemical induction of seizures, such as the pentylenetetrazol (PTZ) and maximal electroshock (MES) tests, to genetically modified animal models such as the Scn1a (NaV1.1) mutant mouse model.

The efficacy of the drug is assessed based on several parameters, such as the onset and duration of seizures, the number of seizures, and the severity of seizures. In addition, side effects and toxicity are evaluated to ensure the safety of the drug.

These screening methods provide a basis for selecting promising candidate drugs for further testing and development. Successful candidates can then move on to clinical trials to evaluate their efficacy in humans.

Some common screening methods used for antiepileptic drugs:

Maximal electroshock seizure (MES) test

Pentylenetetrazol (PTZ) seizure test

6 Hz seizure test

Kindling model of epilepsy

Amygdala kindling model

Hippocampal kindling model

Status epilepticus model

Electrical kindling model

Frings audiogenic seizure-susceptible mouse test

Scn1a (NaV1.1) mutant mouse model

Pilocarpine-induced epilepsy model

These screening methods are used to assess the antiepileptic properties of drugs and can be conducted in various animal models of epilepsy. Each test has its own advantages and limitations, and the choice of a particular test depends on the research question being addressed.

Maximal Electroshock Seizure (MES) Test:

The Maximal Electroshock Seizure (MES) Test is a preclinical animal model used to evaluate the anticonvulsant activity of drugs. The test involves applying a high-intensity electrical shock to induce generalized tonic-clonic seizures, and the effect of the test drug on the seizure threshold is measured.

Methodology

The MES test can be conducted in various animal species, including mice, rats, and guinea pigs. Typically, mice are used for this test.

The MES test requires an electroconvulsive stimulator capable of delivering a high-intensity electrical shock to the animal. The shock electrode should be placed on the corneal surface of one eye, and the reference electrode should be placed on the opposite side of the animal's head.

On the day of the experiment, animals are placed in a restraining device, and the electrodes are attached. The animals are then subjected to a series of electrical shocks, with the intensity of the shock being increased until a generalized tonic-clonic seizure is observed. The threshold intensity required to induce seizures is recorded as the MES threshold.

The test drug can be administered either systemically or directly into the brain, depending on the research question being addressed. The drug can be administered before or after the MES test to assess its effects on seizure threshold.

The MES threshold is used as a measure of seizure susceptibility, and the data obtained from the MES test can be analyzed using various statistical methods, including analysis of variance (ANOVA) and t-tests. The MES test can be used to evaluate the efficacy of drugs in preventing seizures, and the data can be compared to a control group to assess the anticonvulsant activity of the test drug.

Appropriate control groups should be included in the experiment to account for any confounding variables. For example, a group of animals that receive a saline injection or vehicle control should be included to control for the effects of the injection itself.

Overall, the MES test is a commonly used assay for evaluating the anticonvulsant activity of drugs. The test is relatively easy to perform, and the threshold intensity required to induce seizures can be quickly determined.

Pentylenetetrazol (PTZ) seizure test

The Pentylenetetrazol (PTZ) seizure test is a commonly used preclinical assay for screening potential anticonvulsant drugs. It involves the induction of seizures in experimental animals using the convulsant agent PTZ, and the subsequent evaluation of the effects of test compounds on seizure threshold and severity.

Methodology:

The test can be conducted in various animal species, including mice, rats, and guinea pigs. The animals should be healthy and free from any previous seizures or neurological deficits.

PTZ is usually administered via intraperitoneal (i.p.) injection, with a dose that induces generalized convulsions in all animals. The dose can vary depending on the species, strain, and age of the animals.

The test compound can be administered either before or after the PTZ injection, depending on the research question being addressed. The compound can be administered via various routes, including i.p., oral, or intravenous.

Seizure activity is observed and scored based on various behavioral and electroencephalographic (EEG) criteria. Common behavioral criteria include hind limb clonus, forelimb clonus, and Straub tail. EEG recordings can also be used to assess the severity and duration of seizures.

The PTZ seizure threshold is defined as the dose of PTZ required to induce seizures in 50% of animals in a given population. The threshold can be determined using a dose-response curve obtained from animals that The effects of test compounds on seizure threshold and severity can be evaluated by comparing the dose-response curves obtained from animals that receive the compound and those that receive a control substance, such as vehicle or saline.

The data obtained from the PTZ seizure test can be analyzed using various statistical methods, including analysis of variance (ANOVA) and t-tests. The seizure threshold and severity can be analyzed as a function of time to assess changes in seizure activity over the course of the experiment.

The PTZ seizure test is a valuable tool for evaluating the potential anticonvulsant effects of test compounds and for identifying new therapeutic agents for the treatment of epilepsy.

6 Hz seizure test

The 6 Hz seizure test is a preclinical assay used to evaluate the potential antiepileptic activity of drugs against focal seizures. This test involves the induction of seizures using electrical stimulation at a frequency of 6 Hz, which results in a more severe seizure compared to other models.

Methodology:

Experimental animals: The 6 Hz seizure test can be conducted in various animal species, including mice and rats.

Apparatus: A 6 Hz electroshock generator is required for conducting this test. The generator should be capable of delivering a constant current shock of up to 32 mA at a frequency of 6 Hz.

Testing: On the day of the experiment, animals are placed in a testing chamber and allowed to habituate for 30 minutes. After habituation, animals receive electrical stimulation of 6 Hz frequency for 3 seconds, which induces seizures. The severity of the seizures is scored on a 5-point scale according to the Racine scale (from 0 to 5).

Drug administration: The 6 Hz seizure test can be used to assess the effects of various drugs on seizure activity. The drug can be administered either systemically or directly into the brain, depending on the research question being addressed.

Data analysis: The data obtained from the 6 Hz seizure test can be analyzed using various statistical methods, including analysis of variance (ANOVA) and t-tests. The severity of seizures can be analyzed as a function of time to assess changes in seizure activity over the course of the experiment.

Controls: Appropriate control groups should be included in the experiment to account for any confounding variables. For example, a group of animals that receive a saline injection or vehicle control should be included to control for the effects of the injection itself.

Overall, the 6 Hz seizure test is a useful preclinical assay for evaluating the potential antiepileptic activity of drugs against focal seizures. The test can be used to assess the effects of drugs on seizure activity and can be applied in various animal models of neurological disorders.

Kindling model of epilepsy

The kindling model of epilepsy is a widely used animal model of temporal lobe epilepsy. It is based on the phenomenon of kindling, which refers to the progressive development of seizures in response to repeated electrical or chemical stimulation of specific brain regions. The kindling model of epilepsy involves repeated electrical stimulation of certain brain regions in animals until they develop epileptic seizures.

Methodology: The kindling model can be induced in a variety of animal species, including rats and mice. The animals are typically implanted with electrodes in the brain region of interest, such as the amygdala or hippocampus.

The kindling process involves repeated electrical stimulation of the brain region at a subthreshold level, which means the stimulation is not strong enough to initially produce seizures. However, after repeated stimulation sessions, seizures eventually develop and become more severe and frequent with each subsequent stimulation.

The development of seizures is monitored by observing the animal's behavior during and after the stimulation sessions. Seizure severity is often scored using a standardized scale, such as the Racine scale, which assigns a score from 0-5 based on the type and severity of the seizure behavior.

The kindling model can be used to investigate the mechanisms of epileptogenesis and to test the efficacy of potential antiepileptic drugs. The model can also be used to study the effects of various interventions on the development and progression of epilepsy, such as electrical or pharmacological treatments.

The kindling model of epilepsy is a valuable tool for studying the development and progression of epilepsy and for evaluating potential treatments for this disorder. However, it is important to note that the model has limitations and may not fully replicate the human condition of epilepsy.

Amygdala kindling model

The amygdala kindling model is an experimental model of epilepsy that involves the repeated stimulation of the amygdala in order to induce seizures. The amygdala is a brain structure that is involved in the processing and regulation of emotions, including fear and anxiety. The kindling model is a widely used model of epilepsy that is used to investigate the mechanisms underlying seizure generation and to test the efficacy of new antiepileptic drugs.

Methodology:

Animal preparation: The amygdala kindling model is typically conducted using rats or mice. The animals are anesthetized and placed in a stereotaxic frame to stabilize the head. A bipolar electrode is implanted into the amygdala using stereotaxic coordinates. The electrode is then connected to a stimulator.

Stimulation procedure: The stimulation procedure involves repeated stimulation of the amygdala with a series of electrical pulses. The stimulation protocol typically involves a series of daily electrical stimulations at a subconvulsive threshold until the animal develops a fully kindled state.

Behavioral observations: The animals are monitored for the development of seizures following the electrical stimulation. The severity of the seizures is classified using a standardized rating scale, such as the Racine scale. The animals are typically observed for several weeks until they reach a fully kindled state, characterized by the occurrence of generalized seizures.

Data analysis: The data obtained from the amygdala kindling model can be analyzed using various statistical methods, including analysis of variance (ANOVA) and t-tests. The number of stimulations required to reach a fully kindled state can be used as a measure of seizure susceptibility. The latency to the onset of seizures and the severity of the seizures can also be analyzed.

Controls: Appropriate control groups should be included in the experiment to account for any confounding variables. For example, a group of animals that undergoes the same surgical procedure but does not receive electrical stimulation should be included as a control group.

The amygdala kindling model is a useful experimental model of epilepsy that is used to investigate the underlying mechanisms of seizure generation and to test the efficacy of new antiepileptic drugs. The model has been shown to be predictive of the effectiveness of antiepileptic drugs in humans, and is widely used in preclinical drug development.

Hippocampal kindling model

The hippocampal kindling model is a widely used experimental model of temporal lobe epilepsy in rodents. This model involves the repeated application of a weak electrical stimulus to a specific area of the brain, which leads to the development of seizure activity over time.

Methodology:

Animal preparation: The hippocampal kindling model can be performed in various species, including mice, rats, and rabbits. The animal is anesthetized and placed in a stereotaxic frame. A small hole is drilled into the skull to expose the hippocampus.

Electrode placement: A bipolar electrode is inserted into the hippocampus, typically in the CA3 region, and is secured to the skull with dental cement.

Stimulation protocol: The kindling protocol involves the repeated application of a weak electrical stimulus to the hippocampus. The stimulus intensity is initially set below the seizure threshold and is gradually increased over time. The stimulus is applied at regular intervals, typically once per day, until the animal develops seizure activity.

Seizure monitoring: Seizure activity is monitored during each stimulation session and scored according to a standardized scale. The animal's behavior is observed for several minutes after each stimulus, and the intensity and duration of any seizures are recorded.

Endpoint: The kindling process continues until the animal reaches a predetermined endpoint, which is typically the development of stage 5 seizures on the Racine scale. At this point, the animal is sacrificed, and the brain is examined for histological changes.

The hippocampal kindling model is a useful tool for studying the mechanisms underlying epilepsy and for testing the efficacy of potential antiepileptic drugs. It has been widely used to study the effects of various neurotransmitters and signaling pathways on seizure activity, as well as to investigate the potential neuroprotective effects of various drugs.

Status epilepticus model

Status epilepticus (SE) is a neurological emergency and a life-threatening condition characterized by continuous or rapidly repeating seizures lasting for more than 5 minutes without recovery of consciousness between seizures. The SE model is commonly used to study the mechanisms of epileptogenesis, the development of epilepsy, and to test the efficacy of antiepileptic drugs.

Methodology: The SE model is induced by different methods, including chemical, electrical, or environmental means. The most common method for inducing SE in rodents is through the use of chemicals, such as pilocarpine or kainic acid.

Pilocarpine model: In the pilocarpine model, rats are treated with an anticholinergic agent, such as scopolamine, to prevent peripheral side effects of pilocarpine. Pilocarpine is then administered in a dose-dependent manner to induce SE. The pilocarpine causes excessive cholinergic activity, leading to seizures and ultimately SE.

Kainic acid model: In the kainic acid model, kainic acid is administered to the animals to induce SE. Kainic acid is an agonist of the glutamate receptor, leading to excessive glutamate activity, which is a key factor in the pathogenesis of epilepsy.

Electrical stimulation model: In the electrical stimulation model, SE is induced by electrical stimulation of the amygdala or hippocampus, which leads to the development of SE.

Environmental model: In the environmental model, SE is induced by exposing animals to hypoxic or hyperthermic conditions, which can lead to seizures and ultimately SE.

Behavioral analysis: During the SE model, animals are continuously monitored for the development of seizures and the duration of SE. Seizure severity is typically scored according to the Racine scale, which is a five-point scale ranging from 1 (behavioral arrest) to 5 (tonic-clonic seizures).

Pathology and histology: The SE model can lead to structural and molecular changes in the brain that are similar to those observed in patients with epilepsy. These changes can be evaluated through histological analysis of brain tissue, such as assessing neuronal loss, gliosis, and the formation of new synapses.

The SE model is a useful tool for studying the mechanisms of epilepsy and testing the efficacy of new antiepileptic drugs. However, the SE model should be used with caution as it is a highly invasive procedure and can cause significant harm to the animals.

Electrical kindling model

The electrical kindling model is a well-established animal model used to study epilepsy and seizure disorders. In this model, brief electrical stimulation is applied to the brain repeatedly, which leads to the development of chronic seizures. This model is based on the concept of kindling, which suggests that repeated stimulation of the brain can lead to a permanent change in neuronal activity, making the brain more susceptible to seizures.

Methodology:

Animal selection: Rodents, such as rats and mice, are commonly used in the electrical kindling model.

Electrode implantation: The first step in this model is to surgically implant electrodes in the brain. Typically, two electrodes are placed in the brain, one in the hippocampus and one in a control area. The electrodes are fixed to the skull with screws and dental cement.

Seizure induction: After the animals have recovered from surgery, brief electrical pulses are applied to the brain through the implanted electrodes. The electrical stimulation is usually applied once per day, and the duration and intensity of the stimulation are gradually increased over time. The animals are monitored for signs of seizure activity, such as convulsions or behavioral changes.

Seizure scoring: The severity of the seizures is scored using a standardized scoring system, such as the Racine scale. The Racine scale is a 5-point scale that ranges from 0 (no response) to 5 (tonic-clonic convulsions).

Kindling development: With repeated electrical stimulation, the animals eventually develop chronic seizures that are triggered by a variety of stimuli. Once the seizures have been fully kindled, the animals can be used for further experiments to study the pathophysiology of epilepsy and to test the efficacy of potential anti-epileptic drugs.

The electrical kindling model has been widely used in epilepsy research and has provided valuable insights into the mechanisms underlying seizure development and the potential therapeutic targets for epilepsy.

Frings audiogenic seizure-susceptible mouse test

The Frings audiogenic seizure-susceptible mouse test is a behavioral assay used to evaluate susceptibility to sound-induced seizures in mice. This test was originally developed by Frings and colleagues in 1940 and has since been used to investigate the genetic and environmental factors that contribute to susceptibility to audiogenic seizures.

Methodology: The test involves exposing mice to a sound stimulus of a specific frequency and intensity to elicit seizures. Typically, a group of mice is exposed to a sound stimulus at a gradually increasing intensity until seizures are observed in some of the mice. The sound stimulus is usually a pure tone with a frequency of 8-60 kHz and an intensity of 90-130 dB. The mice are observed for the presence of a range of seizure behaviors, including head nodding, forelimb clonus, hindlimb clonus, and loss of posture.

The mice are classified as either seizure-prone or seizure-resistant based on their response to the sound stimulus. Seizure-prone mice are those that exhibit seizures in response to the sound stimulus, while seizure-resistant mice do not exhibit seizures.

The Frings audiogenic seizure-susceptible mouse test is useful for investigating the genetic and environmental factors that contribute to susceptibility to sound-induced seizures. For example, this test has been used to investigate the role of specific genes, such as the LGI1 gene, in susceptibility to audiogenic seizures. It has also been used to study the effects of environmental factors, such as stress, on seizure susceptibility.

Scn1a (NaV1.1) mutant mouse model

The Scn1a mutant mouse model is a genetic mouse model of epilepsy that is created by disrupting the Scn1a gene, which codes for the alpha subunit of the voltage-gated sodium channel NaV1.1. This mouse model is used to study Dravet syndrome, a severe form of epilepsy that is often caused by mutations in the human SCN1A gene.

The Scn1a mutant mouse model displays many of the characteristic features of Dravet syndrome, including spontaneous seizures, increased seizure susceptibility, and impaired cognitive function. These mice also exhibit altered sodium channel function, decreased excitatory synaptic transmission, and altered neuronal excitability.

The Scn1a mutant mouse model is commonly used in research to study the mechanisms of epilepsy and to develop new treatments for Dravet syndrome and other forms of epilepsy. Researchers use a variety of methods to evaluate the effects of different treatments, such as measuring seizure frequency, duration, and severity, as well as assessing cognitive function and other behavioral changes.

Pilocarpine-induced epilepsy model

The pilocarpine-induced epilepsy model is a widely used model of temporal lobe epilepsy in rodents. This model is created by injecting the muscarinic receptor agonist pilocarpine into rodents to induce status epilepticus, which is a prolonged seizure state. The status epilepticus episode can then result in the development of spontaneous recurrent seizures, which resemble human temporal lobe epilepsy. The pilocarpine model is used to study the underlying mechanisms of epilepsy, as well as to test the efficacy of potential antiepileptic drugs.

The methodology for the pilocarpine-induced epilepsy model generally involves the following steps:

Selection of animals: Typically, male rodents such as rats or mice are used. The animals should be healthy, and their age and weight should be within a specific range depending on the study design.

Injection of pilocarpine: Pilocarpine is administered via intraperitoneal injection. The dose and timing of the injection can vary depending on the desired outcome of the study. Generally, a high dose of pilocarpine is used to induce status epilepticus.

Observation of status epilepticus: The animals are monitored for signs of status epilepticus, such as limb clonus, rearing, and falling. Once the animals exhibit these signs, they are typically left to experience the seizure activity for a specific amount of time.

Administration of diazepam: After a set time, an anticonvulsant drug such as diazepam is given to terminate the status epilepticus.

Observation of spontaneous seizures: Following the status epilepticus, the animals are monitored for the development of spontaneous recurrent seizures.

The pilocarpine-induced epilepsy model has been used extensively in research to investigate the pathophysiology of epilepsy and to test the efficacy of potential antiepileptic drugs. However, the model has some limitations, including high mortality rates and variable seizure induction across animals.

Audiogenic seizure model

The audiogenic seizure model is a laboratory animal model of epilepsy that is based on the induction of seizures by exposure to loud noise. In this model, laboratory animals are exposed to loud, sudden noises, such as a loud tone or a clap, which can induce seizures in susceptible animals.

This model has been widely used to study the mechanisms of epilepsy and to evaluate the efficacy of antiepileptic drugs. After the induction of seizures, laboratory animals are observed for the presence and severity of seizures, and the efficacy of antiepileptic drugs can be evaluated by monitoring the frequency, duration, and severity of seizures.

The audiogenic seizure model has provided important insights into the mechanisms of epilepsy and has been useful for the evaluation of antiepileptic drugs. However, it is important to note that this model has some limitations, such as the variability in the response of laboratory animals to loud noise, and that the results obtained from animal studies may not always be directly applicable to human patients.

Despite its limitations, the audiogenic seizure model remains an important tool in the study of epilepsy and the development of new antiepileptic drugs.

Genetic models of epilepsy

Genetic models of epilepsy refer to laboratory animal models of epilepsy that are based on the expression of specific genetic mutations that are associated with epilepsy in humans. In these models, animals are engineered to express specific mutations that are associated with human epilepsy, and then observed for the presence and severity of seizures.

Examples of genetic models of epilepsy include mice that express mutations associated with human genetic epilepsies, such as the mutated alpha-1 subunit of the GABA-A receptor in the GABA(a) receptor mutation mouse model or the mutated Scn1a gene in the Dravet syndrome mouse model.

These models have been widely used to study the mechanisms of epilepsy and to evaluate the efficacy of antiepileptic drugs. After the induction of seizures, laboratory animals are observed for the presence and severity of seizures, and the efficacy of antiepileptic drugs can be evaluated by monitoring the frequency, duration, and severity of seizures.

Genetic models of epilepsy have provided important insights into the mechanisms of epilepsy and have been useful for the evaluation of antiepileptic drugs. However, it is important to note that these models have some limitations, such as the variability in the response of laboratory animals to specific genetic mutations, and that the results obtained from animal studies may not always be directly applicable to human patients.

Despite its limitations, genetic models of epilepsy remain important tools in the study of epilepsy and the development of new antiepileptic drugs.

Traumatic brain injury model

The traumatic brain injury (TBI) model is a laboratory animal model of epilepsy that is based on the induction of seizures by traumatic brain injury. In this model, laboratory animals are subjected to a traumatic injury, such as a controlled cranial impact, to induce seizures.

This model has been widely used to study the mechanisms of epilepsy that can occur after TBI, and to evaluate the efficacy of antiepileptic drugs in this setting. After the induction of seizures, laboratory animals are observed for the presence and severity of seizures, and the efficacy of antiepileptic drugs can be evaluated by monitoring the frequency, duration, and severity of seizures.

The TBI model has provided important insights into the mechanisms of epilepsy after TBI and has been useful for the evaluation of antiepileptic drugs in this setting. However, it is important to note that this model has some limitations, such as the variability in the response of laboratory animals to TBI, and that the results obtained from animal studies may not always be directly applicable to human patients.

Despite its limitations, the TBI model remains an important tool in the study of epilepsy after TBI and the development of new antiepileptic drugs.

There are several screening methods available for evaluating the efficacy and safety of antiepileptic drugs. These include in vitro assays, as well as in vivo animal models such as the MES, PTZ, 6 Hz, kindling, and status epilepticus models. Each of these models has its advantages and limitations, and it is important to use a combination of them to obtain a comprehensive understanding of the drug's effects.

Furthermore, the choice of a screening method for a particular antiepileptic drug depends on various factors such as the drug's mechanism of action, the type of seizures it is intended to treat, and its potential side effects. Overall, the development of new and improved screening methods for antiepileptic drugs is essential to improve the treatment of epilepsy and the quality of life of patients with this disorder.

Antidepressants

Screening methods for antidepressants typically involve testing the ability of a compound to affect behavior in animal models of depression. These models aim to simulate aspects of the human condition of depression, such as altered mood, anhedonia (inability to experience pleasure), and decreased motivation. The ultimate goal is to identify compounds that can reverse or prevent these symptoms, which can inform the development of new antidepressant drugs.

Some commonly used animal models for screening antidepressants include the forced swim test, tail suspension test, novelty suppressed feeding test, and chronic mild stress model. These tests measure various behavioral and physiological changes that occur in response to stress, which is a key component of depression. The specific test or battery of tests chosen can depend on the research question, animal species, and other factors.

The development of effective antidepressants is a complex and ongoing process that requires a combination of animal and human studies to fully understand the mechanisms of depression and identify new therapeutic targets.

List of screening methods for antidepressant drugs

Sure, here are some commonly used screening methods for antidepressant drugs:

Forced swim test (FST)
Tail suspension test (TST)
Open field test (OFT)
Elevated plus maze (EPM)
Novelty suppressed feeding (NSF)
Chronic mild stress (CMS)
Learned helplessness (LH)
Sucrose preference test (SPT)
Social interaction test (SIT)
Resident-intruder test (RIT)

It's worth noting that these tests are used as preclinical models to evaluate potential antidepressant drug candidates and their efficacy. However, none of these tests are perfect and each has its own limitations. Additionally, the translatability of preclinical models to clinical outcomes can be variable, so further clinical studies are necessary to confirm the efficacy of potential antidepressant drugs.

Forced swim test (FST)

The forced swim test (FST) is a commonly used preclinical test for assessing the efficacy of antidepressant drugs. The test is based on the assumption that when exposed to a stressful situation, animals will display characteristic behaviors that can be used to assess their depressive-like state. In the FST, mice or rats are placed in a cylinder filled with water and allowed to swim for a set period, typically 6 minutes. During this time, the animals will display two distinct behaviors: active swimming, and passive floating or immobility. The amount of time the animal spends immobile is thought to reflect its depressive-like state.

The test is typically performed in two sessions. In the first session, the animal is placed in the water and allowed to swim for a set period, after which it is removed and returned to its home cage. The second session is performed 24 hours later and is identical to the first, except that the animal has now been exposed to the test before and may display reduced immobility due to habituation.

Antidepressant drugs are thought to reduce immobility time in the FST, indicating an improvement in the animal's depressive-like state. The test has been used to screen a variety of antidepressant drugs, including selective serotonin reuptake inhibitors (SSRIs), tricyclic antidepressants, monoamine oxidase inhibitors, and others. However, it is important to note that the test has several limitations, including its dependence on animal behavior and the potential for false positive or negative results. Therefore, the FST is typically used in combination with other preclinical tests to assess the efficacy of potential antidepressant drugs.

Tail suspention test

The tail suspension test (TST) is a behavioral test commonly used to assess depressive-like behavior in rodents. In this test, a mouse or rat is suspended by its tail, and the immobility time is recorded. The immobility time is defined as the time during which the animal remains completely immobile, making only movements that are necessary to breathe. The test is based on the assumption that animals showing increased immobility time are experiencing a state of helplessness or hopelessness, which is indicative of depressive-like behavior.

The tail suspension test is a widely used screening tool in the preclinical development of antidepressant drugs, and it is often used in combination with other behavioral tests to assess antidepressant activity. The test is relatively simple to perform and can be completed quickly, making it an efficient way to screen large numbers of compounds.

The test is typically performed by suspending a mouse or rat by its tail from a horizontal bar or support, with the animal's head positioned upwards. The suspension height is typically 25-30 cm above a surface that provides a soft landing. The test session usually lasts for 6 minutes, during which the immobility time is recorded. The immobility time is typically measured manually by an observer who is blind to the treatment condition of the animal.

The tail suspension test is a widely used model to investigate depressive-like behavior, but it has some limitations. The test may be influenced by factors such as stress, fatigue, and pain, and it may not be specific to depression. Additionally, some antidepressant drugs may produce false positive results in the test due to their sedative or motor-impairing effects. Therefore, it is important to use multiple tests to confirm the antidepressant-like activity of a compound.

Open field test

The open field test is a commonly used behavioral assay to evaluate anxiety-like and exploratory behaviors in rodents. The test is based on the natural aversion of rodents to open and brightly lit spaces. The open field apparatus is typically a square or circular arena with high walls to prevent escape, and it is illuminated by bright overhead lights.

The test is conducted by placing the rodent in the center of the open field and recording its behavior for a set period of time (usually 5-10 minutes). The behavior of the animal can be monitored and recorded using a video camera and specialized software.

Typical behaviors observed during the test include locomotion, rearing, and exploratory behaviors. Anxiety-like behaviors, such as decreased locomotion and increased thigmotaxis (i.e., tendency to stay near the walls of the arena), can also be measured. The open field test is often used in conjunction with other tests to evaluate behavioral phenotypes associated with anxiety and depression, such as the elevated plus maze and the forced swim test.

Elevated plus maze

The elevated plus maze is a commonly used behavioral test to measure anxiety-like behavior in laboratory animals, particularly rodents. The test takes advantage of the natural aversion of rodents to open spaces and the tendency to explore new environments.

The elevated plus maze consists of a plus-shaped platform elevated above the ground, with two open arms and two enclosed arms. The open arms are devoid of walls or rails, while the enclosed arms are surrounded by high walls. The test animal is placed in the center of the maze facing one of the open arms and allowed to explore the maze for a set period of time, usually five minutes.

The time spent in the open and enclosed arms, as well as the number of entries into each arm, are recorded and used to evaluate anxiety-like behavior. Anxious animals tend to spend less time in the open arms and make fewer entries into the open arms, while less anxious animals spend more time in the open arms and make more entries into the open arms.

The elevated plus maze is a validated test and has been used to evaluate the anxiolytic or anxiogenic effects of pharmacological agents, as well as the effects of genetic or environmental manipulations on anxiety-like behavior.

Novelty suppressed feeding

Novelty suppressed feeding (NSF) is a behavioral test used to assess anxiety-like behavior and the effects of potential anxiolytic compounds in rodents. The test involves placing a food-deprived rodent in an open arena with a small amount of food in the center of the arena. The latency to approach and begin eating the food is measured as an index of anxiety-like behavior, with longer latencies indicating greater anxiety.

The NSF test typically involves the following methodology:

Food deprivation: The animal is deprived of food for a period of 12-24 hours to increase motivation to eat the food in the test.

Test setup: The animal is placed in an open arena (such as a white plastic box) with a small amount of food in the center of the arena. The arena is brightly lit to increase the anxiety of the animal.

Testing: The latency to approach and eat the food is measured. A cutoff time of typically 5-10 minutes is used to prevent stress from prolonged exposure.

Data analysis: The latency to eat the food is recorded and used as an index of anxiety-like behavior.

NSF test can be performed in both mice and rats and is sensitive to a variety of anxiolytic drugs. However, it is important to note that this test can also be influenced by other factors such as hunger and motivation, and it is always necessary to interpret the results of this test in combination with other behavioral tests to confirm the effects of a potential anxiolytic compound.

Chronic mild stress

Chronic mild stress (CMS) is an animal model used in research to induce depressive-like behavior. It involves subjecting the animal to a series of mild stressors, such as changes in the light-dark cycle, wet or soiled bedding, food or water deprivation, exposure to a novel environment, or social stress. These stressors are applied repeatedly, typically for several weeks, in a randomized fashion to prevent habituation.

The CMS model is thought to induce depression-like behavior by altering the function of neurotransmitter systems in the brain, such as the serotonin, dopamine, and noradrenaline systems, as well as the hypothalamic-pituitary-adrenal (HPA) axis, which is involved in the stress response.

Behavioral changes associated with the CMS model include reduced interest in food, decreased exploratory behavior, anhedonia (reduced ability to experience pleasure), decreased social interaction, and increased immobility in the forced swim test and the tail suspension test.

The CMS model has been used to screen potential antidepressant drugs and to investigate the neurobiological mechanisms underlying depression.

Learned helpless (LH)

Learned helplessness (LH) is a behavioral model used to study depression and other mood disorders in animals. It was first described by Martin Seligman and colleagues in the late 1960s, who discovered that dogs subjected to inescapable electric shocks later showed reduced escape and avoidance behavior even when they had the opportunity to do so. This phenomenon was termed "learned helplessness" as the dogs had learned that they were unable to control the outcome of the situation.

The learned helplessness model in rodents typically involves exposing animals to a series of uncontrollable and unpredictable stressors, such as electric shocks or loud noise, over several days or weeks. The animals are then tested for their response to a subsequent stressor that they can control, such as the ability to escape from an electrified grid. Animals that have learned helplessness are expected to show reduced escape behavior and increased immobility, similar to the behavior observed in depression.

The learned helplessness model has been widely used to study the neural mechanisms underlying depression and to screen potential antidepressant drugs. It has been suggested that the model may have limited face validity, as it does not fully capture the complexity of depression, but it remains a widely used tool in preclinical research.

Sucrose preference test

The sucrose preference test is a widely used preclinical test to evaluate anhedonia, a symptom commonly associated with depression. Anhedonia is a loss of interest or pleasure in activities that would normally be considered enjoyable. In the sucrose preference test, animals are given a choice between water and a 1% to 2% sucrose solution. The reduction of sucrose intake is interpreted as an indication of anhedonia.

The test can be performed in different ways. One of the most common methods involves training the animals to drink from two bottles, one containing water and the other containing sucrose solution. After a few days of training, the animals are food- and water-deprived for a period of time, usually 12-24 hours, to increase their motivation to drink. They are then presented with the two bottles and allowed to drink freely for a set period of time, usually 1-2 hours. The amount of water and sucrose solution consumed is measured, and the preference for sucrose is calculated as the ratio of sucrose intake to total fluid intake.

The test can be modified by adding different stressors before or during the test to assess the impact of stress on anhedonia. For example, animals can be exposed to chronic mild stressors, such as food or water deprivation, cage tilting, or exposure to an unpleasant odor, to induce anhedonia. Alternatively, acute stressors, such as electric shock or forced swim stress, can be applied before the test to assess the impact of stress on the animals' preference for sucrose.

The sucrose preference test is widely used in preclinical research to evaluate the antidepressant effects of drugs or other interventions, such as transcranial magnetic stimulation or deep brain stimulation.

Social interaction test

The social interaction test is a behavioral assay used to measure sociability and social memory in rodents. It is commonly used in preclinical research to study the effects of drugs, genetic modifications, and other manipulations on social behavior.

Methodology

Before the start of the actual test, the rodents are habituated to the empty arena for 10-15 minutes to reduce any initial anxiety.

The test consists of two parts - sociability and social memory.

In the first part of the test, the test subject is placed in one compartment of the arena, and an unfamiliar conspecific (rodent of the same species and sex) is placed in the other compartment. The subject is allowed to explore the arena for a specified time (usually 5 minutes), and the time spent in each compartment is recorded.

In the second part of the test, the same test subject is placed in the arena with the same familiar conspecific as in the sociability phase and a novel conspecific. The subject is allowed to explore the arena for a specified time (usually 5 minutes), and the time spent in each compartment is recorded.

The time spent in each compartment is used to calculate the social interaction ratio (SIR) and the social memory ratio (SMR). The SIR is calculated as the time spent in the compartment with the novel conspecific divided by the total time spent in both compartments during the sociability phase. The SMR is calculated as the time spent in the compartment with the familiar conspecific divided by the total time spent in both compartments during the social memory phase.

The social interaction test is a widely used and reliable tool to evaluate social behavior in rodents. It can help in the development of novel treatments for social impairments associated with various neurological and psychiatric disorders.

Resident intruder test

The resident-intruder test is an animal model used to investigate aggressive behavior, particularly in rodents such as rats and mice. The test involves introducing a new "intruder" animal into the home cage of a resident animal and observing their social interaction. The resident animal typically displays aggressive behavior towards the intruder, such as attacking or chasing, while the intruder animal may display submissive or defensive behavior.

The test is often used to study the neural and behavioral mechanisms of aggression, as well as the effects of experimental manipulations such as drug treatments or genetic modifications. It can also be used to study the impact of environmental factors on aggressive behavior, such as social isolation or exposure to stress.

The test can be modified in various ways, such as varying the sex or strain of the animals or manipulating the duration or frequency of exposure to the intruder. The test can be used in both acute and chronic studies, depending on the research question.

Ethical considerations are important when conducting the resident-intruder test, and appropriate measures should be taken to minimize the distress and harm to the animals involved.

Screening methods for antidepressants are essential for evaluating the efficacy and safety of potential antidepressant drugs. These methods aim to identify novel compounds that can produce rapid and sustained antidepressant effects, have fewer adverse effects, and have better tolerability. Various animal models have been developed to simulate the pathophysiology of depression and to assess the antidepressant potential of new drugs. The most widely used screening methods for antidepressants include the forced swim test, tail suspension test, novelty suppressed feeding test, chronic mild stress model, learned helplessness model, social interaction test, and the sucrose preference test. Each test has its advantages and limitations, and a combination of these tests is often used to evaluate the efficacy of novel antidepressants. Overall, screening methods for antidepressants are critical for the development of safe and effective treatments for depression.

XIV

Screening methods for Anti- Diabetic drugs

Screening for type 1 anti-diabetic drugs

Screening for type 1 anti-diabetic drugs involves a multi-step process to identify potential compounds that could be effective in managing the disease. Type 1 diabetes is characterized by an inability of the body to produce sufficient amounts of insulin, leading to high blood glucose levels. The goal of screening for type 1 anti-diabetic drugs is to identify compounds that can promote insulin production and secretion, as well as improve glucose metabolism.

In general, screening for type 1 anti-diabetic drugs involves a combination of in vitro and in vivo assays, including cell-based assays, animal models, and clinical trials. These assays are designed to evaluate the potential efficacy, safety, and pharmacological properties of compounds, as well as their mechanism of action.

Some of the key considerations in screening for type 1 anti-diabetic drugs include the need for compounds that are specific to the underlying mechanisms of type 1 diabetes, as well as those that are effective at low doses and have a good safety profile. Additionally, compounds that can be administered orally are preferred, as they are more convenient for patients and have better compliance.

The screening process for type 1 anti-diabetic drugs is a complex and multi-step process that requires a deep understanding of the underlying mechanisms of the disease and the potential therapeutic targets. By using a combination of in vitro and in vivo assays, researchers can identify promising compounds and move them towards clinical development.

List of some common screening methods available for Type 1 antidiabetic drugs:

Streptozotocin-induced diabetes model: This is a common model used to induce Type 1 diabetes in animals. Streptozotocin (STZ) is a cytotoxic compound that specifically destroys pancreatic beta cells, resulting in insulin deficiency and hyperglycemia.

Insulin tolerance test (ITT): This test measures the ability of the body to utilize exogenously administered insulin. In this test, insulin is injected into the animal and the blood glucose level is measured over time.

Glucose tolerance test (GTT): This test measures the ability of the body to regulate blood glucose levels in response to a glucose challenge. In this test, a bolus of glucose is administered to the animal and the blood glucose level is measured over time.

Glycosylated hemoglobin (HbA1c) assay: This assay measures the amount of HbA1c, which is an indicator of average blood glucose levels over the past 2-3 months.

Pancreatic islet cell culture: This in vitro model can be used to study the effects of test compounds on pancreatic islet cells and insulin secretion.

Glucose-stimulated insulin secretion (GSIS) assay: This assay measures the ability of pancreatic beta cells to secrete insulin in response to a glucose challenge.

Insulin receptor binding assay: This assay measures the binding affinity of test compounds to the insulin receptor.

Pancreatic beta cell regeneration assay: This assay measures the ability of test compounds to promote regeneration of pancreatic beta cells, which are essential for insulin production.

These are just a few examples of the many screening methods available for Type 1 antidiabetic drugs. The choice of screening method depends on the specific research question and the stage of drug development.

Streptozotocin-induced diabetes model:

The Streptozotocin (STZ)-induced diabetes model is a commonly used animal model of Type 1 diabetes. STZ is a chemical that selectively destroys the insulin-producing beta cells in the pancreas, leading to insulin deficiency and hyperglycemia.

Methodology:

Animal selection and preparation: Typically, rodents such as rats or mice are used for the STZ-induced diabetes model. Before the induction of diabetes, the animals are fasted overnight and their baseline blood glucose levels are measured.

Induction of diabetes: STZ is administered to the animals via a single injection or multiple injections over several days. The dose and route of administration of STZ depend on the species and strain of animal being used.

Monitoring blood glucose levels: Blood glucose levels are measured periodically after the induction of diabetes to monitor the severity and progression of the disease.

Drug treatment: After the induction of diabetes, the test compound is administered to the animals orally or by injection. The effects of the test compound on blood glucose levels are measured and compared to a control group.

The data obtained from the STZ-induced diabetes model can be analyzed to determine the efficacy of the test compound in lowering blood glucose levels in diabetic animals.

The STZ-induced diabetes model has limitations. It is a model of acute-onset diabetes and may not fully recapitulate the pathophysiology of human Type 1 diabetes. Therefore, it is important to use caution when interpreting the results of this model and to use it in combination with other models to fully evaluate the antidiabetic properties of drugs.

Insulin tolerance test (ITT)

The insulin tolerance test (ITT) is a widely used screening method for Type 1 antidiabetic drugs. It measures the ability of the body to utilize exogenously administered insulin and provides information about insulin sensitivity and glucose metabolism.

Methodology:

Animal selection and preparation: Rodents such as rats or mice are commonly used for the ITT. Before the test, the animals are fasted overnight to standardize their metabolic state and baseline blood glucose levels are measured.

Insulin administration: A bolus of insulin is injected into the animal and the blood glucose level is measured over time using a glucometer. The dose and route of insulin administration depend on the species and strain of animal being used.

Blood glucose monitoring: Blood glucose levels are measured at several time points after insulin injection, typically at 15, 30, 60, and 120 minutes. The change in blood glucose levels over time is used to assess the animal's insulin sensitivity and glucose metabolism.

Drug treatment: After the insulin injection, the test compound is administered to the animal orally or by injection. The effects of the test compound on blood glucose levels are measured and compared to a control group.

Data analysis: The data obtained from the ITT can be analyzed to determine the efficacy of the test compound in improving insulin sensitivity and glucose metabolism in diabetic animals.

Limitations: It measures insulin sensitivity in response to a single bolus of insulin and may not fully reflect the complexity of glucose metabolism in the body. Therefore, it is important to use caution when interpreting the results of this test and to use it in combination with other tests to fully evaluate the antidiabetic properties of drugs.

Glucose tolerance test (GTT)

The glucose tolerance test (GTT) is a widely used screening method for Type 2 antidiabetic drugs. It measures the ability of the body to regulate blood glucose levels after the administration of glucose and provides information about insulin sensitivity and glucose metabolism.

Methodology:

1. Rodents such as rats or mice are commonly used for the GTT. Before the test, the animals are fasted overnight to standardize their metabolic state and baseline blood glucose levels are measured.
2. A bolus of glucose is administered to the animal and the blood glucose level is measured over time using a glucometer. The dose and route of glucose administration depend on the species and strain of animal being used.
3. Blood glucose levels are measured at several time points after glucose administration, typically at 15, 30, 60, 90, and 120 minutes. The change in blood glucose levels over time is used to assess the animal's ability to regulate blood glucose levels.
4. After the glucose administration, the test compound is administered to the animal orally or by injection. The effects

of the test compound on blood glucose levels are measured and compared to a control group.

5. The data obtained from the GTT can be analyzed to determine the efficacy of the test compound in improving insulin sensitivity and glucose metabolism in diabetic animals.

Limitations: It measures glucose regulation in response to a single bolus of glucose and may not fully reflect the complexity of glucose metabolism in the body. Therefore, it is important to use caution when interpreting the results of this test and to use it in combination with other tests to fully evaluate the antidiabetic properties of drugs.

Glycosylated hemoglobin (HbA1c) assay:

The glycosylated hemoglobin (HbA1c) assay is a commonly used screening method for Type 2 antidiabetic drugs. It measures the level of HbA1c, which is formed when glucose binds irreversibly to hemoglobin in red blood cells. HbA1c provides information about the average blood glucose levels over the past 2-3 months and is a marker for long-term glycemic control.

Methodology:

1. Rodents such as rats or mice are commonly used for the HbA1c assay. Before the test, the animals are fasted overnight to standardize their metabolic state and baseline blood glucose levels are measured.
2. Blood is collected from the animals using a variety of techniques, such as tail vein puncture or cardiac puncture. The blood is then processed to isolate the red blood cells.
3. The level of HbA1c is measured using a variety of methods, such as high-performance liquid chromatography (HPLC) or immunoassays. The HbA1c level is expressed as a percentage of

the total hemoglobin.

4. The test compound is administered to the animal orally or by injection for a specified period of time. The effects of the test compound on HbA1c levels are measured and compared to a control group.
5. The data obtained from the HbA1c assay can be analyzed to determine the efficacy of the test compound in improving long-term glycemic control in diabetic animals.

The HbA1c assay is a useful tool for assessing long-term glycemic control, but it has some limitations. For example, it may not be suitable for animals with hemolytic anemia or certain genetic variants that affect hemoglobin structure. Therefore, it is important to use caution when interpreting the results of this test and to use it in combination with other tests to fully evaluate the antidiabetic properties of drugs.

Pancreatic islet cell culture

Pancreatic islet cell culture is a laboratory technique used to isolate and culture pancreatic islets, also known as islets of Langerhans, from animals or humans. These islets contain the insulin-secreting beta cells that are responsible for regulating blood glucose levels. Islet cell culture is a useful tool for studying the physiology of pancreatic beta cells and for developing and testing new drugs for diabetes treatment.

Methodology

- The pancreas is removed from an animal or human and the islets are isolated using enzymatic digestion and density gradient centrifugation. The islets are then washed and examined under a microscope to ensure purity and viability.

- The islets are then placed in a specialized culture medium that contains nutrients and growth factors that promote cell survival and proliferation. The culture medium also provides a controlled environment for the islets, with stable temperature, humidity, and pH levels.
- The culture conditions are optimized to maintain the viability and function of the islets. This includes controlling the oxygen and carbon dioxide levels, as well as the glucose and nutrient concentrations in the culture medium.
- The islets can be treated with test compounds to evaluate their effects on insulin secretion and other parameters. These compounds can be added to the culture medium, or the islets can be transplanted into animals to evaluate their efficacy in vivo.
- The function and viability of the islets can be assessed using a variety of techniques, such as glucose-stimulated insulin secretion assays, electrophysiology measurements, and histological analysis.

Pancreatic islet cell culture is a complex and technically challenging technique, and requires specialized equipment and expertise. However, it is a valuable tool for studying the physiology and pharmacology of pancreatic beta cells, and has the potential to accelerate the development of new treatments for diabetes.

Glucose-stimulated insulin secretion (GSIS) assay

The glucose-stimulated insulin secretion (GSIS) assay is a laboratory technique used to evaluate the insulin secretory capacity of pancreatic beta cells. This assay is commonly used to assess the function of beta cells in both healthy individuals and in those with diabetes.

Methodology for the GSIS assay:

1. Islets of Langerhans are isolated from the pancreas of a donor animal or human using enzymatic digestion and density gradient centrifugation. Islets are then cultured in specialized media to ensure their survival.
2. Groups of islets are transferred to a tube or well, and then exposed to a low glucose concentration for a defined period of time. This is often followed by exposure to a high glucose concentration, which stimulates insulin secretion. The islets are then collected, and the amount of insulin secreted is measured using an assay.
3. Alternatively, a dynamic perifusion system can be used, in which islets are continuously exposed to media containing varying glucose concentrations. This allows for the assessment of insulin secretion at different glucose concentrations over time.
4. The amount of insulin secreted by the islets can be measured using a variety of techniques, such as ELISA or radioimmunoassay.

The insulin secretion data can be analyzed to determine the insulin secretory response to varying glucose concentrations. This information can be used to assess the function of beta cells, and to evaluate the effects of different compounds or treatments on insulin secretion.

The GSIS assay is a useful tool for studying the physiology and pharmacology of pancreatic beta cells. It can also be used to evaluate the function of beta cells in animal models of diabetes, and to assess the efficacy of new treatments for diabetes.

Insulin receptor binding assay

The insulin receptor binding assay is a laboratory technique used to measure the binding of insulin to its receptor. This assay is commonly used in diabetes research to evaluate the effects of drugs, hormones, or other compounds on insulin receptor function.

- Insulin and its receptor are purified from animal or human tissues using various biochemical techniques.
- Insulin is radiolabeled with a radioactive isotope, typically iodine-125 or tritium, to enable detection of the insulin-receptor complex.
- The radiolabeled insulin is incubated with a sample of purified insulin receptor for a defined period of time.
- After incubation, the mixture is separated into two fractions, representing the bound and unbound fractions of insulin.
- The amount of radiolabeled insulin bound to the receptor is measured using a scintillation counter or other appropriate equipment.
- The amount of bound insulin is analyzed to determine the binding affinity of the insulin receptor for the radiolabeled insulin, and to assess the effects of different compounds or treatments on insulin receptor binding.

The insulin receptor binding assay is a useful tool for studying the molecular mechanisms of insulin signaling, and for evaluating the effects of drugs or other compounds on insulin receptor function. The assay can be used to identify potential drugs for the treatment of diabetes and other metabolic disorders.

Pancreatic beta cell regeneration assay:

Pancreatic beta cell regeneration assays are laboratory techniques used to evaluate the regenerative capacity of beta cells in the pancreas. This type of assay is important in diabetes research, as the loss of beta cells is a hallmark of both type 1 and type 2 diabetes.

Mehodology

1. An animal model of beta cell regeneration is established. The most commonly used animal models for this type of assay are

rodents, such as mice or rats.

2. Beta cells are ablated by inducing chemical or genetic damage to the pancreas, such as treatment with the toxin streptozotocin, or using a genetic approach to selectively kill beta cells.
3. A regenerative stimulus is then applied to the pancreas, such as treatment with growth factors, small molecules, or other compounds. This stimulus can be applied directly to the pancreas, or delivered systemically via injection.
4. Pancreatic tissue is harvested and analyzed using histological and immunostaining techniques to assess the regeneration of beta cells. This includes staining for insulin and other beta cell markers, as well as evaluating the size and number of islets in the pancreas.
5. The functional capacity of regenerated beta cells is also evaluated, such as assessing insulin secretion in response to glucose stimulation.
6. The regeneration data is analyzed to determine the regenerative capacity of beta cells in response to different stimuli, and to identify potential drugs or other compounds that can enhance beta cell regeneration.

Pancreatic beta cell regeneration assays are important tools in diabetes research, as they can be used to identify potential therapeutic targets for the treatment of diabetes. By understanding the mechanisms of beta cell regeneration, researchers hope to develop new drugs and treatments that can enhance beta cell regeneration and restore pancreatic function in diabetic patients.

Screening for type 1 anti-diabetic drugs is a crucial step in the drug discovery and development process. The primary goal of these screening methods is to identify compounds that can lower blood glucose levels by stimulating insulin secretion or reducing insulin resistance, with minimal side effects. In vivo animal models are commonly used to assess the efficacy and safety of potential drug candidates. These models range from chemically-induced diabetic models to genetically modified animal models. The use of various assays, including glucose tolerance tests, insulin tolerance tests, and HbA1c assays, can provide insight into the drug's effectiveness in regulating blood glucose levels. Overall, the screening process for type 1 anti-diabetic drugs is a complex and challenging process, requiring a multi-disciplinary approach that involves pharmacologists, chemists, biologists, and clinicians. However, the development of effective and safe drugs for type 1 diabetes can significantly improve the quality of life for those affected by this disease.

Screening methods for type 2 antidiabetic drugs

Type 2 diabetes is a complex metabolic disorder characterized by insulin resistance and impaired insulin secretion. It is a major health problem worldwide, and the incidence is increasing rapidly. Current treatments for type 2 diabetes include lifestyle changes, oral antidiabetic drugs, and insulin therapy. However, these treatments have limitations such as side effects, variable efficacy, and the need for frequent monitoring. Therefore, there is a need for the development of new and improved drugs to treat type 2 diabetes.

The screening of potential drug candidates for type 2 diabetes involves a variety of in vitro and in vivo assays. In vitro assays are used to evaluate the effect of a drug candidate on the molecular targets that are involved in the pathogenesis of type 2 diabetes. In vivo assays, on the other hand, are used to evaluate the efficacy of a drug candidate in animal models of type 2 diabetes.

The most commonly used in vivo models for type 2 diabetes are high-fat diet-induced obesity models, streptozotocin-nicotinamide-induced diabetes models, and genetic models such as db/db and ob/ob mouse models. These models have been used to evaluate the effect of drug candidates on blood glucose levels, insulin resistance, and pancreatic beta-cell function, among other parameters.

The screening of potential drug candidates for type 2 diabetes involves a multidisciplinary approach, using a combination of in vitro and in vivo assays to identify promising drug candidates for further development.

Commonly used screening methods for type 2 antidiabetic drugs:

Here are some of the most commonly used in vivo screening methods for type 2 antidiabetic drugs:

Oral glucose tolerance test (OGTT): This test involves administering a dose of glucose to fasted animals and measuring blood glucose levels at specific time points to assess the animal's ability to regulate blood glucose levels.

Insulin tolerance test (ITT): This test involves administering insulin to animals and measuring blood glucose levels at specific time points to assess the animal's sensitivity to insulin.

High-fat diet-induced obesity model: This model involves feeding animals a high-fat diet to induce obesity and insulin resistance, which mimics the pathogenesis of type 2 diabetes.

Streptozotocin-nicotinamide-induced diabetes model: This model involves administering a combination of streptozotocin and nicotinamide to animals to induce hyperglycemia and insulin resistance, which mimics the pathogenesis of type 2 diabetes.

db/db and ob/ob mouse models: These are genetic models of obesity and insulin resistance, which are widely used for studying the pathogenesis of type 2 diabetes.

Glucagon-like peptide-1 (GLP-1) assay: This assay measures the levels of GLP-1, a hormone that regulates blood glucose levels, in response to drug treatment.

HbA1c assay: This assay measures the levels of glycated hemoglobin, which provides an indication of average blood glucose levels over a period of weeks to months.

Pancreatic beta cell mass assay: This assay measures the mass of pancreatic beta cells, which are responsible for insulin production, to assess the potential of a drug to promote beta cell regeneration.

These screening methods can provide valuable information about the potential effects of a drug on type 2 diabetes and related metabolic pathways in vivo.

Few more commonly used in vivo screening methods for type 2 antidiabetic drugs:

Glucose-stimulated insulin secretion (GSIS) assay: This assay measures the ability of a drug to enhance insulin secretion from pancreatic beta cells in response to glucose stimulation.

Hyperinsulinemic-euglycemic clamp: This test involves maintaining a constant blood glucose level while administering insulin to assess the ability of a drug to enhance insulin sensitivity.

Adipocyte differentiation assay: This assay measures the ability of a drug to induce the differentiation of pre-adipocytes into mature adipocytes, which can promote glucose uptake and improve insulin sensitivity.

Lipid metabolism assays: These assays measure the effects of a drug on lipid metabolism, including serum triglyceride levels, adipocyte lipolysis, and hepatic lipid accumulation, which are associated with insulin resistance and type 2 diabetes.

Incretin assays: These assays measure the levels of incretin hormones, such as GLP-1 and glucose-dependent insulinotropic peptide (GIP), which are involved in the regulation of insulin secretion and glucose metabolism.

Gluconeogenesis assay: This assay measures the ability of a drug to inhibit gluconeogenesis, which is the process by which the liver produces glucose, and is a key contributor to hyperglycemia in type 2 diabetes.

These screening methods can provide valuable information about the potential effects of a drug on various metabolic pathways and cellular processes involved in the pathogenesis of type 2 diabetes.

Oral glucose tolerance test (OGTT):

The oral glucose tolerance test (OGTT) is a commonly used in vivo screening method for type 2 antidiabetic drugs. The OGTT involves the administration of a defined amount of glucose to an animal or human subject after an overnight fast, and then measuring the changes in blood glucose levels over time. The test typically involves measuring baseline blood glucose levels before administering the glucose load, and then measuring blood glucose levels at regular intervals after the glucose load, typically at 30, 60, 90, and 120 minutes.

In individuals with normal glucose tolerance, blood glucose levels will rise after the glucose load, but then quickly return to baseline levels as insulin secretion increases and glucose is taken up by cells. In individuals with impaired glucose tolerance or type 2 diabetes, blood glucose levels will remain elevated for a longer period of time after the glucose load, indicating a reduced ability to clear glucose from the blood and/or impaired insulin secretion or sensitivity.

The OGTT can be used to evaluate the effects of a drug on glucose tolerance and insulin secretion and sensitivity. Drugs that improve glucose tolerance may increase insulin secretion, enhance insulin sensitivity, or reduce hepatic glucose production. The OGTT is a useful tool for assessing the efficacy of type 2 antidiabetic drugs and for identifying potential side effects, such as hypoglycemia or impaired glucose tolerance.

Insulin tolerance test (ITT)

The insulin tolerance test (ITT) is a commonly used in vivo screening method for type 2 antidiabetic drugs. The ITT involves administering a bolus injection of insulin to an animal or human subject and measuring the resulting changes in blood glucose levels over time. The test typically involves measuring baseline blood glucose levels before administering the insulin, and then measuring blood glucose levels at regular intervals after the insulin injection, typically at 15, 30, 60, 90, and 120 minutes.

In individuals with normal insulin sensitivity, blood glucose levels will fall rapidly after the insulin injection as insulin promotes glucose uptake by cells. In individuals with impaired insulin sensitivity or type 2 diabetes, blood glucose levels may not fall as rapidly or may not fall as much, indicating a reduced ability of insulin to promote glucose uptake.

The ITT can be used to evaluate the effects of a drug on insulin sensitivity and glucose uptake. Drugs that improve insulin sensitivity may enhance glucose uptake and improve glucose tolerance. The ITT is a useful tool for assessing the efficacy of type 2 antidiabetic drugs and for identifying potential side effects, such as hypoglycemia or impaired insulin sensitivity.

Methodology

1. The mice or rats should be fasted for at least 6 hours prior to the experiment.
2. Before the start of the experiment, a drop of blood is collected from the tail vein of the animal for the measurement of baseline blood glucose level.
3. A small amount of insulin (0.75 to 1 unit/kg body weight) is injected into the peritoneal cavity of the animal.
4. Blood glucose levels are measured at various time points (e.g., 15, 30, 60, 90, 120 minutes) after insulin injection. Blood samples can be collected from the tail vein or by retro-orbital bleeding under anesthesia.
5. Blood glucose levels can be measured using a glucometer or by standard laboratory methods.
6. The rate of blood glucose disappearance (KITT) can be calculated by fitting the blood glucose measurements to a decay curve using a mathematical model. The area under the curve (AUC) can also be calculated to compare the glucose clearance between

different treatment groups.

It's important to note that the ITT is an invasive procedure that should only be performed by trained personnel and under appropriate animal ethics approval.

High-fat diet-induced obesity model:

The high-fat diet-induced obesity model is a commonly used in vivo model for studying type 2 diabetes and obesity. This model involves feeding an animal, typically a rodent, with a diet that is high in fat content (usually 40-60% of total calories) for several weeks or months, which leads to the development of obesity and insulin resistance.

In this model, animals develop a number of metabolic abnormalities that are similar to those seen in humans with type 2 diabetes and obesity, including hyperglycemia, hyperinsulinemia, glucose intolerance, and dyslipidemia. The high-fat diet-induced obesity model is a useful tool for studying the pathophysiology of type 2 diabetes and identifying potential drug targets.

The high-fat diet-induced obesity model can also be used to test the efficacy of type 2 antidiabetic drugs. Drugs that improve insulin sensitivity, reduce hepatic glucose production, or enhance glucose uptake may be effective in reversing or preventing the metabolic abnormalities associated with this model. However, it should be noted that this model may not perfectly replicate the pathophysiology of human type 2 diabetes, and the results obtained from this model should be interpreted with caution.

Mehodology

- Typically, male C57BL/6J mice are used for this model, as they are known to be susceptible to diet-induced obesity.

- The mice are fed a high-fat diet (HFD) consisting of 45-60% calories from fat for a period of 12-16 weeks. A control group of mice can be fed a normal chow diet (NCD) with 10-20% calories from fat.
- The body weight of the mice is monitored weekly to track the development of obesity.
- After 12-16 weeks of HFD feeding, the mice can be subjected to a glucose tolerance test (GTT) to assess their glucose tolerance and insulin sensitivity.

Similarly, an insulin tolerance test (ITT) can be performed to assess insulin sensitivity in the mice.

At the end of the experimental period, the mice can be sacrificed and various tissues (e.g., liver, adipose tissue, skeletal muscle) can be harvested for further analysis.

The collected data can be analyzed to evaluate the effect of HFD on body weight, glucose and insulin tolerance, and various metabolic parameters.

It's important to note that the high-fat diet-induced obesity model is an invasive procedure that should only be performed by trained personnel and under appropriate animal ethics approval. Care should be taken to minimize animal suffering and distress throughout the experiment.

Streptozotocin-nicotinamide

The streptozotocin-nicotinamide model is a commonly used in vivo model for studying type 2 diabetes. This model involves administering a single dose of streptozotocin, a beta cell toxin, to animals following nicotinamide pre-treatment. Nicotinamide protects the beta cells from the cytotoxic effects of streptozotocin, leading to selective destruction of pancreatic beta cells and insulin deficiency.

This model results in the development of hyperglycemia and insulin deficiency, which mimics the pathophysiology of human type 2 diabetes. The streptozotocin-nicotinamide model is useful for studying the mechanisms of beta cell destruction and insulin deficiency, as well as for identifying potential drug targets for the treatment of type 2 diabetes.

The streptozotocin-nicotinamide model can also be used to test the efficacy of type 2 antidiabetic drugs. Drugs that enhance beta cell function, promote insulin secretion, or reduce insulin resistance may be effective in improving glucose homeostasis in this model. However, it should be noted that this model may not perfectly replicate the pathophysiology of human type 2 diabetes, and the results obtained from this model should be interpreted with caution.

Methodology

- Male Wistar rats are commonly used for this model. Animals should be kept on a standard chow diet for at least one week before starting the experiment.
- The rats are fasted overnight before the induction of diabetes. Nicotinamide (110 mg/kg body weight) is injected intraperitoneally, followed by streptozotocin (45 mg/kg body weight) 15 minutes later.
- Blood glucose levels should be monitored regularly using a glucometer, starting from 48 hours after the induction of diabetes. The rats will develop hyperglycemia within a few days of the induction.
- The rats can be used for various experiments related to diabetes research, such as testing the efficacy of antidiabetic drugs or studying the underlying mechanisms of diabetes.
- A control group of rats can be included in the experiment, which receives only nicotinamide injection.

It is important to note that this model has some limitations, including the fact that it only partially replicates the human condition of type 2 diabetes, and that it may not fully represent the chronic, progressive nature of the disease. Therefore, the results obtained from this model should be interpreted with caution and validated using other models and/or clinical studies.

db/db and ob/ob mouse models

The db/db and ob/ob mouse models are two commonly used in vivo models for studying type 2 diabetes and obesity.

The db/db mouse model is a genetic model of type 2 diabetes that is caused by a mutation in the leptin receptor gene. This mutation leads to hyperphagia, obesity, and insulin resistance, which eventually progresses to hyperglycemia and insulin deficiency. The db/db mouse model is useful for studying the mechanisms of beta cell dysfunction and insulin resistance, as well as for identifying potential drug targets for the treatment of type 2 diabetes.

The ob/ob mouse model is another genetic model of type 2 diabetes that is caused by a mutation in the gene encoding leptin, a hormone that regulates energy balance and appetite. This mutation leads to hyperphagia, obesity, and insulin resistance, which eventually progresses to hyperglycemia and insulin deficiency. The ob/ob mouse model is useful for studying the mechanisms of beta cell dysfunction and insulin resistance, as well as for identifying potential drug targets for the treatment of type 2 diabetes.

Both the db/db and ob/ob mouse models are useful for studying the pathophysiology of type 2 diabetes and identifying potential drug targets. These models can also be used to test the efficacy of type 2 antidiabetic drugs. Drugs that improve insulin sensitivity, reduce hepatic glucose production, or enhance glucose uptake may be effective in improving glucose homeostasis in these models. However, it should be noted that these models may not perfectly replicate the pathophysiology of human type 2 diabetes, and the results obtained from these models should be interpreted with caution.

Methodology

The methodology for using the db/db and ob/ob mouse models for studying type 2 diabetes is as follows:

db/db mouse model:

1. Obtain db/db mice, which are homozygous for the leptin receptor mutation and are obese and insulin-resistant.
2. Age-matched wild-type (WT) mice can be used as controls.
3. Feed both groups of mice a normal diet or a high-fat diet for several weeks to induce obesity and insulin resistance.
4. Perform various tests to study the effects of potential antidiabetic drugs on the db/db mice, such as glucose tolerance test (GTT), insulin tolerance test (ITT), and measurement of insulin and glucose levels in blood.
5. Treat the db/db mice with the potential drug and monitor changes in glucose and insulin levels over time.
6. Compare the results to the control group to determine the efficacy of the drug in treating type 2 diabetes.

ob/ob mouse model:

1. Obtain ob/ob mice, which are homozygous for the mutation in the leptin gene and are obese and insulin-resistant.
2. Age-matched WT mice can be used as controls.
3. Feed both groups of mice a normal diet or a high-fat diet for several weeks to induce obesity and insulin resistance.
4. Perform various tests to study the effects of potential antidiabetic drugs on the ob/ob mice, such as GTT, ITT, and measurement of insulin and glucose levels in blood.
5. Treat the ob/ob mice with the potential drug and monitor changes in glucose and insulin levels over time.
6. Compare the results to the control group to determine the efficacy of the drug in treating type 2 diabetes.

Note: The methodology may vary depending on the specific research question and the type of drug being studied. It is important to follow ethical guidelines and obtain necessary approvals before conducting animal experiments.

Glucagon-like peptide-1 (GLP-1) assay

A glucagon-like peptide-1 (GLP-1) assay is a laboratory test that measures the concentration of GLP-1 in blood or other biological samples. GLP-1 is a hormone that is produced in the gut in response to food intake and plays an important role in glucose homeostasis. GLP-1 has several physiological effects that make it an attractive target for the treatment of type 2 diabetes, including stimulating insulin secretion, inhibiting glucagon secretion, slowing gastric emptying, and promoting satiety.

The GLP-1 assay can be used to measure the levels of active GLP-1 in circulation, which can help to assess the effectiveness of GLP-1-based therapies for type 2 diabetes, such as GLP-1 receptor agonists and dipeptidyl peptidase-4 (DPP-4) inhibitors. In addition, the GLP-1 assay can be used to investigate the regulation of GLP-1 secretion and metabolism in different physiological and pathological conditions, such as obesity, insulin resistance, and gut disorders.

The GLP-1 assay can be performed using various techniques, including enzyme-linked immunosorbent assay (ELISA), radioimmunoassay (RIA), and mass spectrometry (MS). ELISA is the most commonly used method and is based on the principle of antibody-antigen binding, where a specific antibody is used to capture GLP-1 from the sample, and a labeled antibody is used to detect the captured GLP-1. RIA is a similar method that uses radioactive isotopes to label the antibodies. MS is a more sensitive and specific method that can measure multiple forms of GLP-1, including intact GLP-1 and its metabolites.

Methodology

The methodology for measuring the levels of GLP-1 in plasma or serum typically involves the following steps:

1. Blood samples are collected from the animals or humans before and after the treatment.
2. The collected samples are centrifuged to obtain plasma or serum, which is used for GLP-1 analysis.
3. The plasma or serum samples are analyzed for GLP-1 levels using ELISA (enzyme-linked immunosorbent assay) or RIA (radioimmunoassay) techniques. These assays involve the use of antibodies specific for GLP-1, which bind to GLP-1 in the sample and generate a signal that is proportional to the amount of GLP-1 present.
4. The GLP-1 levels in the samples are quantified by comparing the signal generated by the samples to that generated by a standard curve generated using known concentrations of GLP-1. The GLP-1 levels are expressed in units of picograms per milliliter (pg/mL) or other appropriate units.

It is important to note that GLP-1 levels can be influenced by a number of factors, including food intake, medication use, and the time of day. Therefore, care should be taken to control these variables when collecting and analyzing samples.

HbA1c assay

The HbA1c assay is a laboratory test that measures the amount of glycosylated hemoglobin in blood. HbA1c is a form of hemoglobin that is formed by the non-enzymatic attachment of glucose to hemoglobin molecules in red blood cells. The HbA1c assay is used to monitor long-term glucose control in individuals with diabetes.

The HbA1c assay reflects the average blood glucose levels over the past 2-3 months, as the lifespan of red blood cells is about 120 days. The HbA1c level is expressed as a percentage of total hemoglobin, and the recommended target level for individuals with diabetes is typically less than 7%.

The HbA1c assay is a reliable and convenient method for monitoring glucose control over time, as it does not require fasting or timed blood glucose measurements. It is also useful for identifying individuals with undiagnosed diabetes or for screening high-risk populations for diabetes. In addition, the HbA1c assay has been shown to be a strong predictor of the risk of diabetes complications, such as retinopathy, nephropathy, and neuropathy.

The HbA1c assay can be performed using various methods, including ion-exchange chromatography, high-performance liquid chromatography (HPLC), and immunoassays. HPLC is the most commonly used method and is based on the separation of different forms of hemoglobin by their charge and size, followed by quantification of the HbA1c fraction. Immunoassays use specific antibodies to detect and quantify the HbA1c fraction. The accuracy and precision of the HbA1c assay can be affected by several factors, such as hemoglobin variants, iron-deficiency anemia, and certain medications.

Methodology for HbA1c assay

The HbA1c assay measures the amount of glycated hemoglobin in the blood, which is a marker for average blood glucose levels over the past 2-3 months. The methodology for the HbA1c assay is as follows:

1. A blood sample is collected from the patient and transferred to a tube containing an anticoagulant.
2. The sample is centrifuged to separate the plasma or serum from the blood cells. The plasma or serum is then used for the assay.
3. There are several methods available for the HbA1c assay, including immunoassays, high-performance liquid chromatography (HPLC), and capillary electrophoresis. In

general, the assay involves the following steps:

a. Hemolysate preparation: The plasma or serum is treated with a lysing agent to release the hemoglobin from the red blood cells.

b. Separation of HbA1c: The HbA1c is separated from other forms of hemoglobin using a specific method, depending on the assay used.

c. Detection: The separated HbA1c is quantified using a detection method, such as immunoassay or UV detection.

The HbA1c level is reported as a percentage of total hemoglobin, with normal values typically ranging from 4-6%. A higher percentage indicates poorer blood glucose control over the past 2-3 months.

Pancreatic beta cell mass assay:

The pancreatic beta cell mass assay is a method for quantifying the total mass of beta cells in the pancreas. Beta cells are the insulin-producing cells of the pancreas, and their loss or dysfunction is a hallmark of diabetes.

The pancreatic beta cell mass assay is typically performed using histological techniques that allow for the visualization and quantification of beta cells in pancreatic tissue sections. The pancreas is dissected and fixed in formalin, embedded in paraffin, and sectioned. The sections are then stained with specific antibodies that recognize and bind to insulin, allowing for the identification of beta cells. The total number of beta cells in each section is counted, and the area of the section is measured to determine the beta cell density. The beta cell density is then multiplied by the total pancreatic volume to obtain the total beta cell mass.

Alternative methods for quantifying beta cell mass include imaging techniques, such as magnetic resonance imaging (MRI) and positron emission tomography (PET), which allow for non-invasive visualization and quantification of beta cells in vivo. These techniques rely on the use of contrast agents or radiolabeled tracers that selectively bind to beta cells.

The pancreatic beta cell mass assay is a valuable tool for understanding the pathophysiology of diabetes and for evaluating the efficacy of interventions aimed at preserving or restoring beta cell mass. It has been used to study the effects of various drugs, such as insulin sensitizers, incretin mimetics, and beta cell regeneration agents, on beta cell mass in animal models of diabetes. In addition, the pancreatic beta cell mass assay has been used to compare the effects of different antidiabetic drugs on beta cell mass and function, and to identify novel targets for drug development.

Methodology

1. Sacrifice the animal and remove the pancreas.
2. Fix the pancreas in 4% paraformaldehyde for at least 24 hours.
3. Embed the pancreas in paraffin or optimal cutting temperature (OCT) compound for sectioning.
4. Cut the pancreas into sections of 5-10 μm thickness.
5. Stain the sections with antibodies specific to insulin, such as anti-insulin antibody.
6. Visualize the stained sections using microscopy and capture digital images.
7. Quantify the beta cell mass by measuring the insulin-positive area or volume of the pancreatic islets.
8. Normalize the beta cell mass to the total pancreas weight to account for variations in pancreas size.

Alternatively, alternative techniques like flow cytometry, image-based analysis, and high-throughput microfluidics can also be used to measure beta cell mass. The specific methodology may vary depending on the technique used.

Glucose uptake assay

A glucose uptake assay is a laboratory method used to measure the ability of cells to take up glucose from the extracellular environment. Glucose uptake is a critical process in glucose metabolism and is essential for maintaining normal blood glucose levels.

The glucose uptake assay is typically performed using cells that are capable of taking up glucose, such as muscle cells or adipocytes. The cells are incubated with a glucose analog, such as 2-deoxy-D-glucose, which is taken up by cells in a manner similar to glucose. After a period of incubation, the cells are washed to remove any residual extracellular glucose analog, and the amount of intracellular glucose analog is measured. This can be done by measuring the radioactivity of a radiolabeled glucose analog or by using a fluorescent glucose analog and measuring the fluorescence.

The glucose uptake assay is used to study the mechanisms of glucose uptake and to evaluate the effects of drugs or other interventions on glucose uptake. It can also be used to screen for potential antidiabetic drugs that increase glucose uptake in cells.

One application of the glucose uptake assay is in the development of insulin sensitizers, which are drugs that increase the ability of cells to respond to insulin and take up glucose. Insulin resistance, a condition in which cells become less responsive to insulin, is a major contributor to the development of type 2 diabetes. Insulin sensitizers work by increasing glucose uptake in cells and lowering blood glucose levels. The glucose uptake assay can be used to identify and optimize insulin sensitizers that enhance glucose uptake in cells.

Insulin secretion assay

Insulin secretion assay is a laboratory method used to measure the amount of insulin secreted by pancreatic beta cells in response to a stimulus such as glucose, amino acids, or other secretagogues. The assay is used to study the regulation of insulin secretion and to evaluate the effects of drugs or other interventions on insulin secretion.

The assay is typically performed using isolated pancreatic islets or cultured beta cells. The cells are incubated in a buffer containing a stimulatory agent such as glucose, and the amount of insulin secreted into the buffer is measured over a period of time. Insulin secretion can be measured by various methods, including radioimmunoassay, enzyme-linked immunosorbent assay (ELISA), or chemiluminescence.

Insulin secretion assays can be used to study the mechanisms of insulin secretion and to identify potential drugs or other interventions that enhance insulin secretion. Insulin secretagogues are drugs that stimulate insulin secretion from beta cells and can be used to treat type 2 diabetes. The insulin secretion assay can be used to screen for and optimize insulin secretagogues that enhance insulin secretion.

In addition to evaluating the effects of drugs or other interventions on insulin secretion, insulin secretion assays can also be used to study the pathophysiology of diabetes. In type 1 diabetes, beta cells are destroyed by the immune system, leading to a loss of insulin secretion. In type 2 diabetes, beta cells become less responsive to glucose and other secretagogues, resulting in impaired insulin secretion. Insulin secretion assays can be used to study these processes and to develop new treatments for diabetes.

Insulin receptor activation assay

An insulin receptor activation assay is a laboratory method used to measure the activation of insulin receptors in response to insulin or other insulin-mimetic agents. The assay is used to study the regulation of insulin receptor signaling and to evaluate the effects of drugs or other interventions on insulin receptor activation.

The insulin receptor is a protein on the surface of many types of cells, including liver, muscle, and fat cells, that binds to insulin and triggers a cascade of intracellular signaling events that ultimately lead to glucose uptake and other metabolic effects. Insulin receptor activation assays typically use cell-based systems that express the insulin receptor and downstream signaling molecules. The cells are stimulated with insulin or other compounds that activate the insulin receptor, and the activation of downstream signaling pathways is measured.

Insulin receptor activation assays can be used to study the mechanisms of insulin signaling and to identify potential drugs or other interventions that enhance insulin receptor activation. Insulin sensitizers are drugs that improve insulin receptor signaling and can be used to treat type 2 diabetes. The insulin receptor activation assay can be used to screen for and optimize insulin sensitizers that enhance insulin receptor activation.

In addition to evaluating the effects of drugs or other interventions on insulin receptor activation, insulin receptor activation assays can also be used to study the pathophysiology of diabetes. In type 2 diabetes, insulin resistance is a hallmark feature of the disease, which is characterized by impaired insulin signaling and glucose uptake. Insulin receptor activation assays can be used to study the mechanisms of insulin resistance and to develop new treatments for diabetes.

PPAR-gamma activation assay

The peroxisome proliferator-activated receptor-gamma (PPAR-gamma) activation assay is a laboratory method used to measure the activation of PPAR-gamma, a nuclear receptor that plays a critical role in regulating glucose and lipid metabolism. PPAR-gamma is a transcription factor that regulates the expression of genes involved in adipogenesis, glucose uptake, and insulin sensitivity.

PPAR-gamma activation assays typically use cell-based systems that express the PPAR-gamma receptor and downstream signaling molecules. The cells are treated with compounds that activate PPAR-gamma, and the activation of downstream signaling pathways is measured. PPAR-gamma activation assays can be used to identify and optimize PPAR-gamma agonists, which are drugs that activate PPAR-gamma and can be used to treat type 2 diabetes and other metabolic disorders.

PPAR-gamma agonists, also known as thiazolidinediones (TZDs), have been shown to improve insulin sensitivity and glucose uptake in peripheral tissues such as adipose tissue, skeletal muscle, and liver. PPAR-gamma activation assays can be used to screen for and optimize TZDs that enhance PPAR-gamma activation and improve insulin sensitivity.

In addition to evaluating the effects of drugs or other interventions on PPAR-gamma activation, PPAR-gamma activation assays can also be used to study the pathophysiology of metabolic disorders such as type 2 diabetes. PPAR-gamma is involved in the regulation of adipocyte differentiation, glucose and lipid metabolism, and inflammation. Dysregulation of PPAR-gamma signaling has been linked to the development of insulin resistance and other metabolic abnormalities. PPAR-gamma activation assays can be used to study the mechanisms of PPAR-gamma dysfunction and to develop new treatments for metabolic disorders.

The development of type 2 anti-diabetic drugs is a complex process that involves several stages of screening, testing, and validation. Screening methods for type 2 anti-diabetic drugs are designed to identify compounds that can lower blood glucose levels and improve insulin sensitivity without causing significant adverse effects. In vivo models such as high-fat diet-induced obesity models, streptozotocin-nicotinamide-induced diabetes models, and db/db and ob/ob mouse models are commonly used for the screening of type 2 anti-diabetic drugs.

Other in vitro methods such as glucose uptake assays, insulin secretion assays, insulin receptor activation assays, and PPAR-gamma activation assays are also used to identify potential drug candidates. Once a promising compound has been identified, it undergoes preclinical and clinical testing to establish its safety and efficacy.

The development of type 2 anti-diabetic drugs is a challenging and complex process that requires a multidisciplinary approach, including chemistry, biology, pharmacology, and clinical research. However, the potential benefits of these drugs in treating and managing type 2 diabetes are significant, and the continued development of new and effective drugs is crucial for improving the health and quality of life of millions of people worldwide.

XV

Screening Methods For Anti Ulcer Drugs

Antiulcer drugs are a class of medications that are used to treat ulcers in the stomach and small intestine. Peptic ulcers, caused by the overproduction of gastric acid, are a common gastrointestinal condition. The development of antiulcer drugs has revolutionized the treatment of this condition.

Screening methods for antiulcer drugs involve testing the efficacy of potential compounds to decrease gastric acid secretion, protect the gastric mucosa, and promote ulcer healing. These screening methods include both in vitro and in vivo assays.

In vitro assays include testing for the inhibition of gastric acid secretion, the promotion of mucus and bicarbonate secretion, and the evaluation of cytoprotective properties. In vivo assays include the assessment of ulcer formation in animal models and the evaluation of the effect of test compounds on acid secretion and ulcer healing. These assays aim to identify the most effective compounds that can be further developed for clinical use.

The development of antiulcer drugs has significantly improved the management of peptic ulcers, and the use of screening methods plays an important role in identifying effective compounds for this purpose.

There are several types of animal models that are commonly used in the screening of anti-ulcer drugs, including:

Acute Ulcer Models in Anti-Ulcer Drug Screening

Acute ulcer models are widely used in the screening of anti-ulcer drugs. These models involve the induction of acute ulcers in laboratory animals (usually rats or mice), and the evaluation of the effect of the drug on the healing of the ulcers.

There are several methods for inducing acute ulcers in laboratory animals, including:

Ethanol-induced ulcers: Ethanol is used to damage the mucosal lining of the stomach, leading to the formation of acute ulcers.

Stress-induced ulcers: Physical or psychological stress can induce acute ulcers in laboratory animals.

Chemical-induced ulcers: Certain chemicals, such as indomethacin, can be used to induce acute ulcers in laboratory animals.

Once the acute ulcers have been induced, researchers evaluate the effect of the drug on the healing of the ulcers. This can be done using various methods, including histological analysis, measurement of ulcer size, and assessment of the rate of ulcer healing.

Chronic Ulcer Models

Chronic ulcer models are used in the screening of anti-ulcer drugs to evaluate the long-term efficacy and safety of a drug. These models involve the induction of chronic ulcers in laboratory animals, and the evaluation of the drug's ability to promote healing and prevent recurrence of the ulcers.

There are several methods for inducing chronic ulcers in laboratory animals

Helicobacter pylori infection: H. pylori is a bacterium that is a common cause of peptic ulcer disease in humans. Researchers can induce chronic ulcers in laboratory animals by infecting them with H. pylori.

Chemical-induced ulcers: Certain chemicals, such as cysteamine, can be used to induce chronic ulcers in laboratory animals.

Once the chronic ulcers have been induced, researchers evaluate the effect of the drug on the healing of the ulcers and on the prevention of ulcer recurrence. This can be done using various methods, including histological analysis, measurement of ulcer size, and assessment of the rate of ulcer healing and recurrence.

Pain Models

Pain is a common symptom of peptic ulcer disease, and is often a major concern for patients. As such, the evaluation of pain relief is an important aspect of the screening of anti-ulcer drugs.

There are several methods for inducing pain in laboratory animals

- **Chemical-induced pain:** Certain chemicals, such as acetic acid, can be used to induce pain in laboratory animals.
- **Inflammation-induced pain:** Inflammation of the stomach or small intestine can induce pain in laboratory animals.

Once pain has been induced, researchers evaluate the effect of the drug on pain relief. This can be done using various methods, including observation of pain behaviors (such as writhing or licking) and measurement of pain-related physiological responses (such as changes in heart rate or blood pressure).

Gastroprotective Effect Models

Gastroprotective effect is the ability of a drug to protect the stomach and small intestine from damage caused by various stimuli, such as acid or non-steroidal anti-inflammatory drugs (NSAIDs). Evaluation of the gastroprotective effect of a drug is an important aspect of the screening of anti-ulcer drugs.

There are several methods for inducing gastric damage in laboratory animals

Acid-induced damage: Hydrochloric acid can be used to induce gastric damage in laboratory animals.

NSAID-induced damage: Non-steroidal anti-inflammatory drugs, such as indomethacin, can be used to induce gastric damage in laboratory animals.

Once gastric damage has been induced, researchers evaluate the effect of the drug on the protection of the stomach and small intestine. This can be done using various methods, including measurement of gastric secretion, assessment of histological changes, and measurement of ulcer size.

Commonly used techniques to evaluate the anti-ulcer activity of drugs

Indomethacin -Induced Ulcer Model

The Indomethacin-induced ulcer model is a commonly used experimental model to study the pathophysiology and treatment of peptic ulcers. Indomethacin is a non-steroidal anti-inflammatory drug (NSAID) that is widely used as an analgesic and anti-inflammatory agent. However, prolonged use of NSAIDs can cause damage to the gastrointestinal mucosa, leading to the development of peptic ulcers. The Indomethacin-induced ulcer model mimics this condition by inducing acute or chronic ulcers in the gastric or intestinal mucosa of animals using Indomethacin. This model has been used to study the role of various factors, such as oxidative stress, inflammation, and gastric acid secretion, in the development and healing of peptic ulcers. It has also been used to evaluate the efficacy of various drugs, such as proton pump inhibitors, histamine H2-receptor antagonists, and natural compounds, in the prevention and treatment of peptic ulcers. Overall, the Indomethacin-induced ulcer model is a useful tool for researchers to investigate the mechanisms underlying the pathogenesis of peptic ulcers and to test the efficacy of potential therapeutic agents.

Methodology

1. The experiment is typically performed on healthy male rats, usually Wistar or Sprague-Dawley rats, with a weight of around 200-250g.
2. Indomethacin is administered to the rats to induce gastric ulcers. The usual dose of indomethacin is 30-40 mg/kg body weight, which can be administered either orally or intraperitoneally.
3. The test compound, either a drug or a natural product, is administered before or after indomethacin to evaluate its anti-ulcer activity. Different doses and routes of administration may be used for test compounds, depending on the nature of the compound and the research question.
4. After a specified period of time, typically 4-6 hours after indomethacin administration, the rats are sacrificed by cervical dislocation or other approved method. The stomachs are then excised and opened along the greater curvature to examine the ulcer index.
5. The stomach is examined under a dissecting microscope and the number of ulcers is counted, along with the size and severity of each ulcer. The ulcer index is calculated as the sum of the average number of ulcers and the severity score. The severity score is calculated as the product of the severity of each ulcer (graded from 0 to 3 based on its size and depth) and the number of ulcers in each category.

6. The data are analyzed using statistical software to evaluate the anti-ulcer activity of the test compound. The results can be expressed as the percentage inhibition of ulcer index, which is calculated as (1-T/C) x 100, where T is the ulcer index in the treated group and C is the ulcer index in the control group.

The Ethanol-induced ulcer model

it is a commonly used experimental model to study acute gastric injury and the pathophysiology of peptic ulcers. Ethanol is a chemical agent that is widely used as a disinfectant, solvent, and fuel. However, when ingested orally, ethanol can cause damage to the gastric mucosa, leading to the development of gastric ulcers. The Ethanol-induced ulcer model mimics this condition by inducing acute ulcers in the gastric mucosa of animals using ethanol. This model has been used to study the role of various factors, such as oxidative stress, inflammation, and mucosal blood flow, in the development and healing of gastric ulcers. It has also been used to evaluate the efficacy of various drugs, such as proton pump inhibitors, histamine H2-receptor antagonists, and natural compounds, in the prevention and treatment of gastric ulcers. Overall, the Ethanol-induced ulcer model is a useful tool for researchers to investigate the mechanisms underlying the pathogenesis of gastric ulcers and to test the efficacy of potential therapeutic agents.

Methodology

1. The experiment is typically performed on healthy male rats or mice, usually Wistar or Sprague-Dawley rats or Swiss mice, with a weight of around 200-250g.
2. Ethanol is administered to the animals to induce gastric ulcers. The usual dose of ethanol is 1-2 mL of 95% ethanol per animal,

which can be administered orally or by gavage.

3. he test compound, either a drug or a natural product, is administered before or after ethanol to evaluate its anti-ulcer activity. Different doses and routes of administration may be used for test compounds, depending on the nature of the compound and the research question.
4. After a specified period of time, typically 1-2 hours after ethanol administration, the animals are sacrificed by cervical dislocation or other approved method. The stomachs are then excised and opened along the greater curvature to examine the ulcer index.
5. The stomach is examined under a dissecting microscope and the number of ulcers is counted, along with the size and severity of each ulcer. The ulcer index is calculated as the sum of the average number of ulcers and the severity score. The severity score is calculated as the product of the severity of each ulcer (graded from 0 to 3 based on its size and depth) and the number of ulcers in each category.
6. The data are analyzed using statistical software to evaluate the anti-ulcer activity of the test compound. The results can be expressed as the percentage inhibition of ulcer index, which is calculated as (1-T/C) x 100, where T is the ulcer index in the treated group and C is the ulcer index in the control group.

The Acetic acid-induced ulcer model

It is an experimental model that is widely used to study the pathophysiology and treatment of gastric ulcers. Acetic acid is a corrosive agent that is used in various industrial processes and has been shown to cause gastric mucosal injury when administered orally. The Acetic acid-induced ulcer model mimics this condition by inducing acute or chronic ulcers in the gastric mucosa of animals using acetic acid. This model has been used to study the role of various factors, such as oxidative stress, inflammation, and mucosal blood flow, in the development and healing of gastric ulcers. It has also been used to evaluate the efficacy of various drugs, such as proton pump inhibitors, histamine H2-receptor antagonists, and natural compounds, in the prevention and treatment of gastric ulcers. Overall, the Acetic acid-induced ulcer model is a useful tool for researchers to investigate the mechanisms underlying the pathogenesis of gastric ulcers and to test the efficacy of potential therapeutic agents.

Methodology

1. The experiment is typically performed on healthy male rats or mice, usually Wistar or Sprague-Dawley rats or Swiss mice, with a weight of around 200-250g.
2. Acetic acid is administered to the animals to induce gastric ulcers. The usual dose of acetic acid is 0.2-0.3 mL of 50-60% acetic acid solution, which can be administered orally or by gavage.
3. The test compound, either a drug or a natural product, is administered before or after acetic acid to evaluate its anti-ulcer activity. Different doses and routes of administration may be used for test compounds, depending on the nature of the compound and the research question.
4. After a specified period of time, typically 20-30 minutes after acetic acid administration, the animals are sacrificed by cervical dislocation or other approved method. The stomachs are then excised and opened along the greater curvature to examine the ulcer index.
5. The stomach is examined under a dissecting microscope, and the number and size of ulcers are recorded. The severity of each ulcer is scored using a grading system, usually from 0 to 4 based on its size and depth. The ulcer index is calculated as the sum of the scores for all ulcers, and the results are expressed as mean ± standard error of the mean (SEM).

The data are analyzed using statistical software to evaluate the anti-ulcer activity of the test compound. The results can be expressed as the percentage inhibition of ulcer index, which is calculated as (1-T/C) x 100, where T is the ulcer index in the treated group and C is the ulcer index in the control group.A higher percentage of inhibition indicates a stronger anti-ulcer activity of the test compound.

The Aspirin-induced gastric ulcer model

The Aspirin-induced gastric ulcer model in rats is widely used to evaluate the gastro-protective potential of various drugs. Aspirin or acetylsalicylic acid (ASA) is a non-steroidal anti-inflammatory drug (NSAID) that has been reported to cause gastric ulcers in experimental animals and humans. This model mimics the pathophysiology of NSAID-induced gastropathy in humans, which is a major side effect of these drugs. In this model, ASA is administered orally to fasted rats, which leads to gastric mucosal damage and ulcer formation. The severity of ulceration is evaluated using various parameters such as ulcer index, ulcer score, and percent ulcer inhibition.

Methodology:

1. Male Wistar rats weighing 180-220 g are fasted overnight with free access to water.
2. The rats are randomly divided into different groups, each consisting of 6-8 animals.
3. ASA is dissolved in saline and administered orally to the test groups at a dose of 200 mg/kg body weight.
4. The control group receives an equivalent volume of saline.
5. In some experiments, test drugs or potential gastro-protective agents are administered orally to the rats 30 minutes before ASA treatment.

6. The rats are sacrificed 4 hours after ASA administration.
7. The stomachs are excised, opened along the greater curvature, and the ulcerated mucosa is gently rinsed with saline.
8. The ulcerated area is measured using a digital vernier caliper or planimeter, and the severity of ulceration is evaluated using parameters such as ulcer index, ulcer score, and percent ulcer inhibition.
9. In some experiments, the gastric tissue is fixed in 10% formalin, processed, and stained with hematoxylin and eosin for histopathological examination.

This model allows for the evaluation of the anti-ulcerogenic potential of various drugs and natural products, and can be used to identify potential gastro-protective agents for further development. The Aspirin-induced gastric ulcer model in rats is a reliable, cost-effective, and easy-to-perform model for screening anti-ulcer agents.

Stress-induced ulcermodel

Stress - induced ulcers are a common type of peptic ulcer that develop in response to physical or emotional stress. The Stress-induced ulcer model is an experimental model used to study the pathophysiology and treatment of stress-induced ulcers. In this model, animals are exposed to various types of stress, such as immobilization, cold, or electric shock, to induce gastric ulceration. The model has been used to investigate the mechanisms underlying the development of stress-induced ulcers, such as alterations in mucosal blood flow, gastric acid secretion, and inflammation. It has also been used to evaluate the efficacy of various drugs, such as proton pump inhibitors, histamine H2-receptor antagonists, and natural compounds, in the prevention and treatment of stress-induced ulcers. Overall, the Stress-induced ulcer model is a useful tool for researchers to investigate the mechanisms underlying the pathogenesis of stress-induced ulcers and to test the efficacy of potential therapeutic agents.

Methodology

1. The experiment is typically performed on healthy male rats or mice, usually Wistar or Sprague-Dawley rats or Swiss mice, with a weight of around 200-250g.
2. The animals are subjected to physical restraint stress, which is a common method for inducing stress-induced ulcers. The animals are placed in restrainers, which restrict their movement and prevent them. The test compound, either a drug or a natural product, is administered before or after the restraint stress to evaluate its anti-ulcer activity. Different doses and routes of administration may be used for test compounds, depending on the nature of the compound and the research question.
3. After a specified period of time, typically 4-6 hours after the restraint stress, the animals are sacrificed by cervical dislocation or other approved method. The stomachs are then excised and opened along the greater curvature to examine the ulcer index.
4. The stomach is examined under a dissecting microscope and the number of ulcers is counted, along with the size and severity of each ulcer. The ulcer index is calculated as the sum of the average number of ulcers and the severity score. The severity score is calculated as the product of the severity of each ulcer (graded from 0 to 3 based on its size and depth) and the number of ulcers in each category.
5. The data are analyzed using statistical software to evaluate the anti-ulcer activity of the test compound. The results can be expressed as the percentage inhibition of ulcer index, which is calculated as (1-T/C) x 100, where T is the ulcer index in the treated group and C is the ulcer index in the control group.

The Pylorus ligation-induced ulcer model

The Pylorus ligation-induced ulcer model is an experimental model that is widely used to study the pathophysiology and treatment of peptic ulcers. The pylorus is a muscular ring that controls the passage of food from the stomach to the small intestine. In the Pylorus ligation-induced ulcer model, the pylorus is surgically ligated to prevent the passage of food from the stomach to the small intestine, which leads to an increase in gastric acid secretion and the development of gastric ulcers. This model has been used to study the role of various factors, such as gastric acid secretion, mucosal blood flow, and inflammatory mediators, in the development and healing of peptic ulcers. It has also been used to evaluate the efficacy of various drugs, such as proton pump inhibitors, histamine H2-receptor antagonists, and natural compounds, in the prevention and treatment of peptic ulcers. Overall, the Pylorus ligation-induced ulcer model is a useful tool for researchers to investigate the mechanisms underlying the pathogenesis of peptic ulcers and to test the efficacy of potential therapeutic agents.

Methodology

- The experiment is typically performed on healthy male rats or mice, usually Wistar or Sprague-Dawley rats or Swiss mice, with a weight of around 200-250g.
- The animals are anesthetized and a midline abdominal incision is made to expose the pylorus. The pylorus is then ligated using a surgical thread to prevent gastric emptying, and the abdomen is closed.
- The test compound, either a drug or a natural product, is administered before or after pylorus ligation to evaluate its anti-ulcer activity. Different doses and routes of administration may be used for test compounds, depending on the nature of the compound and the research question.

- After a specified period of time, typically 4-6 hours after pylorus ligation, the animals are sacrificed by cervical dislocation or other approved method. The stomachs are then excised and opened along the greater curvature to examine the ulcer index.
- The stomach is examined under a dissecting microscope, and the number and size of ulcers are recorded. The severity of each ulcer is scored using a grading system, usually from 0 to 4 based on its size and depth. The ulcer index is calculated as the sum of the scores for all ulcers, and the results are expressed as mean ± standard error of the mean (SEM).
- The data are analyzed using statistical software to evaluate the anti-ulcer activity of the test compound. The results can be expressed as the percentage inhibition of ulcer index, which is calculated as (1-T/C) x 100, where T is the ulcer index in the treated group and C is the ulcer index in the control group. A higher percentage of inhibition indicates a stronger anti-ulcer activity of the test compound.

NSAID-induced enteropathy model

It is a pathological condition characterized by the development of ulcers and inflammation in the small intestine due to the long-term use of nonsteroidal anti-inflammatory drugs (NSAIDs). NSAIDs are commonly used for pain relief and have anti-inflammatory properties, but they can cause adverse effects such as gastric ulcers, bleeding, and enteropathy. The NSAID-induced enteropathy model is an experimental model used to study the pathophysiology of this condition. In this model, animals are treated with NSAIDs, such as aspirin or indomethacin, for a prolonged period to induce enteropathy. This model has been used to investigate the mechanisms underlying the development of NSAID-induced enteropathy, such as oxidative stress, inflammation, and alterations in gut microbiota. It has also been used to evaluate the efficacy of various drugs and natural compounds in preventing or treating

NSAID-induced enteropathy. Overall, the NSAID-induced enteropathy model is a valuable tool for researchers to study the pathogenesis of this condition and to develop new strategies for its prevention and treatment.

NSAID-induced enteropathy is a condition that can occur with long-term use of nonsteroidal anti-inflammatory drugs (NSAIDs), leading to small intestinal mucosal injury, inflammation, and ulceration. Here is an overview of the methodology used in the NSAID-induced enteropathy model:

1. The experiment is typically performed on healthy male rats or mice, usually Sprague-Dawley rats or C57BL/6 mice, with a weight of around 200-250g.
2. NSAIDs such as indomethacin or aspirin are administered orally to induce enteropathy. Different doses and durations of administration may be used for different research questions. It's important to note that the doses used in animals are typically higher than those used in humans, and the duration of administration is often longer.
3. After a specified period of time, typically 3-5 days of NSAID administration, the animals are sacrificed by cervical dislocation or other approved method. The small intestine is then excised, flushed with saline, and examined macroscopically and microscopically.
4. The small intestine is examined for gross changes such as edema, bleeding, or ulceration. The severity of these changes is graded using a scoring system, and the results are expressed as mean ± standard error of the mean (SEM).
5. Tissue samples from the small intestine are collected and fixed in formalin. Sections are then prepared and stained with hematoxylin and eosin for microscopic evaluation. The degree of villous damage, crypt hyperplasia, and inflammatory cell infiltration is assessed using a scoring system, and the results are expressed as mean ± SEM.

The data are analyzed using statistical software to evaluate the severity of enteropathy induced by NSAIDs. The results can be expressed as the percentage change in villus height, the percentage of villi with complete denudation, or the histological score. A higher score or percentage indicates a more severe enteropathy.

Helicobacter pylori (H. pylori) infection is one of the most common causes of gastric ulcers. The H. pylori-induced gastric ulcer model in mice is a widely used model for studying the pathogenesis of H. pylori-induced gastric ulcers and for screening potential anti-ulcer agents.

Methodology:

1. Inoculation of H. pylori: H. pylori is grown on a selective agar medium, and bacterial cells are harvested and suspended in PBS. Mice are inoculated with H. pylori via oral gavage at a concentration of 1 × 10^8 CFU/mL.
2. Monitoring of gastric inflammation: After 1 week of H. pylori infection, mice are euthanized and their stomachs are removed. The stomach is opened along the greater curvature, and the severity of gastric inflammation is determined macroscopically and histologically.
3. Assessment of gastric ulceration: The degree of ulceration is assessed by measuring the ulcer index, which is calculated by multiplying the ulcer area by the severity score. The ulcer area is measured using a planimeter, and the severity score is assigned based on the severity of inflammation and the extent of necrosis.
4. Evaluation of anti-ulcer agents: The potential anti-ulcer agents are administered to the H. pylori-infected mice via oral gavage. The degree of ulceration is assessed as described above, and the ulcer index is compared between the treated and control groups.
5. Overall, the H. pylori-induced gastric ulcer model in mice is a reliable and well-established model for studying the pathogenesis of H. pylori-induced gastric ulcers and for

screening potential anti-ulcer agents.

Helicobacter pylori-induced gastric ulcer model in mice

Helicobacter pylori (H. pylori) infection is one of the most common causes of gastric ulcers. The H. pylori-induced gastric ulcer model in mice is a widely used model for studying the pathogenesis of H. pylori-induced gastric ulcers and for screening potential anti-ulcer agents.

Methodology:

1. Inoculation of H. pylori: H. pylori is grown on a selective agar medium, and bacterial cells are harvested and suspended in PBS. Mice are inoculated with H. pylori via oral gavage at a concentration of 1×10^8 CFU/mL.
2. Monitoring of gastric inflammation: After 1 week of H. pylori infection, mice are euthanized and their stomachs are removed. The stomach is opened along the greater curvature, and the severity of gastric inflammation is determined macroscopically and histologically.
3. Assessment of gastric ulceration: The degree of ulceration is assessed by measuring the ulcer index, which is calculated by multiplying the ulcer area by the severity score. The ulcer area is measured using a planimeter, and the severity score is assigned based on the severity of inflammation and the extent of necrosis.
4. Evaluation of anti-ulcer agents: The potential anti-ulcer agents are administered to the H. pylori-infected mice via oral gavage. The degree of ulceration is assessed as described above, and the ulcer index is compared between the treated and control groups.

The H. pylori-induced gastric ulcer model in mice is a reliable and well-established model for studying the pathogenesis of H. pylori-induced gastric ulcers and for screening potential anti-ulcer agents.

Cysteamine-induced duodenal ulcer model in rats

Cysteamine-induced duodenal ulcer model is a commonly used experimental model to induce duodenal ulcers in rats. Cysteamine is a sulfhydryl compound that increases the production of hydroxyl radical in the intestinal mucosa leading to mucosal injury. This model is useful to study the pathogenesis and therapeutic interventions for duodenal ulcers.

Methodology:

1. Male Wistar rats weighing between 200-250g are commonly used for this model.
2. Rats are acclimatized in the laboratory for at least a week before the experiment.
3. ICysteamine is administered to rats either orally or subcutaneously at a dose of 300 mg/kg body weight. This is usually followed by fasting for 2-3 hours to facilitate the uptake of cysteamine.
4. Rats are euthanized 3-4 hours after cysteamine administration, and the duodenum is removed and examined for the presence of ulcers.
5. The number, size, and severity of ulcers are evaluated macroscopically and microscopically. The severity of ulcers can be scored based on the size, depth, and extent of the lesion.
6. The efficacy of drugs for treating duodenal ulcers can be evaluated by administering the drug before or after cysteamine induction and assessing the severity of ulcers. Several drugs have been evaluated using the cysteamine-induced duodenal ulcer

model in rats, including proton pump inhibitors, H2 receptor antagonists, and cytoprotective agents. For example, omeprazole, a proton pump inhibitor, was shown to significantly reduce the number of ulcers and the severity of lesions when administered prior to cysteamine induction. Similarly, ranitidine, an H2 receptor antagonist, was found to significantly reduce ulcer severity when administered prior to cysteamine. Cytoprotective agents such as sucralfate have also been tested in this model and have shown promising results. The cysteamine-induced duodenal ulcer model in rats is a useful tool for evaluating the efficacy of potential anti-ulcer drugs and may help in the development of new treatments for duodenal ulcers.

The water immersion stress-induced gastric ulcer model

The water immersion stress-induced gastric ulcer model in mice is a commonly used preclinical model to evaluate the potential anti-ulcer activity of drugs. The model is based on the fact that stress is one of the major risk factors for the development of gastric ulcers. In this model, mice are subjected to water immersion stress by immersing them in water at 20°C for 3.5 hours. This stress causes the gastric mucosa to become more susceptible to damage, resulting in the development of gastric ulcers. The severity of the ulcer can be evaluated by measuring the ulcer index, which is the sum of the length and width of each ulcer in the stomach. The efficacy of drugs can be evaluated by administering the drug before or after stress induction and assessing the severity of the ulcer.

The water immersion stress-induced gastric ulcer model is a relatively simple and inexpensive model that can be used to screen a large number of compounds for their anti-ulcer activity. However, it has some limitations, such as the lack of reproducibility and the fact that it does not mimic the complex etiology of human gastric ulcers. Therefore, it is often used in combination with other preclinical models to evaluate the potential anti-ulcer activity of drugs.

Mehodolgy

The water immersion stress-induced gastric ulcer model in mice is a commonly used model to study stress-induced ulcers. In this model, mice are deprived of food and water for a period of 24 hours, after which they are subjected to water immersion stress by placing them in a container of water maintained at a temperature of 25-30°C for a period of 3-4 hours. The mice are then sacrificed, and the stomach is removed and examined for the presence of ulcers. The severity of the ulcers can be assessed by measuring the length and width of each ulcer, as well as the number of ulcers per stomach. The model can be used to evaluate the efficacy of drugs for preventing or treating stress-induced gastric ulcers. The administration of test drugs can be carried out before or after water immersion stress induction, and the severity of the ulcers can be compared with a control group to evaluate the drug's effectiveness. This model is useful in studying the underlying mechanisms of stress-induced ulcers and in screening potential drugs for the treatment of stress-related gastric ulcers.

ꕤ

The screening methods for antiulcer drugs involve a range of in vitro, ex vivo, and in vivo assays. The in vitro assays are useful in determining the mechanisms of action of antiulcer drugs and identifying novel compounds, while ex vivo and in vivo assays provide a more realistic assessment of drug efficacy and safety. The in vivo models include chemically-induced ulcer models, stress-induced ulcer models, and bacterial infection models, which are the most commonly used. The choice of screening method will depend on the specific research question, the type of antiulcer drug being investigated, and the resources available. Overall, these screening methods are essential in identifying potential candidates for the treatment of various ulcer-related disorders, including peptic ulcer, gastroesophageal reflux disease, and stress-induced ulceration.

XVI
Antihypertensive Drugs

Screening methods for antihypertensive drugs are essential in the development of effective treatments for hypertension. Hypertension is a major risk factor for cardiovascular disease, stroke, and renal disease, and affects a significant proportion of the global population. As a result, the development of new and effective antihypertensive drugs is a critical goal in the field of pharmacology.

Screening methods for antihypertensive drugs typically involve in vitro and in vivo assays that evaluate the effectiveness of drug candidates in lowering blood pressure. In vitro assays may use isolated tissues or cells to assess the effects of drugs on key enzymes and receptors involved in blood pressure regulation, such as angiotensin-converting enzyme (ACE), angiotensin II receptors, and calcium channels. In vivo assays may involve the use of animal models of hypertension to evaluate the effects of drugs on blood pressure, as well as on the underlying mechanisms of hypertension.

In order to screen for potential antihypertensive drugs, researchers may use a range of animal models of hypertension, such as the spontaneously hypertensive rat (SHR), the Dahl salt-sensitive rat, and models of chronic renal hypertension. These models provide valuable tools for studying the mechanisms of hypertension and evaluating the potential benefits of new drugs.

In vitro assays for screening antihypertensive drugs may include the measurement of enzyme activity, receptor binding, and intracellular signaling pathways involved in blood pressure regulation. In vivo assays may involve the use of techniques such as the tail cuff method, telemetry, and invasive blood pressure monitoring to measure changes in blood pressure in response to drug treatments.

Screening methods for antihypertensive drugs are critical in the development of effective treatments for hypertension, and the use of in vitro and in vivo assays can provide valuable insights into the mechanisms of hypertension and the potential benefits of new drug treatments.

Let us discuss most common screening methods used to screen antihypertensive drugs

The Deoxycorticosterone acetate (DOCA)-salt model

It is a widely used animal model of hypertension that is induced by the administration of DOCA and a high-salt diet. The DOCA-salt model is used to simulate the human condition of mineralocorticoid-induced hypertension, which is characterized by elevated levels of aldosterone and sodium retention.

The DOCA-salt model has been used to investigate the pathophysiology of hypertension and to screen for potential antihypertensive drugs. The model induces hypertension by causing sodium retention, volume expansion, and increased sympathetic nervous system activity. These factors lead to increased peripheral resistance and elevated blood pressure.

The DOCA-salt model can be induced in a variety of animal species, including rats and mice. The administration of DOCA is typically done via subcutaneous injection, and the high-salt diet is usually provided in the drinking water. The duration of the DOCA-salt treatment can vary, but typically lasts several weeks to several months.

Researchers use a variety of techniques to monitor blood pressure in the DOCA-salt model, including tail-cuff plethysmography, radiotelemetry, and invasive blood pressure monitoring. In addition to blood pressure, researchers may also monitor other physiological parameters, such as heart rate, renal function, and electrolyte balance.

The DOCA-salt model is a valuable tool for studying the mechanisms of hypertension and for screening potential antihypertensive drugs. By inducing hypertension in animals and evaluating the effects of various treatments, researchers can gain insights into the pathophysiology of hypertension and identify potential new drug targets. The DOCA-salt model has been used to evaluate a range of drugs, including ACE inhibitors, angiotensin receptor blockers, calcium channel blockers, and diuretics.

The DOCA-salt model is a well-established and useful tool for studying hypertension and for screening potential antihypertensive drugs. The model provides a valuable insight into the pathophysiology of hypertension and can aid in the development of new and effective treatments for this prevalent condition.

Methodology

1. Animal selection: Select male Wistar or Sprague-Dawley rats weighing between 200 and 250 grams.
2. Surgery for implantation of catheter: Prior to the start of the study, implant a catheter into the carotid artery for direct measurement of arterial blood pressure. This involves:
3. Anesthetize the rat with an intraperitoneal injection of pentobarbital sodium (60 mg/kg).
4. Shave and clean the neck area, and make a midline incision.
5. Dissect the carotid artery, ligate the surrounding vessels, and place a catheter in the artery.

6. Tunnel the catheter under the skin to the back of the rat and attach it to a subcutaneously implanted port.
7. Close the incision with sutures.
8. DOCA and salt administration: After a 5-day recovery period, induce hypertension in the rats using the following protocol:
9. Administer DOCA (25 mg/kg, subcutaneously) dissolved in mineral oil twice a week for 4 weeks.
10. Provide rats with 1% sodium chloride solution as their only source of drinking water for the entire 4-week period.
11. Monitoring blood pressure: Measure blood pressure using the following methods:
12. At the end of the 4-week treatment period, measure baseline blood pressure by recording arterial pressure for at least 30 minutes using the arterial catheter.
13. Monitor blood pressure weekly during the treatment period using the arterial catheter.
14. Measure tail-cuff blood pressure at baseline and weekly during the treatment period using a non-invasive tail-cuff method.
15. Euthanasia and tissue collection: At the end of the treatment period, euthanize the rats using an overdose of pentobarbital sodium (200 mg/kg) and collect the following tissues:
16. Heart: Weigh the heart and record its weight as a measure of hypertrophy.
17. Kidney: Weigh the kidneys and measure their length as a measure of renal hypertrophy.
18. Blood: Collect blood for analysis of plasma renin activity and electrolyte levels.

The DOCA-salt model involves the induction of hypertension in rats by the administration of DOCA and a high-salt diet, with monitoring of blood pressure and collection of tissues for analysis at the end of the treatment period. This model provides a valuable tool for studying the pathophysiology of hypertension and for evaluating the effects of potential antihypertensive drugs.

ACE inhibition in rats Model

ACE (angiotensin-converting enzyme) inhibition in rats is a commonly used experimental model for studying the effects of drugs on blood pressure and cardiovascular function. ACE inhibitors are a class of drugs commonly used to treat hypertension and other cardiovascular diseases by inhibiting the activity of ACE, an enzyme that converts angiotensin I to angiotensin II, a potent vasoconstrictor.

In this model, rats are administered an ACE inhibitor drug and changes in blood pressure and cardiovascular function are measured. The effects of the drug on ACE activity in various tissues, such as the heart, aorta, and kidney, can also be studied. This model can provide valuable information about the efficacy and safety of ACE inhibitors and other drugs for treating hypertension and related conditions.

ACE inhibition in rats can be studied using various methods, including enzyme activity assays, blood pressure measurements, and cardiovascular function assessments. The specific methodology used may depend on the research question being investigated and the specific drug being tested. It is important to follow all applicable ethical guidelines and regulations when working with animals in research.

General Methodology

Animal selection: Select male rats of a suitable age and weight (e.g. 6-8 weeks and 150-250 grams, respectively). Use rats that are healthy and free of any pre-existing medical conditions.

1. Drug administration: Administer the test drug, such as an ACE inhibitor, to the rats via oral gavage or intraperitoneal injection. The dose and frequency of administration can vary depending on the specific drug being tested.

2. Blood pressure measurement: Measure the rats' blood pressure using a non-invasive method, such as a tail-cuff system or radiotelemetry. Blood pressure should be measured before and after drug administration.
3. Tissue collection: Sacrifice the rats and collect tissue samples, such as the heart, aorta, or kidney, for further analysis.
4. Enzyme activity assay: Use an enzyme activity assay to determine the level of ACE inhibition in the collected tissue samples. For example, use a fluorometric assay to measure the conversion of a synthetic substrate by ACE in the tissue sample in the presence or absence of the test drug.
5. Statistical analysis: Use appropriate statistical methods to analyze the data and determine the significance of any observed changes in blood pressure or ACE activity.

It's important to note that this is a general methodology and that specific details may vary depending on the specific drug being tested and the research question being investigated. Additionally, it is important to follow all applicable ethical guidelines and regulations when working with animals.

Gold balt hypertension modal

The Goldblatt hypertension model is an experimental model for studying hypertension, a condition characterized by high blood pressure. The model was developed by Walter Goldblatt in the 1930s and involves the partial occlusion of one or both renal arteries to simulate renal artery stenosis, a common cause of hypertension in humans.

In this model, the renal artery is surgically constricted or clamped to induce chronic renal ischemia, which in turn leads to an increase in renin production and activation of the renin-angiotensin-aldosterone system (RAAS), a key pathway involved in blood pressure regulation. This increase in RAAS activity leads to elevated blood pressure and other physiological changes.

The Goldblatt hypertension model has been used to study the pathophysiology of hypertension and to test the efficacy and safety of drugs for treating hypertension. Methods for inducing renal artery stenosis in animal models include surgical procedures such as partial renal artery ligation, complete renal artery occlusion, and placement of an occlusive cuff around the renal artery.

This model has some limitations, as the hypertension induced in this model may not fully replicate the pathophysiology of hypertension in humans, and the surgical procedures required can be invasive and potentially harmful to the animals. However, the model remains a valuable tool for studying hypertension and the RAAS pathway and can provide important insights into the development and treatment of hypertension.

Methodolgy

The Goldblatt hypertension model is a widely used experimental model for inducing hypertension in animals. The model involves the partial occlusion of one or both renal arteries to simulate renal artery stenosis, which is a common cause of hypertension in humans. The method for inducing renal artery stenosis in this model may vary depending on the specific research question being investigated, but generally involves the following steps:

1. Anesthesia: The animal is anesthetized using an appropriate anesthetic agent. The choice of agent and the dosage used may vary depending on the animal species and individual animal characteristics. For example, in rats, a common anesthetic agent is ketamine-xylazine.
2. Surgical preparation: The animal is prepared for surgery by shaving and cleaning the surgical site, typically the left or right flank, and by administering analgesics and antibiotics as needed to minimize pain and prevent infection.
3. Exposure of the renal artery: A small incision is made in the flank to expose the renal artery. The method for exposing the

renal artery may vary depending on the animal species and individual animal characteristics. For rats, the renal artery can be accessed through the retroperitoneal space, which is located behind the peritoneal cavity. The peritoneal cavity is opened, and the retroperitoneal space is accessed by gently pushing the bowel to the side. The renal artery can then be identified and exposed.

4. Partial occlusion of the renal artery: The renal artery is partially occluded using techniques such as the placement of a constricting device, ligation, or embolization. One common technique involves placing a silver clip around the renal artery to create a stenosis. The extent of occlusion may vary depending on the research question being investigated.
5. Postoperative care: The animal is carefully monitored and provided with appropriate postoperative care. This includes pain management, fluid and electrolyte balance, and wound care. Pain management can include the use of analgesics such as buprenorphine, while fluid and electrolyte balance can be maintained by providing the animal with adequate water and electrolyte solutions. Wound care may involve cleaning the surgical site and applying antibiotics to prevent infection.
6. Blood pressure monitoring: Blood pressure is measured at various time points after induction of renal artery stenosis. This can be done using techniques such as tail-cuff plethysmography, where a cuff is placed around the tail and inflated to measure blood pressure non-invasively, or radiotelemetry, where a small device is implanted in the animal to measure blood pressure continuously.

The Goldblatt hypertension model is a valuable tool for studying the pathophysiology of hypertension and for testing the efficacy and safety of drugs for treating hypertension. However, it is important to follow all applicable ethical guidelines and regulations when working with animals in research.

CHRONIC RENAL HYPERTENSION (1 Kidney- I -Clip Method)

The chronic renal hypertension model using the one-kidney, one-clip (1K1C) method is a widely used experimental model to study hypertension and its related complications such as renal dysfunction, cardiac hypertrophy, and vascular remodeling. This model involves the surgical placement of a clip on one of the renal arteries, leading to a reduction in renal perfusion and activation of the renin-angiotensin-aldosterone system (RAAS). The activation of RAAS leads to vasoconstriction and sodium retention, ultimately resulting in elevated blood pressure.

The 1K1C model is a reliable and reproducible method for inducing hypertension, and it can be used to study the mechanisms of hypertension, as well as test the efficacy of antihypertensive drugs. This model is particularly useful for investigating the role of the RAAS in hypertension, as well as its potential as a therapeutic target.

Methodology

Animal preparation: a. Male Sprague-Dawley rats weighing 250-300 g are housed under standard laboratory conditions with a 12-hour light/dark cycle and free access to food and water. b. Animals are acclimatized for 7 days before the start of the experiment.

1. Surgical procedure: a. Rats are anesthetized with a mixture of ketamine (60 mg/kg) and xylazine (7.5 mg/kg) by intraperitoneal injection. b. A midline abdominal incision is made, and the left renal artery is isolated. c. A silver clip (0.25 mm) is placed around the renal artery, occluding it and reducing the renal blood flow by approximately 70%. d. The abdomen is closed in layers, and animals are allowed to recover.
2. Blood pressure measurement: a. Blood pressure is measured using a tail-cuff system at baseline and weekly thereafter. b.

Systolic blood pressure is measured in conscious animals, and the average of three readings is taken for each measurement.

3. Assessment of renal function: a. Twenty-four-hour urine collections are obtained from animals in metabolic cages at baseline and after 4 weeks of clipping. b. Urine samples are analyzed for proteinuria, creatinine clearance, and electrolyte excretion.
4. Assessment of cardiac hypertrophy: a. At the end of the experiment, animals are euthanized, and the heart is excised and weighed. b. The ratio of heart weight to body weight is calculated as an index of cardiac hypertrophy.
5. Assessment of vascular remodeling: a. The aorta is excised and fixed in 4% paraformaldehyde for histological analysis. b. Transverse sections of the aorta are stained with hematoxylin and eosin to assess vascular morphology and with Masson's trichrome to assess collagen deposition.
6. Statistical analysis: a. Data are expressed as mean ± standard deviation. b. Statistical analysis is performed using one-way analysis of variance (ANOVA) followed by Tukey's post hoc test.

Note: The above methodology is provided for information purposes only. Animal experiments should be conducted in accordance with institutional and national guidelines for the care and use of laboratory animals, and all procedures should be approved by the appropriate animal ethics committee.

TAIL CUFF METHOD (Blood Pressure in Conscious rats)

The tail cuff method is a non-invasive technique used to measure blood pressure in conscious rats. It is a widely used method for the evaluation of the antihypertensive effects of drugs in preclinical studies. The method is based on the principle that the blood pressure in the tail artery of a rat is proportional to the pressure in the carotid artery, which is the major artery supplying blood to the brain.

The tail cuff method involves placing a rat in a restrainer, and then placing a cuff around the base of its tail. The cuff is connected to a pressure transducer that detects the blood pressure in the tail artery. The tail is heated to promote vasodilation and increase blood flow, and then the cuff is inflated to a pressure that occludes the blood flow. The pressure is gradually released, and the point at which the blood flow resumes is recorded as the systolic pressure. The pressure at which blood flow becomes turbulent is recorded as the diastolic pressure.

The tail cuff method can provide reliable and accurate measurements of blood pressure in rats, and it has the advantage of being non-invasive, which reduces the stress and discomfort experienced by the animals. However, the method requires adequate training and skill to perform, and it may be affected by various factors such as ambient temperature, humidity, and noise, which can influence the measurements. Therefore, careful attention to experimental conditions and proper training of personnel are essential for obtaining valid and reproducible results.

Methodology

Equipment and Supplies:

1. Tail-cuff blood pressure system (e.g. CODA Non-Invasive Blood Pressure System)
2. Heating pad or lamp
3. Animal restrainer
4. Alcohol swabs
5. Sterile saline solution
6. Paper towels

Preparation of Animals:

1. Use conscious rats with a body weight between 200-400 g

2. Train the rats to the restrainer for several days before the experiment
3. Do not feed the rats on the day of the experiment to avoid fluctuations in blood pressure due to food intake
4. Place the rats on a heating pad or under a lamp to induce vasodilation of the tail vessels

Procedure:

1. Place the rat in the restrainer and allow it to calm down for at least 5 minutes before beginning the measurements
2. Clean the tail with alcohol swabs and apply a small amount of sterile saline to the tail to facilitate contact with the cuff
3. Position the tail cuff at the base of the tail and secure it with tape or a clamp
4. Inflate the cuff to occlude the blood flow in the tail and gradually release the pressure
5. Record the systolic and diastolic pressures, which correspond to the pressures at which the blood flow resumes and becomes turbulent, respectively
6. Repeat the measurements several times (e.g. 3-5 times) and calculate the mean value
7. Allow a rest period of at least 5 minutes between each measurement to avoid the effects of stress or handling
8. Data Analysis:Calculate the mean values of systolic and diastolic pressures for each rat.Analyze the data using appropriate statistical methods (e.g. t-test, ANOVA) to determine the effects of the treatments or interventions

Note: The tail cuff method is a highly technical and sensitive technique that requires proper training and calibration of the equipment. The accuracy and reproducibility of the results can be influenced by various factors such as the age, strain, and sex of the animals, ambient temperature and humidity, and the experience of the operator. Therefore, it is important to carefully follow the established protocols and to perform the measurements under standardized conditions to ensure reliable and valid results.

Salt- sensitive Dahl Rats

The Salt-sensitive Dahl rat is an established model of hypertension that is genetically prone to develop hypertension when fed a high salt diet. This model has been used to study the mechanisms involved in the development and progression of hypertension, as well as for evaluating the efficacy of antihypertensive drugs. The Salt-sensitive Dahl rat model is widely accepted and utilized due to the similarities between the hypertension in these rats and human hypertension. The model has been used extensively in studying the pathophysiology of hypertension and to assess the effectiveness of various drugs in controlling hypertension.

General methodology

1. Housing: The rats are housed in a controlled environment with a 12-hour light/dark cycle and temperature ranging from 22-24°C. They are fed a normal salt diet for at least one week before the start of the experiment.
2. Induction of hypertension: The hypertension in Salt-sensitive Dahl rats is typically induced by feeding them a high salt diet. The rats are randomly assigned to either a high salt diet group or a normal salt diet group. The high salt diet typically contains 8% NaCl and the normal salt diet contains 0.3% NaCl. The duration of feeding the high salt diet may vary, but typically ranges from 4-6 weeks. Blood pressure is monitored throughout the feeding period.
3. Blood pressure monitoring: Blood pressure can be measured in conscious rats using a tail-cuff method or by implanting

telemetry devices. Blood pressure should be measured at regular intervals throughout the experiment.

4. Endpoints: At the end of the experiment, the rats are sacrificed and various tissues such as the heart, kidneys, and aorta are collected for histological and biochemical analysis. Blood samples may also be collected for analysis of various markers such as renin, aldosterone, and endothelin-1.
5. The methodology for the Salt-sensitive Dahl rat model of hypertension can be further modified depending on the specific research questions being addressed.

ANGIOTENSIN - II ANTAGONISM

Testing Angiotensin-II antagonism involves evaluating the ability of a drug to block the activity of Angiotensin II, a hormone that plays a central role in regulating blood pressure. Angiotensin II receptor blockers (ARBs) are a class of drugs that selectively block the effects of Angiotensin II on the renin-angiotensin-aldosterone system, thereby reducing blood pressure and protecting against cardiovascular and renal disease.

The testing of ARBs involves various experimental models, including both in vitro and in vivo assays. These models aim to measure the activity of ARBs in blocking Angiotensin II receptors and reducing blood pressure.

In vitro assays include receptor-binding studies, which assess the ability of ARBs to bind to Angiotensin II receptors, and functional assays, which measure the ability of ARBs to inhibit Angiotensin II-induced vasoconstriction or aldosterone secretion.

In vivo assays involve the use of animal models of hypertension, such as spontaneously hypertensive rats (SHR) or Angiotensin II-infused rats. These models are used to evaluate the ability of ARBs to lower blood pressure and prevent target organ damage. Other in vivo assays include the measurement of urinary albumin excretion as a marker of renal damage and the assessment of cardiac and vascular remodeling.

Overall, the testing of Angiotensin II antagonism involves a variety of experimental models that aim to evaluate the ability of ARBs to block the activity of Angiotensin II and reduce blood pressure, as well as protect against cardiovascular and renal disease.

Methodology

Animal selection: Male Wistar or Sprague Dawley rats weighing 250-350 g are used for the experiment.

Diet: The rats are maintained on a standard laboratory diet with free access to tap water.

Drug administration: The rats are randomly divided into different groups, and drugs are administered according to the treatment schedule.

Blood pressure measurement: Blood pressure is measured in conscious rats using a non-invasive tail-cuff method.

Induction of hypertension: Hypertension is induced by subcutaneous infusion of angiotensin-II for 14 days using osmotic minipumps.

Treatment: The rats are treated with test drugs for 14 days, starting from the day of angiotensin-II infusion.

Blood pressure measurement: Blood pressure is measured again on the 14th day of drug treatment.

Sacrifice: The rats are euthanized, and blood and tissue samples are collected for biochemical and histological analysis.

Data analysis: The blood pressure and biochemical parameters are analyzed statistically to assess the efficacy of the test drug in antagonizing the effects of angiotensin-II.

Here are some additional details that may be useful:

The dose and route of administration of the test drug should be determined based on the pharmacokinetics and pharmacodynamics of the drug.

The dose and duration of angiotensin-II infusion should be determined based on the desired level of hypertension and the experimental design.

The tail-cuff method should be calibrated and validated before use, and the rats should be acclimatized to the procedure before the actual measurement.

The biochemical parameters that can be measured include plasma renin activity, plasma angiotensin-II levels, and urinary excretion of sodium and potassium.

The tissue samples that can be collected include the heart, kidney, and aorta, which can be used for histological examination and molecular analysis of gene expression.

Monocrotaline Induced Pulmonary Hyperyension

Monocrotaline-induced pulmonary hypertension (MCT-PH) is an extensively studied preclinical model of pulmonary hypertension. In this model, a single injection of monocrotaline, a pyrrolizidine alkaloid derived from the plant Crotalaria spectabilis, leads to progressive pulmonary vascular remodeling and increased pulmonary arterial pressure, ultimately leading to right ventricular hypertrophy and heart failure. The MCT-PH model is widely used to evaluate the efficacy of novel treatments for pulmonary hypertension and to study the pathophysiological mechanisms underlying the disease.

Methodology

Animals: Male rats weighing between 150-200g are typically used for this model. The animals are housed in a controlled environment with a temperature of 22-24°C and 12 hours light/dark cycle. Standard rat chow and water are provided ad libitum.

Monocrotaline administration: Monocrotaline (MCT) is dissolved in sterile saline and administered as a single subcutaneous injection at a dose of 60 mg/kg body weight. The injection is usually given on day 1 of the experiment.

Monitoring: Rats are monitored daily for the first 5-7 days for signs of morbidity or mortality. These include lethargy, loss of appetite, weight loss, and difficulty breathing.

Hemodynamic measurements: After 21 days, hemodynamic measurements are taken to assess the extent of pulmonary hypertension. Rats are anesthetized with ketamine and xylazine, and the right jugular vein is cannulated for the measurement of right ventricular systolic pressure (RVSP). The RVSP is recorded using a pressure transducer connected to a PowerLab data acquisition system.

Tissue harvesting: After hemodynamic measurements, the animals are euthanized, and the lungs and heart are harvested for further analysis. The ratio of right ventricular weight to left ventricular plus septal weight (RV/LV+S) is often used as an indicator of right ventricular hypertrophy.

Histology: Lung tissues are fixed in formalin, embedded in paraffin, and sectioned. Sections are stained with hematoxylin and eosin (H&E) to evaluate the degree of pulmonary vascular remodeling.

Biochemical analysis: Enzyme-linked immunosorbent assay (ELISA) and Western blotting can be used to evaluate the expression of proteins involved in the development of pulmonary hypertension.

It's important to note that this is a highly invasive and complicated model, and expertise is required to perform it properly. Additionally, various modifications and variations of the protocol can be made based on the specific research questions and goals.

Renal Artery Stenosis (RAS) Model in rats

Renal Artery Stenosis (RAS) Model in rats, which is used to study the effects of chronic hypertension on the kidneys. The methodology involves the surgical preparation of male Sprague-Dawley rats by inducing renal artery stenosis using a silver clip, and measuring blood pressure using a tail-cuff method. The degree of stenosis produced by the clip determines the level of hypertension, which can be modified by changing the size of the clip used. The rats are allowed to recover for a period of 7-10 days before blood pressure measurement is taken, and then sacrificed for histological and biochemical analysis. It is important to note that this model induces chronic hypertension, which can lead to renal damage over time, and that care should be taken to ensure the welfare of the animals during the experiment.

Methodology

1. Male Sprague-Dawley rats weighing 200-250 g are used in this model.
2. The rats are anesthetized with ketamine and xylazine (90 mg/kg and 10 mg/kg, respectively). A flank incision is made to expose the left kidney, and a silver clip (0.20 mm internal diameter) is placed on the renal artery to create stenosis. The right kidney is left intact.
3. The rats are allowed to recover for 7-10 days before blood pressure measurement is taken. During the recovery period, they are kept in individual cages with food and water available ad libitum.
4. Blood pressure is measured in conscious rats using a tail-cuff method. The rats are placed in a restrainer, and a cuff is placed around the tail. The cuff is inflated to occlude blood flow, and then slowly released while blood pressure is measured using a pressure transducer and a computerized system.
5. The mean arterial blood pressure (MAP) is calculated by averaging the blood pressure measurements taken over a period of 3-5 days. The rats are then sacrificed, and the kidneys are harvested for histological and biochemical analysis.

Note: In this model, the degree of stenosis produced by the clip determines the level of hypertension. The severity of hypertension can be modified by changing the size of the clip used. It is important to note that this model induces chronic hypertension, which can lead to renal damage over time. Care should be taken to ensure the welfare of the animals during the experiment.

CHRONIC RENAL HYPERTENSION (1 Kidney- I -Clip Method)

The one-kidney, one-clip (1K1C) Goldblatt model is a commonly used method for inducing chronic renal hypertension in experimental animals. The method involves placing a silver clip around the renal artery of one kidney, thereby reducing blood flow to the kidney and increasing renin production. This results in the development of hypertension that is sustained over several weeks. The model is useful for studying the pathophysiology of renovascular hypertension and testing the efficacy of drugs used to treat hypertension. The 1K1C model can be performed in various animal species, including rats and rabbits. The model is considered to be a reliable and reproducible method for inducing hypertension in experimental animals.

Methodology

The one-kidney, one-clip (1K-1C) model of hypertension is a well-established experimental model of renovascular hypertension in rats. In this model, a renal artery is partially occluded with a silver clip, leading to decreased blood flow to the kidney and subsequent activation of the renin-angiotensin-aldosterone system, resulting in hypertension.

Here is a detailed methodology for inducing chronic renal hypertension using the 1K-1C method in rats:

Animal selection: Male Wistar or Sprague-Dawley rats weighing 200-300 g are commonly used for this model.

Anesthesia: The rat is anesthetized with an intraperitoneal injection of a mixture of ketamine (50 mg/kg) and xylazine (5 mg/kg). The depth of anesthesia is monitored by the absence of a pedal withdrawal reflex.

Surgery: A left flank incision is made, and the left renal artery is exposed. A silver clip with an internal diameter of 0.20 mm is placed around the renal artery, leaving the right kidney and the adrenal gland untouched.

Postoperative care: The rat is given an analgesic (e.g., buprenorphine) for pain relief, and antibiotics (e.g., enrofloxacin) to prevent infection. The animal is kept warm and allowed to recover from anesthesia.

Verification of hypertension: After the surgery, the rats are kept in metabolic cages and blood pressure is monitored by a radiotelemetry system or tail-cuff method. Hypertension is usually confirmed after one to two weeks and maintained for several weeks to months.

Experimental protocols: The effects of various drugs on hypertension can be tested in this model. The test drug can be administered orally or intravenously, and the blood pressure can be monitored over time. In addition, blood and tissue samples can be collected for further analysis.

Overall, the 1K-1C model is a widely used experimental model of chronic renal hypertension, and it can be used to investigate the mechanisms underlying hypertension and to evaluate the efficacy of novel antihypertensive drugs.

ATIHYPERTENSIVE & VASODILATIOR ACTIVITY IN GANGLION BLOCKED ANG II SUPPORTED RATS.

To demonstrate the direct vasodilator activity of antihypertensive agent The ganglion-blocked Angiotensin II (Ang II) supported rat model is used to evaluate the vasodilatory activity of antihypertensive agents. This model involves the administration of ganglionic blocking agents such as hexamethonium, which block the transmission of nerve impulses between the sympathetic nervous system and the peripheral vasculature. This results in a significant reduction in arterial blood pressure. However, the administration of Ang II is used to maintain the blood pressure within a range similar to hypertensive patients. This model is useful in assessing the direct vasodilatory activity of antihypertensive agents, which can lower blood pressure independent of the sympathetic nervous system. The results from this model can provide valuable insights into the potential use of antihypertensive agents in the treatment of hypertension.

GANGLION BLOCKED ANG II SUPPORTED RATS Model

The ganglion-blocked Angiotensin II (Ang II) supported rat model is used to evaluate the vasodilatory activity of antihypertensive agents. This model involves the administration of ganglionic blocking agents such as hexamethonium, which block the transmission of nerve impulses between the sympathetic nervous system and the peripheral vasculature. This results in a significant reduction in arterial blood pressure. However, the administration of Ang II is used to maintain the blood pressure within a range similar to hypertensive patients. This model is useful in assessing the direct vasodilatory activity of antihypertensive agents, which can lower blood pressure independent of the sympathetic nervous system. The results from this model can provide valuable insights into the potential use of antihypertensive agents in the treatment of hypertension

Methodology for the ganglion-blocked Ang II supported rat model for evaluating antihypertensive and vasodilatory activity:

1. Animal preparation: Male Wistar rats (250-300 g) are housed in a temperature-controlled room with a 12-hour light/dark cycle and given free access to food and water. The rats are anesthetized with ketamine (50 mg/kg) and xylazine (5 mg/kg) intraperitoneally.
2. Surgical procedure: The right femoral vein and artery are cannulated with polyethylene tubing for the administration of drugs and measurement of arterial blood pressure, respectively. The left jugular vein is also cannulated for the administration of hexamethonium, a ganglionic blocker. The surgical procedure is performed under aseptic conditions.
3. Measurement of baseline blood pressure: After a 30-minute stabilization period, the baseline arterial blood pressure is measured using a PowerLab system with a tail-cuff sensor.
4. Administration of ganglionic blocker: Hexamethonium (10 mg/kg) is administered through the jugular vein to block the transmission of nerve impulses between the sympathetic nervous system and the peripheral vasculature.
5. Maintenance of blood pressure with Ang II: Ang II (50 ng/kg/min) is administered through the femoral vein to maintain the blood pressure within a range similar to hypertensive patients.
6. Administration of test agent: After a 30-minute stabilization period, the test agent is administered through the femoral vein. The dose and duration of administration depend on the specific agent being tested.
7. Measurement of blood pressure and heart rate: The arterial blood pressure and heart rate are continuously monitored and recorded for 2 hours after the administration of the test agent.
8. Data analysis: The results are expressed as mean arterial pressure and heart rate. Statistical analysis is performed using appropriate tests to compare the results of the test agent to a control group.

Note: The specific values and duration of the procedures may vary depending on the experimental design and the specific agents being tested. It is important to follow appropriate ethical guidelines and obtain approval from institutional animal care and use committees before conducting animal experiments.

IN VITRO MODELS -MONOCROTALINE INDUCED HYPERTENSION

Monocrotaline-induced pulmonary hypertension (MCT-PH) is a commonly used in vitro model for studying the pathophysiology of pulmonary hypertension. This model involves exposing pulmonary arterial smooth muscle cells (PASMCs) to monocrotaline, which induces damage to the endothelial cells lining the pulmonary vasculature, leading to an increase in pulmonary vascular resistance and pulmonary arterial pressure. The model is useful for investigating the cellular and molecular mechanisms involved in the development of pulmonary hypertension, as well as for testing the efficacy of novel pharmacological interventions. MCT-PH has been used to study the effects of various drugs on pulmonary vascular remodeling, such as endothelin receptor antagonists, phosphodiesterase inhibitors, and potassium channel openers.

Methodolgy

The Monocrotaline (MCT) induced pulmonary hypertension (PH) model is an in vitro model that is commonly used to study the pathophysiology of pulmonary hypertension and test the efficacy of drugs used to treat the disease. The method involves exposing cultured pulmonary arterial smooth muscle cells (PASMCs) to monocrotaline, which is a toxic pyrrolizidine alkaloid that causes injury to the endothelial cells and smooth muscle cells of the pulmonary vasculature, leading to the development of PH.

To perform the MCT-induced PH model, PASMCs are cultured in 96-well plates and exposed to monocrotaline at varying concentrations for a period of 24-48 hours. After the exposure period, the cells are analyzed for various parameters such as cell viability, proliferation, migration, and apoptosis. In addition, the expression levels of proteins and genes involved in the pathogenesis of PH are also analyzed using techniques such as western blotting, immunofluorescence, and quantitative PCR.

The MCT-induced PH model is a useful tool for investigating the cellular and molecular mechanisms underlying the development of PH and for evaluating the efficacy of new treatments for the disease. However, it is important to note that the in vitro model has its limitations and that the results obtained from this model may not always translate to the in vivo setting.

ACE INHIBITION IN ISOLATED GUINEA PIG ILEUM

ACE (angiotensin-converting enzyme) inhibition in isolated guinea pig ileum is an experimental model used to study the effects of ACE inhibitors on smooth muscle contractility. The method involves isolating the guinea pig ileum and suspending it in an organ bath containing Krebs buffer solution. The ileum is then stimulated with a contractile agent, typically acetylcholine, to induce contraction. The contraction is then measured using force displacement transducers.

ACE inhibitors are then added to the organ bath to evaluate their inhibitory effects on angiotensin II-induced smooth muscle contraction. The concentration-response curve for angiotensin II is first determined, followed by the addition of the ACE inhibitor to the organ bath. The concentration of the ACE inhibitor is increased incrementally to determine its inhibitory effects on angiotensin II-induced contraction. The potency and efficacy of the ACE inhibitor can be determined by analyzing the degree of inhibition of angiotensin II-induced contraction.

This model is useful for studying the mechanisms of ACE inhibition and for evaluating the potency and efficacy of ACE inhibitors. It is a reliable and reproducible model that can be used to investigate the effects of ACE inhibitors on smooth muscle contraction and to develop new antihypertensive drugs.

Methodolgy

The ACE inhibition assay in isolated guinea pig ileum is a commonly used in vitro method for testing the efficacy of ACE inhibitors. The method involves dissecting a segment of the guinea pig ileum and suspending it in a tissue bath containing oxygenated Krebs solution at 37°C. The tissue is connected to an isometric transducer to measure changes in tension. After allowing the tissue to equilibrate, a concentration-response curve is generated using a contractile agent such as angiotensin I or angiotensin II. The ACE inhibitor being tested is added to the bath and allowed to equilibrate before generating a second concentration-response curve. The degree of inhibition of the contractile response to angiotensin I or angiotensin II is then measured and compared to a control group that received no ACE inhibitor. The degree of inhibition can be expressed as the IC50, which is the concentration of the ACE inhibitor required to inhibit 50% of the response to angiotensin I or angiotensin II. The results of this assay can provide valuable information about the potency and efficacy of ACE inhibitors in vitro.

GUENIA PIG ATRIA Model

The guinea pig atria model is a commonly used in vitro model for studying the β1 sympatholytic activity of drugs. This model involves the use of isolated guinea pig atria, which are sensitive to β1 receptor agonists and antagonists. The model is useful for studying the effects of drugs on cardiac function and the sympathetic nervous system, and for identifying potential new drugs for the treatment of cardiovascular diseases.

Methodology:

The β1 sympatholytic activity in guinea pig atria can be measured by the Langendorff method. The guinea pig is anesthetized and the heart is quickly removed and placed in a Langendorff apparatus. The atria are isolated and stimulated with an electrical field to induce contraction. The contractions are then recorded using a force transducer. The β1 adrenergic receptor agonist isoproterenol is added to the atria to induce a maximal contraction. The β1 sympatholytic activity of a test drug is determined by measuring its ability to reduce the isoproterenol-induced contraction. The concentration-response relationship of the test drug can also be determined to calculate its potency and efficacy.

Alternatively, the isolated atria can be placed in an organ bath and connected to a force transducer. The atria are then stimulated with electrical field or agonist to induce contraction, and the contractions are recorded. The test drug is added to the bath and its effect on the contraction is measured.

The concentration of the test drug required to inhibit 50% of the maximal contraction induced by isoproterenol is calculated as the IC50 value. The β1 sympatholytic activity of a test drug can be quantified by comparing its IC50 value to that of a reference drug with known β1 sympatholytic activity, such as metoprolol.

Chronic renal hypertension in Dogs

Chronic renal hypertension is a condition in which high blood pressure results from renal dysfunction. In dogs, this condition can be induced experimentally to study the pathophysiology of renovascular hypertension and test the efficacy of drugs used to treat hypertension. The two-kidney, one-clip (2K1C) Goldblatt model is a commonly used method for inducing chronic renal hypertension in dogs.

Methodology: The 2K1C Goldblatt model involves the placement of a silver clip around one renal artery, thereby reducing blood flow to one kidney and activating the renin-angiotensin system. This results in the development of hypertension, which is sustained over several weeks. The model can be performed in various dog breeds, including beagles and mongrels. Prior to the surgery, the dogs are screened for general health and blood pressure. The surgical procedure involves anesthesia and a midline abdominal incision. The renal artery is isolated and a silver clip is placed around it to induce stenosis. The other kidney is left unclipped to serve as a control. Following surgery, the dogs are monitored for blood pressure and renal function, and treated with antihypertensive drugs as necessary.

The 2K1C model in dogs is considered to be a reliable and reproducible method for inducing hypertension and evaluating the efficacy of drugs used to treat hypertension. However, the use of dogs in research can raise ethical concerns and should be conducted with appropriate oversight and adherence to ethical guidelines.

Renin inhibition in Monkeys

Renin is an enzyme that plays a crucial role in the regulation of blood pressure and fluid balance. Inhibition of renin activity is one approach for the treatment of hypertension. Monkeys have been used as an animal model to study the pharmacological effects of renin inhibitors.

The monkey is a commonly used animal model for preclinical studies of drugs targeting the renin-angiotensin system. Renin inhibitors are a class of drugs that block the activity of renin, an enzyme that plays a key role in the regulation of blood pressure. The use of monkeys in this research is important, as they share many physiological similarities with humans, making them an ideal model for studying drug effects and safety.

The methodology for renin inhibition in monkeys could include the following steps:

1. Animal preparation: The monkeys are acclimatized to the laboratory environment and are housed in individual cages with

access to food and water.

2. Surgery: The monkeys are anesthetized and a surgical procedure is performed to implant catheters in the femoral artery and vein for blood sampling and drug administration.
3. Baseline measurements: Baseline measurements of blood pressure, heart rate, and renin activity are obtained.
4. Drug administration: The renin inhibitor drug is administered either orally or intravenously at a predetermined dose.
5. Follow-up measurements: Blood pressure, heart rate, and renin activity are monitored at regular intervals over a period of several hours.
6. Data analysis: The data is analyzed to determine the effect of the renin inhibitor drug on blood pressure, heart rate, and renin activity in the monkeys.

Screening methods play a critical role in the drug discovery process by enabling the identification of potential drug candidates. There are several screening methods used to identify drugs that are effective in treating hypertension.In conclusion, there are various animal models available for screening the efficacy of antihypertensive drugs. Each model has its advantages and disadvantages, and the choice of the appropriate model depends on the research question and the drug being tested. The in vitro assays also provide valuable information on the mechanism of action of the drugs and their potential side effects. Overall, a combination of in vitro and in vivo screening methods is necessary to identify potential antihypertensive drug candidates and to determine their safety and efficacy. The use of appropriate animal models and in vitro assays is crucial for the development of safe and effective antihypertensive drugs for the treatment of hypertension and its associated complications.

XVII

Drug Used in Congestive Heart Failure

Heart failure is a debilitating condition that affects millions of people worldwide, and the search for effective treatments is ongoing. In order to develop new drugs to treat heart failure, researchers rely on a variety of screening methods to identify potential candidates for further study. These screening methods typically involve the use of animal models or in vitro assays to evaluate the effects of potential drug candidates on various aspects of heart function, such as contractility, relaxation, and cardiac output. By using these screening methods, researchers can identify promising drug candidates that can then be further tested in preclinical and clinical studies. The ultimate goal of these screening methods is to identify new drugs that can improve the quality of life and survival of patients with heart failure.

Some commonly used screening techniques for Drugs to treat CHF

1. Transverse aortic constriction-induced heart failure model in mice
2. Pressure overload-induced heart failure model in rats
3. Myocardial infarction-induced heart failure model in rats
4. Coronary artery ligation-induced heart failure model in rats
5. Doxorubicin-induced cardiotoxicity model in mice
6. Pressure overload-induced heart failure model in rats

Transverse aortic constriction (TAC)

Transverse aortic constriction (TAC) is a widely used model for studying heart failure in mice. In this model, the aorta is constricted by placing a ligature around it, which leads to increased resistance to blood flow and pressure overload in the heart, resulting in cardiac dysfunction and heart failure. This model is useful for studying the pathophysiology of heart failure and for evaluating the efficacy of drugs for treating heart failure.

Methodology:

Animal preparation: Male mice (8-12 weeks old) are anesthetized using isoflurane, and the chest is opened to expose the aortic arch. The transverse aorta is constricted using a ligature, and the chest is closed.

Sham surgery: A sham group is used as a control, in which the chest is opened, but the aorta is not constricted.

Echocardiography: Echocardiography is performed before and after the surgery to assess cardiac function.

Treatment intervention: Drugs or other interventions are administered to the mice to evaluate their efficacy in treating heart failure.

Assessment of heart function: Heart function is assessed by echocardiography, pressure-volume analysis, histology, and molecular analysis.

Data analysis: Data is analyzed to evaluate the efficacy of the treatment intervention.

Overall, the TAC model is a valuable tool for studying heart failure and for evaluating potential treatments for this condition. It is a complex and technically challenging model that requires expertise in surgical techniques, echocardiography, and data analysis.

Myocardial infarction modal (MI)

Myocardial infarction (MI), commonly known as a heart attack, is a serious medical condition that occurs when blood flow to a part of the heart is blocked, resulting in damage or death of heart muscle cells. MI is typically caused by the rupture of a plaque in a coronary artery, leading to the formation of a blood clot that obstructs blood flow. The resulting ischemia and lack of oxygen to the affected area can cause chest pain, shortness of breath, and other symptoms.

MI is a major cause of morbidity and mortality worldwide, and the development of new treatments to improve patient outcomes is an active area of research. Animal models of MI are important tools in this research, allowing scientists to study the pathophysiology of the disease and test the efficacy of potential treatments.

There are various animal models of MI, including the ligation of coronary arteries, chemical-induced injury, and genetic models. These models can be performed in different species, including mice, rats, rabbits, and pigs. The choice of model depends on the research question and the specific characteristics of the model being used. The use of animal models has contributed significantly to our understanding of the mechanisms underlying MI and the development of new treatments for the disease.

Methodology

The methodology for inducing myocardial infarction (MI) in animals typically involves surgically occluding a major coronary artery to produce ischemia and subsequent infarction of the myocardium. The details of the procedure can vary depending on the animal species and specific research goals, but here is a general overview of the methodology:

1. Anesthetize the animal with an appropriate anesthetic agent.
2. Intubate the animal to maintain airway and respiration.
3. Place the animal on a heating pad to maintain body temperature.
4. Position the animal in the supine position, and expose the heart by making a midline sternotomy.
5. Identify the coronary artery to be occluded.
6. Occlude the artery using a surgical ligature, clip, or suture. The duration of occlusion can vary depending on the study design.
7. After a predetermined period of time, remove the occlusion to allow reperfusion of the myocardium.
8. Close the chest incision and monitor the animal for recovery.
9. Animals may be sacrificed at various time points after the procedure to evaluate the extent of myocardial damage, inflammation, and other relevant endpoints.

It is important to note that inducing MI in animals is a highly invasive and potentially lethal procedure, and should only be performed by trained and experienced personnel in accordance with ethical guidelines and animal welfare regulations.

Pressure overload method

The pressure overload method is a widely used experimental model to induce cardiac hypertrophy and heart failure in animal studies. This model involves increasing the workload on the heart by surgically inducing pressure overload in the left ventricle of the heart. The resulting hypertrophy and remodeling of the heart mimics the pathophysiology of human heart failure caused by pressure overload conditions, such as hypertension and aortic stenosis.

In this model, the pressure overload is achieved through the surgical constriction of the aorta, which results in increased afterload on the left ventricle. This increased afterload causes the ventricular walls to thicken and the ventricular chamber to become smaller. Over time, this can lead to heart failure.

The pressure overload method can be performed in various animal species, including mice, rats, and rabbits. It is useful for studying the mechanisms involved in the development and progression of cardiac hypertrophy and heart failure, as well as for testing potential therapeutic interventions.

Methodology

The pressure overload method is a commonly used experimental model to induce cardiac hypertrophy and heart failure in animals. The most commonly used technique for inducing pressure overload in rodents involves the surgical constriction of the aorta (also known as aortic banding) to create a pressure gradient across the constriction. The procedure involves exposing the aorta through a midline incision and placing a ligature or clip around the aorta to create a stenosis.

The degree of constriction can be adjusted to produce varying levels of pressure overload and cardiac hypertrophy. The model can be performed in mice and rats, and can be used to study the molecular mechanisms of cardiac hypertrophy, the progression to heart failure, and the efficacy of therapeutic interventions.

The methodology for the pressure overload model typically involves the following steps:

- Anesthetize the animal using an appropriate anesthetic agent.
- Make a midline incision in the chest to expose the aorta.
- Place a ligature or clip around the aorta to create a stenosis.
- Close the chest incision and monitor the animal for recovery.

- Assess the degree of pressure overload and cardiac hypertrophy using echocardiography, histological analysis, or other techniques.
- Perform interventions such as drug treatments to evaluate their effects on cardiac function and hypertrophy.

Coronary artery ligation-induced heart failure model in rats

Coronary artery ligation-induced heart failure model in rats is a widely used animal model for studying heart failure. This model involves the surgical occlusion of the left anterior descending coronary artery, which results in the infarction of a significant portion of the left ventricular myocardium, leading to heart failure. The method is highly reproducible, and the degree of myocardial infarction can be adjusted by varying the location and severity of the ligation.

Methodology:

- Anesthetize the rat using an appropriate anesthetic agent such as ketamine or isoflurane.
- Intubate the rat and maintain anesthesia with a mechanical ventilator.
- Create a left thoracotomy incision to expose the heart.
- Identify the left anterior descending coronary artery.
- Place a suture around the artery, and occlude it to induce myocardial infarction.
- Close the thoracotomy incision and allow the animal to recover.
- Monitor the animal for signs of heart failure, such as shortness of breath, lethargy, and decreased activity.
- Administer the test drug to the animal and monitor its effect on heart function.

This model is useful for testing the efficacy of drugs for treating heart failure and for studying the underlying mechanisms of heart failure. It has been used to identify new drug targets and to test the effectiveness of various pharmacological interventions.

Doxorubicin-induced cardiotoxicity model in mice

Doxorubicin is a widely used chemotherapeutic agent for the treatment of various types of cancers. However, its use is limited due to the development of cardiotoxicity, which can lead to heart failure. Animal models are used to study the mechanisms underlying doxorubicin-induced cardiotoxicity and to evaluate potential treatments.

The doxorubicin-induced cardiotoxicity model in mice is a commonly used preclinical model for studying drug-induced cardiac toxicity. The model involves the administration of doxorubicin to mice, which induces cardiac damage and dysfunction. This model is used to evaluate the efficacy of potential treatments for doxorubicin-induced cardiotoxicity and to investigate the underlying mechanisms of the disease.

Methodology

- Male or female mice are usually used in this model. The mice should be healthy and free of pre-existing cardiac disease.
- Doxorubicin is administered to the mice by injection, usually at a dose of 10-20 mg/kg. The frequency and duration of doxorubicin administration can vary depending on the study design.
- Echocardiography is used to evaluate cardiac function and structure in the mice. This is typically done before and after doxorubicin administration.
- Blood samples are collected from the mice before and after doxorubicin administration to measure biomarkers of cardiac

damage and dysfunction. Common biomarkers include cardiac troponins and brain natriuretic peptide (BNP).

- The hearts of the mice are collected and examined for histological changes. This can include the assessment of cardiac fibrosis, inflammation, and cell death.
- Potential treatments for doxorubicin-induced cardiotoxicity can be evaluated by administering the drug before or after doxorubicin administration and assessing its effect on cardiac function, biomarkers, and histology.
- Data obtained from echocardiography, biomarker analysis, and histopathology are analyzed using statistical methods to evaluate the efficacy of potential treatments and to investigate the underlying mechanisms of doxorubicin-induced cardiotoxicity.

Pressure overload-induced heart failure model in rats

Pressure overload-induced heart failure model in rats is a widely used experimental model for studying heart failure. This model is induced by the application of pressure overload on the heart, leading to ventricular hypertrophy and eventually heart failure.

The methodology

- Anesthetize the rats with an appropriate anesthetic agent. Make a small incision in the skin of the chest and expose the aortic arch. Place a ligature around the aortic arch and a small metallic clip on the aorta just below the left subclavian artery. This creates a pressure gradient and increased afterload on the left ventricle.
- Administer antibiotics and analgesics after the surgery to prevent infection and reduce pain. Monitor the rats regularly for

signs of distress or complications.

- Perform echocardiography at regular intervals to assess the development of ventricular hypertrophy and dysfunction.
- After the desired duration of pressure overload, sacrifice the rats and harvest the hearts for histological analysis. Measure the left ventricular mass and perform histological staining to assess the extent of hypertrophy and fibrosis.
- Analyze the expression of various genes and proteins involved in the pathogenesis of heart failure, such as inflammatory cytokines, fibrotic markers, and apoptotic pathways.

This model can be used to screen and evaluate the efficacy of drugs for the treatment of heart failure by administering the drugs before or after the induction of pressure overload and assessing the functional and histological changes in the heart.

Isolated heart preparation

Isolated heart preparation is a widely used method for screening drugs to treat cardiovascular diseases, including heart failure. The method involves removing the heart from an anesthetized animal and setting it up in a Langendorff perfusion system, where it is perfused with oxygenated, temperature-controlled buffer solution. The preparation can be used to assess various cardiac parameters, including heart rate, contractility, and coronary flow.

The procedure for isolated heart preparation typically involves the following steps:

1. Anesthetize the animal and remove the heart.
2. Quickly place the heart in ice-cold buffer solution to prevent damage.
3. Attach the aorta to a cannula and perfuse the heart with buffer solution until it is completely free of blood.
4. Connect the cannula to a Langendorff perfusion system, which maintains the heart at a constant flow rate and temperature.

5. Measure baseline cardiac parameters, such as heart rate and contractility, before administering any drugs.
6. Administer the drug of interest and monitor the changes in cardiac parameters.
7. At the end of the experiment, perfuse the heart with a fixative solution to preserve the tissue for histological analysis.

Isolated heart preparation has the advantage of allowing direct measurement of cardiac function in a controlled environment. It also allows for the study of the effects of drugs on specific cardiac parameters, which can help identify potential targets for drug development. However, this method does not account for the effects of systemic factors, such as the autonomic nervous system, that can influence cardiac function in vivo. Additionally, the use of animal models raises ethical considerations.

Screening methods for drugs to treat CHF are diverse and often involve the use of animal models. These models provide important information on the efficacy and safety of potential drugs. The choice of model depends on the specific research question and the stage of drug development. In vitro assays, isolated heart preparations, and hemodynamic monitoring provide useful information on drug mechanisms of action, while in vivo models of heart failure allow for the evaluation of drug effects in a physiological context. Ultimately, the combination of multiple screening methods is often necessary to comprehensively evaluate the potential of a drug to treat CHF.

XVIII

Anti-Inflammatory Drugs

Anti-inflammatory drugs are pharmacological agents that are used to alleviate inflammation, a process in which the immune system responds to injury, infection, or tissue damage. Inflammation is associated with pain, swelling, redness, and heat in the affected area. Inflammation can be acute or chronic, and when chronic, it is associated with various diseases such as rheumatoid arthritis, Crohn's disease, psoriasis, and asthma, among others. Anti-inflammatory drugs are an essential class of drugs used to manage these conditions.

The screening methods for anti-inflammatory drugs are designed to evaluate the effectiveness of drugs in reducing inflammation in different models. These models may involve chemical or physical induction of inflammation in animal models, and the drugs are tested for their ability to reduce inflammation in these models. The tests measure different parameters such as edema, pain, and leukocyte migration. The most commonly used tests for screening anti-inflammatory drugs include the carrageenan-induced paw edema test, the formalin-induced paw edema test, the cotton pellet-induced granuloma test, and the acetic acid-induced vascular permeability test, among others. These tests can provide important information about the pharmacological properties of drugs, including their anti-inflammatory activity.

Common screening methods used for anti-inflammatory drugs:

Carrageenan-induced paw edema test: In this test, inflammation is induced by injecting carrageenan into the paw of an animal. The degree of paw swelling is then measured over time and compared to a control group.

Formalin-induced paw edema test: Similar to the carrageenan-induced paw edema test, this test involves injecting formalin into the paw to induce inflammation and then measuring paw swelling over time.

Cotton pellet-induced granuloma test: This test involves implanting cotton pellets into the subcutaneous tissue of an animal, which induces granuloma formation and subsequent inflammation. The weight of the granuloma is measured to assess the degree of inflammation.

Acetic acid-induced vascular permeability test: In this test, the permeability of blood vessels is assessed by injecting acetic acid into the peritoneal cavity of an animal and measuring the amount of fluid that leaks out of the vessels.

Lipopolysaccharide (LPS)-induced endotoxemia test: LPS is a component of the cell wall of gram-negative bacteria and can induce systemic inflammation when injected into an animal. This test involves measuring various markers of inflammation in response to LPS injection.

Histamine-induced edema test: Histamine is a compound involved in the inflammatory response, and this test involves injecting histamine into the paw of an animal and measuring paw swelling over time.

Air pouch model: In this test, a sterile air pouch is created in the subcutaneous tissue of an animal and an inflammatory agent is introduced into the pouch. The degree of inflammation is then assessed by measuring the number and type of immune cells present in the pouch.

These are just a few examples, and there are many other screening methods used for anti-inflammatory drugs depending on the specific mechanism of action being studied.

Other methods

Dextran-induced edema test

Formaldehyde-induced arthritis test

Kaolin-carrageenan-induced arthritis test

TPA-induced ear edema test

Xylene-induced ear edema test

Croton oil-induced ear edema test

Freund's adjuvant-induced arthritis test

Acute lung injury model

Cytokine-induced neutrophil chemoattraction test

Glucocorticoid-induced thymocyte apoptosis test

Granulomatous tissue-induced angiogenesis test

Mycobacterium tuberculosis-induced granuloma test

Each of these tests has its specific methodology and experimental design for evaluating the anti-inflammatory potential of drugs.

Carrageenan-induced paw edema test:

The carrageenan-induced paw edema test is a widely used method to evaluate the anti-inflammatory activity of drugs. It involves the injection of carrageenan, a naturally occurring sulfated polysaccharide, into the paw of a rodent, typically a rat or mouse, to induce inflammation. The injection results in edema, or swelling, of the paw, which is then measured at regular intervals using a plethysmometer. The degree of edema is indicative of the inflammatory response, and the reduction in edema following administration of a drug is taken as a measure of its anti-inflammatory activity.

The test is often performed with a single dose of the drug administered either before or after the induction of inflammation. The degree of inflammation is typically quantified by measuring the paw volume using a plethysmometer or by histological analysis of the tissue. The test can also be performed using a variety of other inflammatory agents, such as carrageenan mixed with dextran, formalin, or kaolin.

Methodology

1. Use male rats or mice (weighing between 150-250 g) for the test.
2. Randomly divide the animals into control and test groups, with at least 5 animals in each group.
3. Administer the test drug orally or intraperitoneally (i.p.) at the desired dose 1 hour before carrageenan injection. The control group should receive a similar volume of vehicle (saline or distilled water).
4. Anesthetize the animal using isoflurane or ether, and then inject 0.1 mL of 1% carrageenan solution (dissolved in saline) into the subplantar region of the left hind paw using a 30-gauge needle.
5. Measure the paw volume using a plethysmometer before carrageenan injection (baseline) and at 1, 2, 3, 4, and 5 hours after injection. Place the paw in the plethysmometer and record the volume displacement value.
6. Calculate the percentage increase in paw volume for each animal at each time point using the formula:

% increase in paw volume = (Vt - V0) / V0 x 100

where V0 is the paw volume before carrageenan injection and Vt is the paw volume at a given time point.

Analyze the data using one-way analysis of variance (ANOVA) followed by post-hoc tests such as Dunnett's test or Tukey's test to determine the significance of differences between groups.

Note: The carrageenan-induced paw edema test is a widely used method for evaluating the anti-inflammatory activity of drugs, and is based on the principle that inflammation induced by carrageenan injection results in increased paw volume due to increased vascular permeability and accumulation of fluid in the tissue.

Formalin-induced paw edema test:

The formalin-induced paw edema test is a widely used animal model for evaluating the anti-inflammatory potential of drugs. The test involves the injection of formalin into the subplantar region of the hind paw of the animal, which causes edema and pain. The test is usually carried out in rats or mice and involves the following methodology:

- The animals used for the test are usually male rats or mice weighing between 150-250 g. The animals are kept under standard laboratory conditions with access to food and water ad libitum. The animals are acclimatized to the laboratory environment for at least a week before the experiment.
- Formalin solution (1% or 2.5%) is injected into the subplantar region of the hind paw of the animal, usually in a volume of 50 µl per paw. The injection is carried out using a microsyringe with a fine gauge needle.
- The paw volume is measured immediately before and after formalin injection using a plethysmometer. The paw volume is measured at 0, 1, 2, 3, 4, and 24 hours after the injection.
- The degree of paw swelling is calculated as the difference between the paw volume before and after the injection of formalin. The percentage of inhibition of paw edema is calculated by comparing the paw volume of the treated group with that of the control group. The data obtained are usually analyzed using statistical methods such as one-way analysis of variance (ANOVA) followed by post-hoc tests.

The test is a reliable and sensitive method for evaluating the anti-inflammatory activity of drugs. However, it should be noted that the test only measures the acute inflammatory response and may not reflect the chronic inflammatory response seen in some diseases.

Cotton pellet induced granuloma test

The cotton pellet-induced granuloma test is a widely used preclinical screening method to evaluate the anti-inflammatory potential of test compounds. This test involves the induction of a foreign body reaction in an animal model, which is characterized by the formation of granuloma tissues.

Methodology

- Typically, male rats or mice are used for this test, which should be healthy, age-matched, and of similar weight.
- The animals are divided into control and treatment groups. The treatment group is further divided into groups receiving different doses of the test compound. The test compound can be administered orally or intraperitoneally, depending on the experimental design.
- After the initial treatment with the test compound, sterile cotton pellets (10 mg each) are implanted subcutaneously in the dorsal region of the animal.
- The test compound administration continues daily for 7 to 10 days.
- At the end of the experimental period, the animals are sacrificed, and the cotton pellets and surrounding tissues are collected for further analysis.
- The cotton pellets are dried and weighed, and the weight of the granuloma formed around the pellet is determined. The extent of granuloma formation is expressed as the weight of the granuloma per 100 g of the animal's body weight.
- The anti-inflammatory potential of the test compound can be evaluated by comparing the extent of granuloma formation in

the control and treatment groups. The test compound is considered to have anti-inflammatory activity if it reduces the extent of granuloma formation in a dose-dependent manner.

Acetic acid- induced vascular permeability test

The acetic acid-induced vascular permeability test is a preclinical screening method to evaluate the anti-inflammatory activity of test compounds. This test is based on the principle that acetic acid induces an inflammatory response by increasing the permeability of the capillaries, leading to the leakage of plasma proteins and fluids from the blood vessels into the surrounding tissues.

Methodology:

1. The test animals (usually mice or rats) are divided into groups, and each group is treated with the test compound or vehicle control (e.g., saline).
2. After 30 minutes of treatment, a 0.6% solution of acetic acid is injected intraperitoneally into each animal.
3. After 10-15 minutes, a dye solution (e.g., Evans blue) is injected intravenously into the animals.
4. After another 30 minutes, the animals are sacrificed, and the peritoneal cavity is washed with saline to collect the extravasated dye solution.
5. The amount of dye present in the peritoneal wash fluid is quantified spectrophotometrically.
6. The results are expressed as the amount of dye extravasation (µg) per gram of tissue.
7. The test compound is considered to have anti-inflammatory activity if it significantly reduces the amount of dye extravasation compared to the vehicle control group.

Note: This test is relatively simple and inexpensive, but it has limitations in terms of specificity and sensitivity. It can provide useful information about the anti-inflammatory potential of a test compound but should be interpreted in conjunction with other tests and preclinical models.

Lipopolysaccharide (LPS)-induced endototaxemia test

The lipopolysaccharide (LPS)-induced endotoxemia test is a preclinical screening method for anti-inflammatory drugs that are intended to treat sepsis and septic shock. LPS, a component of the cell wall of gram-negative bacteria, can induce the release of cytokines and other inflammatory mediators that contribute to the pathogenesis of sepsis. In this test, LPS is administered to experimental animals to mimic the inflammatory response that occurs during sepsis.

Methodology

- The test is typically performed in rodents (mice or rats) of either sex. Animals are fasted overnight before the experiment, with free access to water. The animals are anesthetized (e.g. by isoflurane inhalation), and a catheter is inserted into a peripheral vein for drug administration and blood collection.
- LPS is dissolved in sterile saline or another appropriate vehicle and is administered intravenously at a dose that produces a systemic inflammatory response. The dose can vary depending on the species, strain, and sex of the animal, as well as the desired endpoint of the experiment. Typically, doses range from 1 to 20 mg/kg.
- After LPS administration, animals are monitored for clinical signs of inflammation, such as fever, hypothermia, lethargy, or anorexia. Blood samples are collected at various time points after LPS administration, and the levels of inflammatory mediators (e.g. cytokines, chemokines, and acute-phase proteins) are measured using various techniques (e.g. ELISA, multiplex assays, Western blotting, qPCR).

- The results are typically presented as the time-course of the inflammatory response, showing the levels of various inflammatory mediators as a function of time after LPS administration. The effect of the test drug on the inflammatory response can be assessed by comparing the data from drug-treated and control animals. The endpoints of the experiment can vary, depending on the research question and the goals of the study, and can include mortality, morbidity, organ dysfunction, histopathology, or other relevant parameters.

Histamine- induced edema test

The histamine-induced edema test is a screening method used to evaluate the potential anti-inflammatory effects of drugs. The test is typically performed in rodents, such as mice or rats, and involves the injection of histamine into a localized area, such as the paw, to induce inflammation and edema.

Here is a brief methodology for the histamine-induced edema test:

- Select the appropriate species and strain of animal based on the research question and availability. Typically, mice or rats are used in this test.
- Randomly divide the animals into groups based on treatment.
- Administer the drug or vehicle solution to each group of animals via an appropriate route of administration. The drug should be administered at a dose and timepoint appropriate for the research question.
- Induce edema by injecting histamine into the paw or other localized area. The concentration of histamine and the volume of injection can vary depending on the experimental design.
- Measure the paw volume at predetermined timepoints (e.g. 1, 2, and 4 hours after injection) using a plethysmometer. The difference in paw volume between the baseline and post-

injection measurements reflects the degree of edema.

- Analyze the data by comparing the paw volume changes between the treatment and control groups. Statistical tests such as the t-test or ANOVA can be used to determine the significance of the results.

It is important to note that the histamine-induced edema test is only one of many screening methods used to evaluate the potential anti-inflammatory effects of drugs, and should be used in conjunction with other tests to provide a comprehensive understanding of a drug's therapeutic potential.

Air pouch model

The air pouch model is a screening method for evaluating the anti-inflammatory activity of test compounds. The model involves the creation of an air pouch, which is a cavity formed by subcutaneously injecting air into the back of an animal. The air pouch is filled with exudate, which is collected and used for analysis of inflammatory parameters.

Methodology

- Small laboratory animals such as mice, rats or guinea pigs are used in the air pouch model.
- The animal is anesthetized and its back is shaved and sterilized. A 20- to 25-gauge needle is used to inject 3-5 mL of sterile air subcutaneously on the back of the animal. The air is injected in such a way that a cavity is formed.
- The test compound is administered via intraperitoneal (i.p.), subcutaneous (s.c.), or oral (p.o.) routes. The route of administration may depend on the nature of the compound being tested.
- After 1-2 hours of administration of the test compound, an inflammatory stimulus such as lipopolysaccharide (LPS) or carrageenan is injected into the air pouch. The amount of LPS or

carrageenan may vary depending on the experimental design.

- After 4-6 hours of the inflammatory stimulus injection, the animal is euthanized, and the air pouch is washed with sterile saline to collect exudate. The volume of exudate collected is measured.
- The collected exudate is used to determine various inflammatory parameters such as leukocyte count, cytokine levels, and prostaglandin levels. These parameters can help in evaluating the anti-inflammatory activity of the test compound.

The air pouch model is a useful tool for evaluating the anti-inflammatory activity of test compounds and can provide valuable information for drug development.

Dextran-induced edema test

The dextran-induced edema test is a preclinical screening method for evaluating the anti-inflammatory activity of drugs. It involves the induction of edema by subcutaneous injection of dextran into a hind paw of the animal. The test is commonly used to assess the effect of nonsteroidal anti-inflammatory drugs (NSAIDs) and other anti-inflammatory agents on edema formation.

The following is a brief outline of the methodology for the dextran-induced edema test:

- The test is commonly performed in rodents, such as rats or mice, of either sex.
- Animals are randomly assigned to different treatment groups (usually 6-10 animals/group).
- The test drug is administered either orally or intraperitoneally at a dose and time specified by the investigator. A negative control group is treated with the vehicle alone (e.g., saline, distilled water), while a positive control group is treated with a standard anti-inflammatory agent.

- After the test drug has been administered, edema is induced by subcutaneous injection of dextran (e.g., 0.1 mL of 1% dextran solution) into the hind paw of the animal.The volume of edema is measured using a plethysmometer at specified time points after the induction of edema (e.g., 1, 2, 3, and 4 hours). The difference between the paw volume before and after the injection of dextran represents the volume of edema.
- The percent inhibition of edema formation by the test drug is calculated and compared to the positive control group. A drug is considered to have anti-inflammatory activity if it significantly inhibits edema formation compared to the negative control group.

The methodology for the dextran-induced edema test can vary depending on the specific experimental design and the animal species used. The test should be conducted in compliance with ethical guidelines and regulations for the use of animals in scientific research.

Formaldehyde-induced arthritis test

Formaldehyde-induced arthritis test is a preclinical model used to evaluate the anti-inflammatory and anti-arthritic potential of test drugs. It involves the induction of arthritis in rats by injecting formaldehyde into the subplantar surface of the right hind paw.

Methodology

1. Albino Wistar rats of either sex weighing 150-200 g are used for the study.
2. The animals are divided into six groups with six animals in each group.
3. Arthritis is induced by injecting 0.1 mL of 2% formaldehyde in saline into the subplantar surface of the right hind paw of each

animal on day 0.

4. Test drugs are administered orally from day 1 to day 21. A standard anti-inflammatory drug such as indomethacin is used as a positive control.
5. The paw volume of each animal is measured on days 0, 7, 14, and 21 using a plethysmometer. The percentage increase in paw volume is calculated by comparing the paw volume of each animal on days 7, 14, and 21 with the paw volume on day 0.
6. On day 21, the animals are sacrificed, and the hind paws are dissected out for histopathological evaluation.
7. The data obtained are analyzed statistically using one-way analysis of variance (ANOVA) followed by Dunnett's test.

The test drug is considered to have anti-inflammatory and anti-arthritic potential if it shows a significant reduction in paw volume and histopathological changes compared to the control group.

Kaolin-carrageenan-induced arthritis test

The kaolin-carrageenan-induced arthritis test is a preclinical screening method for anti-inflammatory drugs. In this test, arthritis is induced by the injection of a mixture of kaolin and carrageenan into the subplantar region of the hind paw. The kaolin-carrageenan mixture causes inflammation in the paw, resulting in edema and hyperalgesia. The test is conducted on rats or mice.

The test involves the following steps:

1. Male or female rats or mice are used in this test. The animals are randomized into different groups, each consisting of 6 to 10 animals.
2. The kaolin-carrageenan mixture is prepared by suspending 1.5% kaolin and 2% carrageenan in saline solution. The mixture is injected into the subplantar region of the hind paw using a 27-gauge needle.

3. Paw volume is measured using a plethysmometer at baseline and at various time points after injection (e.g., 1, 2, 3, 4, 6, and 24 hours). The difference between the paw volume after injection and the baseline paw volume is used to assess the degree of paw edema.
4. The degree of hyperalgesia is assessed using the paw withdrawal threshold or latency in response to mechanical or thermal stimulation. The paw withdrawal threshold or latency is measured at baseline and at various time points after injection (e.g., 1, 2, 3, 4, 6, and 24 hours).
5. Test drugs or reference drugs are administered orally or by injection at various time points after induction of arthritis.
6. The paw volume and paw withdrawal threshold or latency are analyzed statistically to determine the degree of edema and hyperalgesia, respectively. The test drug is considered to be effective if it significantly reduces paw edema and hyperalgesia compared to the control group.

The kaolin-carrageenan-induced arthritis test is a reliable and sensitive method for evaluating the anti-inflammatory effects of test drugs in preclinical studies.

TPA-induced ear edema test

The TPA (12-O-tetradecanoylphorbol-13-acetate) induced ear edema test is used to evaluate the anti-inflammatory effects of drugs. TPA is a potent inflammatory agent that can induce inflammation in the mouse ear. The test involves the following steps:

- The test substance is dissolved in an appropriate solvent (e.g. DMSO, acetone) to obtain the desired concentration.
- TPA is dissolved in acetone to obtain a stock solution of 10 μg/mL.
- The test animals (usually mice) are divided into different groups, and each group is treated with a different dose of the test

substance. After 30 minutes, 20 µl of TPA solution is applied to the inner and outer surface After 6 hours, the mice are sacrificed, and the ears are removed and weighed. The thickness of the ear is The increase in ear thickness in the TPA-treated ear is calculated by subtracting the thickness of the left ear from the thickness of the right ear. The test substance is considered to have anti-inflammatory activity if it reduces the increase in ear thickness caused by TPA.

- The TPA-induced ear edema test is a widely used method for screening drugs with anti-inflammatory properties. The test is simple, quick, and relatively inexpensive, and can provide valuable information about the anti-inflammatory activity of test compounds.

Xylene-induced ear edema test

The xylene-induced ear edema test is a method for assessing the anti-inflammatory activity of test substances in mice. It involves applying a solution of xylene to the surface of the ear, which induces an inflammatory response characterized by edema or swelling of the ear. The degree of edema can be measured using a caliper or by weighing the ear tissue.

The test involves the following steps:

1. A solution of xylene is prepared in a suitable solvent, such as acetone or olive oil.
2. Test animals (usually mice) are divided into groups, with each group receiving a different treatment (e.g., the test substance or a control).
3. The xylene solution is applied to the surface of one ear of each animal in each group, while the other ear is left untreated as a control.
4. After a specified time period (usually 4 hours), the animals are euthanized, and the ears are removed and weighed or measured

using a caliper to determine the degree of swelling.

5. The degree of edema is expressed as the increase in ear weight or ear thickness compared to the untreated control ear.
6. The anti-inflammatory activity of the test substance can be assessed by comparing the degree of edema in the test group to that of the control group. A reduction in edema in the test group compared to the control group indicates anti-inflammatory activity.

Croton oil-induced ear edema test

The Croton oil-induced ear edema test is a method used to evaluate the anti-inflammatory activity of compounds in a topical formulation using a mouse model. In this test, Croton oil is applied topically to the inner and outer surfaces of the ear of the mouse, which leads to edema formation within 6 hours. The degree of edema can be measured by weighing the ear of the mouse before and after the induction of inflammation. The difference between the weight of the edematous ear and the weight of the untreated ear is taken as a measure of the extent of inflammation. This method can be used to screen the topical anti-inflammatory activity of compounds such as plant extracts or synthetic drugs.

Freund's adjuvant-induced arthritis test

The Freund's adjuvant-induced arthritis test is a commonly used animal model to study rheumatoid arthritis. The test involves injecting an adjuvant, usually Freund's adjuvant, into the paw of a rodent, which causes an immune response leading to inflammation and edema in the injected paw. The test can be used to evaluate the effects of anti-inflammatory drugs on the severity of arthritis.

Brief methodology for the test:

- Typically rats or mice are used for this test.

- Freund's adjuvant (typically Complete Freund's Adjuvant, CFA) is injected into the base of the tail or hind paw of the animal.
- The development of arthritis is assessed by measuring the paw volume or weight, and scoring the animals for the degree of inflammation, edema, and pain.
- Anti-inflammatory drugs are administered to test their efficacy in reducing the severity of the arthritis.
- The effects of the drugs are evaluated by measuring the paw volume or weight, and scoring the animals for the degree of inflammation, edema, and pain.

Note: The methodology and specific details of the test can vary depending on the researcher's needs and preferences.

Acute lung injury model

Acute lung injury (ALI) is a condition in which there is inflammation and damage to the lungs, leading to difficulty in breathing and decreased oxygen levels in the blood. There are various models of ALI that have been developed in animals to study the pathophysiology and test potential treatments.

One commonly used model of ALI involves inducing injury to the lungs by intratracheal instillation of a solution containing lipopolysaccharide (LPS), a component of the cell wall of gram-negative bacteria. The LPS triggers an immune response in the lungs, leading to inflammation, alveolar damage, and impaired gas exchange. The severity of the injury can be controlled by varying the dose of LPS administered.

Other models of ALI include the use of mechanical ventilation to induce lung injury, administration of bacterial or viral pathogens to the lungs, and exposure to injurious agents such as smoke or chemicals.

The severity of ALI can be assessed by measuring various parameters such as lung histology, levels of inflammatory cytokines, arterial blood gas levels, and lung compliance. Potential treatments for ALI can also be tested using these models, including anti-inflammatory drugs, antioxidants, and mechanical ventilation strategies.

Cytokine-induced neutrophil chemoattraction test

The cytokine-induced neutrophil chemoattraction test, also known as the Boyden chamber assay or the transwell assay, is a widely used in vitro assay to study the ability of various stimuli to induce the migration of neutrophils, which are a type of white blood cell, across a membrane.

The assay involves the use of a specialized chamber, called a Boyden chamber, which consists of two compartments separated by a porous membrane. The bottom compartment contains a chemoattractant stimulus, such as a cytokine, while the top compartment contains a suspension of neutrophils. The neutrophils are allowed to migrate across the membrane towards the chemoattractant stimulus in the bottom compartment.

After a set amount of time, the membrane is removed and the number of neutrophils that have migrated across the membrane is quantified. This can be done by counting the number of cells in a given area under a microscope or by measuring the amount of a neutrophil-specific enzyme, such as myeloperoxidase, in the bottom compartment.

The cytokine-induced neutrophil chemoattraction test can be used to assess the potency and efficacy of various cytokines or other stimuli in inducing neutrophil migration. It is also useful for studying the mechanisms of neutrophil migration and for screening potential anti-inflammatory or anti-migratory compounds.

Glucocorticoid-induced thymocyte apoptosis test

The glucocorticoid-induced thymocyte apoptosis test is a widely used in vitro screening assay for potential anti-inflammatory compounds, specifically those that may act as glucocorticoid receptor agonists.

In this assay, thymocytes are isolated from mice or rats and exposed to a synthetic glucocorticoid hormone, such as dexamethasone. The thymocytes are then stained with annexin V and propidium iodide, which allows for the identification and quantification of apoptotic cells. The percentage of apoptotic thymocytes is determined by flow cytometry, and this serves as an indicator of the potential anti-inflammatory activity of the compound being tested.

The test can be used to screen a large number of compounds in a relatively short period of time and can be modified to test for specific mechanisms of action, such as the involvement of specific cytokines or signaling pathways in the apoptotic response.

Granulomatous tissue-induced angiogenesis test

The granulomatous tissue-induced angiogenesis test is used to evaluate the angiogenic response of new blood vessel formation induced by the implantation of granulomatous tissue in an animal model. The test is a modification of the chick chorioallantoic membrane (CAM) assay, which is widely used to study angiogenesis in vivo.

Here is the general methodology for the granulomatous tissue-induced angiogenesis test:

- Typically, rats or mice are used for this test. The animals are housed in a controlled environment with a 12-hour light/dark cycle and allowed free access to food and water.
- A sterile sponge or other foreign body is implanted subcutaneously in the animal to induce the formation of granulomatous tissue. The sponge or foreign body is typically soaked in an inflammatory agent (such as After a specified period (usually 7-14 days), the granulomatous tissue is harvested from the animal and cut into small pieces.
- A small piece of the harvested granulomatous tissue is placed onto the chorioallantoic membrane (CAM) of a fertilized chicken

egg. The CAM is a highly vascularized tissue that surrounds the developing chick embryo.

- The eggs are incubated for a specified period (usually 3-7 days) and the angiogenic response is observed by examining the blood vessels that grow around the implanted tissue. The response can be quantified by measuring the length or number of blood vessels.
- Data obtained from the angiogenic response can be analyzed statistically to determine the significance of the response and to compare the effects of different treatments or conditions.

The granulomatous tissue-induced angiogenesis test can be used to evaluate the angiogenic response of anti-inflammatory drugs or other compounds that may affect blood vessel formation.

Mycobacterium tuberculosis-induced granuloma test

The Mycobacterium tuberculosis-induced granuloma test is a preclinical screening method used for the evaluation of potential anti-tuberculosis drugs. In this test, M. tuberculosis is inoculated into the animal model, and after some time, the granulomatous response is observed. The test measures the ability of the drug to reduce the formation of granulomas, which are characteristic of tuberculosis infection.

Methodology

- The most commonly used animal model for this test is the guinea pig, but other models such as the rabbit and mouse can also be used.
- A suspension of M. tuberculosis is inoculated into the animal model, typically by intradermal or intravenous injection.
- After the establishment of the infection, the animals are treated with the test drug or a control drug. Treatment duration and

dosage may vary based on the study design.

- At the end of the treatment period, the animals are euthanized, and the granulomas are harvested and examined for size and number. The efficacy of the drug is determined by comparing the size and number of granulomas in the treated animals to those in the control group.
- This test is a well-established model for evaluating the efficacy of potential anti-tuberculosis drugs and can provide valuable information in the preclinical development of new drugs.

Te screening methods for anti-inflammatory drugs aim to evaluate the potential of new compounds to reduce inflammation and related pathologies. These assays provide valuable information on the efficacy and safety of the compounds, allowing for the identification of promising candidates for further development. However, it is important to note that no single assay can fully predict the clinical efficacy of an anti-inflammatory drug. Thus, a combination of different models and assays that capture various aspects of the inflammatory response should be employed to increase the predictability and reliability of the preclinical evaluations. Overall, these screening methods play a critical role in the drug discovery process and the development of new and effective treatments for inflammatory diseases.

XIX

Screening Methods for Analgesics and Antipyretic Drugs

Introduction:

Screening drugs for antipyretic and analgesic properties is an essential step in drug discovery and development. Antipyretic drugs are used to reduce fever, while analgesic drugs are used to relieve pain. Effective antipyretic and analgesic drugs must be able to target specific pathways involved in the regulation of fever and pain without causing unwanted side effects. To identify potential antipyretic and analgesic drugs, a variety of in vitro and in vivo screening assays are used to evaluate their efficacy and safety.

In vitro screening assays can include binding assays, enzyme inhibition assays, and cell-based assays, among others. These assays are used to assess the potential of a drug candidate to bind to a target receptor, block the activity of an enzyme involved in the pathway of interest, or affect cellular responses relevant to fever and pain.

In vivo screening assays are performed in animal models and can include the acetic acid-induced writhing test, formalin test, hot plate test, and other assays that evaluate the ability of a drug candidate to reduce pain or fever. These assays are used to assess the pharmacodynamic and pharmacokinetic properties of a drug candidate in a living organism and to evaluate its potential toxicity.

Common Screening Methods:

There are several common screening methods used to test the antipyretic and analgesic properties of drugs. Here are a few examples:

Acetic Acid-Induced Writhing Test:

The acetic acid-induced writhing test is a common method used to evaluate the analgesic properties of drugs. This test induces pain in laboratory animals by injecting a small amount of acetic acid into the peritoneal cavity, which causes abdominal contractions or "writhing." The test substance is then administered, and the number of writhes is counted over a specific time period. A reduction in the number of writhes indicates analgesic activity.

Methodology:

Animals: The test is typically performed on mice or rats of either sex. Animals should be healthy and free of any signs of illness or injury.

Preparation of test substances: The test substance should be dissolved in a suitable vehicle, such as saline or distilled water, to the desired concentration. A positive control drug such as aspirin may also be used to validate the test.

Acetic acid injection: A small volume of acetic acid (usually 0.7-1.0%) is injected into the peritoneal cavity of the animal using a fine needle. The animal is then observed for a period of 5-15 minutes for the development of writhing responses. The number of writhes is counted and recorded.

Administration of test substance: The test substance is administered via the desired route (e.g., oral, intraperitoneal, subcutaneous, etc.) either before or after the acetic acid injection. The number of writhes is then counted over a specific time period (usually 5-30 minutes) and recorded.

The number of writhes in the control group and treatment group(s) are compared using statistical methods such as one-way ANOVA, followed by post-hoc tests. A reduction in the number of writhes in the treatment group compared to the control group indicates analgesic activity.

It is important to note that this test has limitations, as it is a non-specific test for pain and does not distinguish between different types of pain. Additionally, the test relies on the subjective observation of writhing responses, which can be affected by factors such as animal age, gender, and strain. Therefore, it is important to use caution when interpreting the results of this test and to use it in combination with other tests to fully evaluate the analgesic properties of drugs.

Formalin Test:

The formalin test is a widely used method to evaluate the analgesic properties of drugs. This test induces pain in laboratory animals by injecting a small amount of formalin into the hind paw, which produces a biphasic pain response. The first phase occurs immediately after injection and lasts for 5-10 minutes, while the second phase occurs after a delay of approximately 15-20 minutes and lasts for 20-60 minutes. The test substance is administered before or after the formalin injection, and the duration of paw licking or biting is measured as an indication of pain.

Methodology:

Animals: The test is typically performed on mice or rats of either sex. Animals should be healthy and free of any signs of illness or injury.

Preparation of test substances: The test substance should be dissolved in a suitable vehicle, such as saline or distilled water, to the desired concentration. A positive control drug such as morphine may also be used to validate the test.

Formalin injection: A small volume of formalin (usually 2-5%) is injected into the hind paw of the animal using a fine needle. The animal is then observed for a period of 60 minutes for the development of paw licking or biting responses. The duration of paw licking or biting is recorded for each 5-minute interval during the observation period.

Administration of test substance: The test substance is administered via the desired route (e.g., oral, intraperitoneal, subcutaneous, etc.) either before or after the formalin injection. The duration of paw licking or biting is then measured and recorded as described in step 3.

The duration of paw licking or biting in the control group and treatment group(s) are compared using statistical methods such as two-way ANOVA, followed by post-hoc tests. A reduction in the duration of paw licking or biting in the treatment group compared to the control group indicates analgesic activity.

This test has limitations, as it is a non-specific test for pain and does not distinguish between different types of pain. Additionally, the test relies on the subjective observation of paw licking or biting responses, which can be affected by factors such as animal age, gender, and strain. Therefore, it is important to use caution when interpreting the results of this test and to use it in combination with other tests to fully evaluate the analgesic properties of drugs.

Hot Plate Test

The hot plate test is a widely used method to evaluate the analgesic properties of drugs. This test measures the reaction time of laboratory animals to a thermal stimulus, such as a heated metal plate. The test substance is administered, and the reaction time is measured as an indication of pain.

Hot Plate test

Methodology:

Animals: The test is typically performed on mice or rats of either sex. Animals should be healthy and free of any signs of illness or injury.

Preparation of test substances: The test substance should be dissolved in a suitable vehicle, such as saline or distilled water, to the desired concentration. A positive control drug such as morphine may also be used to validate the test.

Hot plate apparatus: The animal is placed on a hot plate apparatus, which consists of a metal surface heated to a constant temperature (usually 50-55°C). The animal is observed for a period of 60 seconds, and the time taken for the animal to show a response (e.g., paw licking, jumping, vocalization) is recorded. The animal is then removed from the hot plate to prevent tissue damage.

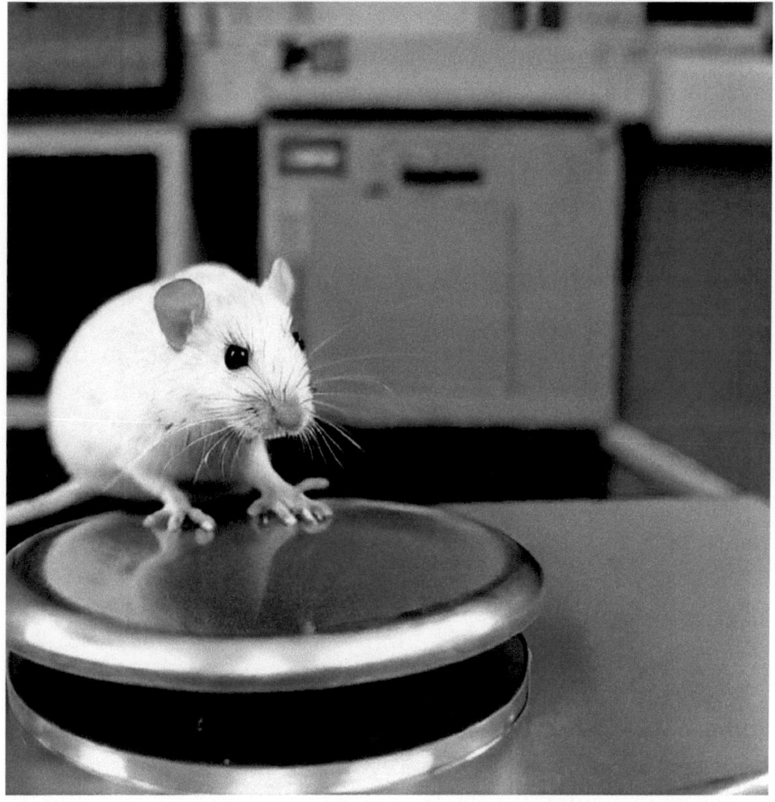

Hot Plate test- animal response

Administration of test substance: The test substance is administered via the desired route (e.g., oral, intraperitoneal, subcutaneous, etc.). The animal is then placed back on the hot plate, and the reaction time is measured and recorded as described in step 3.

The reaction time in the control group and treatment group(s) are compared using statistical methods such as one-way ANOVA, followed by post-hoc tests. An increase in the reaction time in the treatment group compared to the control group indicates analgesic activity.

It is a non-specific test for pain and does not distinguish between different types of pain. Additionally, the test relies on the subjective observation of pain responses, which can be affected by factors such as animal age, gender, and strain. Therefore, it is important to use caution when interpreting the results of this test and to use it in combination with other tests to fully evaluate the analgesic properties of drugs.

Brewer's Yeast-Induced Pyrexia Test

The Brewer's yeast-induced pyrexia test is a widely used method to evaluate the antipyretic properties of drugs. This test induces fever in laboratory animals by injecting Brewer's yeast subcutaneously or intraperitoneally, which produces a fever response. The test substance is administered before or after the yeast injection, and the rectal temperature is measured as an indication of fever.

Methodology:

Animals: The test is typically performed on rats of either sex. Animals should be healthy and free of any signs of illness or injury.

Preparation of test substances: The test substance should be dissolved in a suitable vehicle, such as saline or distilled water, to the desired concentration. A positive control drug such as aspirin may also be used to validate the test.

Brewer's yeast injection: A suspension of Brewer's yeast (usually 20-30% w/v) is injected subcutaneously or intraperitoneally into the animal. The animal is then observed for a period of 18-24 hours for the development of fever.

Administration of test substance: The test substance is administered via the desired route (e.g., oral, intraperitoneal, subcutaneous, etc.) either before or after the yeast injection. The rectal temperature is measured at regular intervals (e.g., 1, 2, 4, and 6 hours) after the yeast injection using a rectal thermometer. The rectal temperature is also measured in a control group that receives only the vehicle or saline.

The rectal temperature in the control group and treatment group(s) are compared using statistical methods such as two-way ANOVA, followed by post-hoc tests. A reduction in the rectal temperature in the treatment group compared to the control group indicates antipyretic activity.

It relies on the induction of fever by Brewer's yeast, which may not be a clinically relevant model for fever. Additionally, the test may be affected by factors such as animal age, gender, and strain. Therefore, it is important to use caution when interpreting the results of this test and to use it in combination with other tests to fully evaluate the antipyretic properties of drugs.

Cytokine-Induced Pyrexia Test

The cytokine-induced pyrexia test is a method used to evaluate the antipyretic properties of drugs. This test induces fever in laboratory animals by injecting cytokines, such as interleukin-1 (IL-1), subcutaneously or intravenously, which produces a fever response. The test substance is administered before or after the cytokine injection, and the rectal temperature is measured as an indication of fever.

Methodology:

Animals: The test is typically performed on rats of either sex. Animals should be healthy and free of any signs of illness or injury.

Preparation of test substances: The test substance should be dissolved in a suitable vehicle, such as saline or distilled water, to the desired concentration. A positive control drug such as aspirin may also be used to validate the test.

Cytokine injection: Cytokines such as interleukin-1 (IL-1) are injected subcutaneously or intravenously into the animal. The animal is then observed for a period of 2-4 hours for the development of fever.

Administration of test substance: The test substance is administered via the desired route (e.g., oral, intraperitoneal, subcutaneous, etc.) either before or after the cytokine injection. The rectal temperature is measured at regular intervals (e.g., 1, 2, and 4 hours) after the cytokine injection using a rectal thermometer. The rectal temperature is also measured in a control group that receives only the vehicle or saline.

The rectal temperature in the control group and treatment group(s) are compared using statistical methods such as two-way ANOVA, followed by post-hoc tests. A reduction in the rectal temperature in the treatment group compared to the control group indicates antipyretic activity.

This test has limitations, as it relies on the induction of fever by cytokines, which may not be a clinically relevant model for fever. Additionally, the test may be affected by factors such as animal age, gender, and strain. Therefore, it is important to use caution when interpreting the results of this test and to use it in combination with other tests to fully evaluate the antipyretic properties of drugs.

Tail Flick Test:

The tail flick test is a widely used method to evaluate the analgesic properties of drugs. This test is based on the observation that animals will reflexively flick their tails when subjected to a painful stimulus, such as heat. The latency to tail flick is measured before and after administration of a test substance, and an increase in the latency to tail flick indicates analgesic activity.

Methodology:

Animals: The test is typically performed on rats or mice of either sex. Animals should be healthy and free of any signs of illness or injury.

Preparation of test substances: The test substance should be dissolved in a suitable vehicle, such as saline or distilled water, to the desired concentration. A positive control drug such as morphine may also be used to validate the test.

Tail flick apparatus: The animal is restrained in a tail flick apparatus, which consists of a box with an opening at one end that allows access to the tail. The tail is exposed to a radiant heat source, such as a lamp or laser, that is applied to the distal end of the tail.

Baseline measurement: The latency to tail flick is measured by applying the heat source to the tail and measuring the time it takes for the animal to flick its tail in response. The baseline measurement is typically repeated three times, with a minimum of 5 minutes between each measurement to allow the animal to recover.

Administration of test substance: The test substance is administered via the desired route (e.g., oral, intraperitoneal, subcutaneous, etc.). The latency to tail flick is measured at regular intervals (e.g., 15, 30, 60, and 120 minutes) after the administration of the test substance. The latency to tail flick is also measured in a control group that receives only the vehicle or saline.

The latency to tail flick in the control group and treatment group(s) are compared using statistical methods such as two-way ANOVA, followed by post-hoc tests. An increase in the latency to tail flick in the treatment group compared to the control group indicates analgesic activity.

The tail flick test has limitations, as it is based on the response of an animal to a painful stimulus, which may not be a clinically relevant model for pain. Additionally, the test may be affected by factors such as animal age, gender, and strain, as well as the intensity and duration of the heat source. Therefore, it is important to use caution when interpreting the results of this test and to use it in combination with other tests to fully evaluate the analgesic properties of drugs.

Paw Pressure Test

The paw pressure test, also known as the Randall-Selitto test, is a commonly used method to assess the mechanical sensitivity and pain response of animals. This test applies pressure to the paw of an animal and measures the threshold at which the animal experiences pain.

Methodology:

Animals: The test is typically performed on rats or mice of either sex. Animals should be healthy and free of any signs of illness or injury.

Preparation of test substances: The test substance should be dissolved in a suitable vehicle, such as saline or distilled water, to the desired concentration. A positive control drug such as morphine may also be used to validate the test.

Paw pressure apparatus: The animal is placed in a restrainer and the paw is placed on a pressure plate connected to a mechanical force transducer. The pressure plate is gradually pressed against the paw until the animal withdraws its paw, indicating the threshold at which pain is experienced. The pressure can be applied manually or by a motorized device.

Baseline measurement: The baseline paw withdrawal threshold is determined by measuring the pressure at which the animal withdraws its paw in response to the pressure. The baseline measurement is typically repeated three times, with a minimum of 5 minutes between each measurement to allow the animal to recover.

Administration of test substance: The test substance is administered via the desired route (e.g., oral, intraperitoneal, subcutaneous, etc.). The paw withdrawal threshold is measured at regular intervals (e.g., 15, 30, 60, and 120 minutes) after the administration of the test substance. The paw withdrawal threshold is also measured in a control group that receives only the vehicle or saline.

The paw withdrawal threshold in the control group and treatment group(s) are compared using statistical methods such as two-way ANOVA, followed by post-hoc tests. An increase in the paw withdrawal threshold in the treatment group compared to the control group indicates analgesic activity.

The paw pressure test has limitations, as it is based on the response of an animal to a mechanical stimulus, which may not be a clinically relevant model for pain. Additionally, the test may be affected by factors such as animal age, gender, and strain, as well as the intensity and duration of the pressure. Therefore, it is important to use caution when interpreting the results of this test and to use it in combination with other tests to fully evaluate the analgesic properties of drugs.

Radioligand Binding Assay

Radioligand binding assays are widely used in pharmacology and drug discovery to investigate the interaction between drugs and their target receptors. The assay involves the use of radiolabeled ligands that bind specifically to the receptor of interest, allowing for the quantification of binding affinity, potency, and selectivity of the test compound.

Methodology:

Preparation of radioligand: The radioligand is prepared by labeling a ligand of interest with a radioactive isotope (e.g., tritium, carbon-14, or iodine-125). The radioligand should have a high specific activity, which is the amount of radioactivity per unit mass of ligand.

Preparation of tissue homogenate: Tissue samples containing the receptor of interest are homogenized and centrifuged to obtain a crude membrane fraction. The membrane fraction is then resuspended in a buffer solution to create a tissue homogenate.

Incubation: The tissue homogenate is incubated with the radioligand in the presence or absence of a range of concentrations of the test compound. The reaction mixture is incubated for a specific period at a specific temperature to allow for binding equilibrium to be reached.

Separation of bound and unbound radioligand: After the incubation period, the reaction mixture is separated into bound and unbound fractions using a suitable technique such as filtration or centrifugation. The amount of radioligand bound to the receptor is quantified using a scintillation counter or gamma counter, which measures the radioactivity.

The data obtained from the radioligand binding assay can be analyzed to determine the binding affinity (Kd) and the maximum binding capacity (Bmax) of the radioligand to the receptor. The data can also be used to determine the potency and selectivity of the test compound.

Radioligand binding assays have limitations, as they do not always provide information about the functional activity of the test compound at the receptor, and may not accurately reflect the in vivo efficacy or pharmacokinetic properties of the compound. Therefore, it is important to use caution when interpreting the results of this assay and to use it in combination with other assays to fully evaluate the pharmacological properties of drugs.

Prostaglandin E2-Induced Hyperalgesia Test:

Prostaglandin E2 (PGE2) is a potent inflammatory mediator that is released during tissue damage or inflammation. PGE2 can induce hyperalgesia, a heightened sensitivity to pain, by sensitizing nociceptors, the pain-sensing neurons. The PGE2-induced hyperalgesia test is a widely used model to study the effects of analgesic drugs on the sensitization of nociceptors.

Methodology:

Animal selection and preparation: Typically, rodents such as mice or rats are used for the PGE2-induced hyperalgesia test. Before the test, the animals are habituated to the testing environment.

Injection of PGE2: PGE2 is injected subcutaneously into the paw of the animal. The injection site is usually marked to ensure that subsequent measurements are taken at the same location.

Measurement of hyperalgesia: The sensitivity to pain is measured by quantifying the withdrawal threshold of the injected paw using a mechanical or thermal stimulus. Mechanical stimuli are typically applied using a series of calibrated von Frey filaments, and the threshold for paw withdrawal is recorded. Alternatively, thermal stimuli are applied using a radiant heat source, and the latency for paw withdrawal is recorded.

Drug treatment: After the injection of PGE2, the test compound is administered orally or by injection to the animal. The effects of the test compound on the PGE2-induced hyperalgesia are measured by repeating the measurements of paw withdrawal threshold or latency.

The data obtained from the PGE2-induced hyperalgesia test can be analyzed to determine the efficacy of the test compound in reversing or reducing the PGE2-induced hyperalgesia.

The PGE2-induced hyperalgesia test has limitations, as it is a model of acute inflammatory pain and may not reflect the clinical efficacy of the test compound for treating chronic pain. Therefore, it is important to use caution when interpreting the results of this test and to use it in combination with other tests to fully evaluate the analgesic properties of drugs.

Screening methods for antipyretic and analgesic drugs are essential for identifying potential new therapies and evaluating the efficacy of existing drugs. These screening methods are designed to simulate the conditions of inflammation and pain in animal models, allowing for the measurement of changes in pain and inflammation in response to treatment.

The most commonly used screening methods include the acetic acid-induced writhing test, formalin test, hot plate test, and paw pressure test for assessing pain, while the brewer's yeast-induced pyrexia test, cytokine-induced pyrexia test, and PGE2-induced hyperalgesia test are commonly used for assessing fever and inflammation.

In addition to these methods, several other in vitro and in vivo assays are also available to assess antipyretic and analgesic activities of drugs, including radioligand binding assay, prostaglandin E2-induced hyperalgesia test, and others. These methods provide a wide range of options for researchers to evaluate the potential.The development of new and effective antipyretic and analgesic drugs is essential for improving the quality of life for patients suffering from pain and inflammation. The use of appropriate screening methods is critical in identifying and selecting the most promising candidates for further development and clinical testing.

Printed by Libri Plureos GmbH in Hamburg, Germany